Since Flannery O'Connor
Essays on the Contemporary American Short Story

Edited by
Loren Logsdon and Charles W. Mayer

An Essays in Literature Book

The editors gratefully acknowledge the support of the *Essays in Literature* Board and EL Editor Thomas P. Joswick. We would also like to thank Fred Jones of the Western Illinois University Art Department for the cover design, Ruth Siedenburg for her editorial assistance, and Mitzae Mullens for her secretarial skills. Finally, we are grateful to the old and new English Department heads, Beth Stiffler and Ronald G. Walker, for their support, and to Mary Logsdon and Sue Mayer for their help and understanding.

Printed by Yeast Printing, Inc. • Macomb, Illinois

Contents

Introduction   5

Flannery O'Connor's Consecration
of the End   Richard Giannone   9

From "The Geranium" to
"Judgement Day":
Retribution in the Fiction
of Flannery O'Connor   John L. Darretta   21

Commentary by John L. Darretta
and Richard Giannone   29

Cheever's "Metamorphoses":
Myth and Postmodern
Short Fiction   E. P. Walkiewicz   32

Eudora Welty's Nostalgic
Imagination   Sally Wolff   45

From Time Immemorial: Native
American Traditions in
Contemporary Short Fiction   Helen Jaskoski   54

Donald Barthelme's Existential
Acts of Art   Clarke Owens   72

Doctorow's *Lives of the Poets* and
the Problem of Witness   Arthur M. Saltzman   83

Cynthia Ozick and Grace Paley:
Diverse Visions in Jewish
and Women's Literature   Jeanne Salladé Criswell   93

Cynthia Ozick, Rewriting Herself:
The Road from "The Shawl"
to "Rosa"   Joseph Lowin   101

Photographs and Fantasies in the
Stories of Ann Beattie   Stacey Olster   113

Neorealism, Postmodern Fantasy,
and the American Short Story   Lance Olsen   124

The Freak Endures: The
Southern Grotesque from
Flannery O'Connor to
Bobbie Ann Mason   Linda Adams Barnes   133

Narrative Displacement and
Literary Faith: Raymond
Carver's Inheritance from
Flannery O'Connor   Barbara C. Lonnquist   142

Contributors   151

*These essays are dedicated to
the memory of Flannery O'Connor,
who gave us so much laughter
and so much light.*

Introduction

This book focuses on the years since the publication of Flannery O'Connor's first story collection, *A Good Man Is Hard to Find* (1955). If the interest and activity of our writers during this period is any indication, the great love affair between American authors and the short story continues apace. The relationship has always been special. In Britain, for instance, attention has been given in this century to the shorter form by such important writers as Joyce, Lawrence, Forster, Woolf, and Greene; but there were few short story writers among the great Victorians to match the likes of Poe, Hawthorne, Melville, James, and Crane, as well as several distinguished local talents like Jewett, Chopin, Cable, and Garland whose work emerged from many hundreds of stories by writers eager to show the rest of the country what the special texture of their region was like. The commitment has been persistent and pervasive. America has seldom produced a first-rate novelist who was not also deeply interested in the story. Think of those closer to us: Dreiser, Wharton, Hemingway, Fitzgerald, Faulkner, Steinbeck, Bellow, Malamud, Welty, Singer, Updike, Oates. Others could be added to the list, all of them, like those mentioned, intensely engaged in creating good things in the shorter form. Mailer might be the only major figure of our time who has been only mildly fascinated, possibly because he has been more fascinated by creating new forms of his own.

Some American writers have cultivated the smaller canvas while neglecting or ignoring the novel altogether. Until now, Raymond Carver has been one of these, and Peter Taylor was until the appearance just the other day of his much-heralded novel, *A Summons to Memphis.* The underrated J. F. Powers is a third, although he too once wrote an interesting novel. Most of the Americans, however, are women who have preferred to work almost exclusively in the short story. It seems reasonable to suggest that some later women writers were drawn to short narratives by the example of the dominant role played by their sex in those proliferating local stories already alluded to. Or is it more significant that women formerly had neither time nor opportunity for full-blown literary careers and, except for a Wharton or a Cather, quite naturally gravitated to the form that could be managed in short bursts? If these things were true, they are true no longer; new ways have slowly evolved, and many of the women discussed in this volume find themselves fully engaged and at home in both longer and shorter structures: Welty, Beattie, Ozick, Mason. And, of course, Joyce Carol Oates's output has been prodigious in both novel and story. Yet we must believe that many women will continue, as in the past, to do their best work in the story, like those twin towers, Porter and O'Connor, who knew that their true métier was the short story and from it, almost alone among Americans of either sex, fashioned major literary reputations. Whether or not the new women alternate their genres, it is clear from such sources as Susan Cahill's *New Women and New Fiction* (1986) that the strong link between American women and the short story is certain to continue for some time to come. Among those showing great promise are Mary Robison, Jayne Anne Phillips, Joanne Greenberg, and Ellen Wilbur.

The chief trend in the American story is not directly related to gender. Perhaps it is only a slight exaggeration to say that, since Flannery O'Connor, a polarizing process has taken place between the traditional "realistic" story and the radical new "experimental" story. Following a few years in the wake of the novel, experimental stories, whether they are called superfiction, surfiction, metafiction, fabulation, postmodern fantasy, or just plain postmodern fiction, nearly always seem to have a common purpose: an abandonment of the bell-cow principle of fiction—trusted since the time of Defoe, except during romantic cycles—that authors can faithfully and more or less accurately represent, imitate, mirror, or reflect the reality of life "out there." Many of the newer writers who have lost the mimetic instinct object to "Jamesian realism" on philosophical grounds. To the modern mind devoted to the idea that the world is both chaotic and incomprehensible, even remarks like Frost's that poetry is a "momentary stay against confusion" seem to assert too much; if there is no discernible order in the universe, a narrator advancing an ordered set of characters and actions moving logically through time and anchored in space must necessarily falsify reality. That reality itself, moreover, is to be challenged on the grounds that only the subjective—imaginative—mind is real, the world being no more than a projection of the author's mind. Hence the relationship of his narrator's consciousness to the work becomes of paramount interest to the experimental writer, with the result that many stories are focused more on how they are being written than on what they say about life. Often the conclusion is that the story is not an image of the world at all, not even a "created work," but an artifact—just another "something" in the world and of it.

Objection to mimesis is made on political as well as philosophical grounds. Joe David Bellamy has referred to the new realistic short fiction as a "downpour of literary Republicanism." Called "neorealism" by Lance Olsen in this volume, the stories of such writers as Raymond Carver, Ann Beattie, and Tobias Wolff are more traditional in technique than the experimental narratives, more conservative in vision, and more successful in gaining admission to the University anthologies. These writers, like the successful realists who came before from Twain to Porter, believe that a sense of actual life must be rendered, consciously and with craft and diligence. They are often looked at askance for having too little to say, for daring even less in their low-keyed "minimalist" structures—qualities that are said to reflect a conservative mood in the nation's capital and across the land.

Yet we must not make too much of this split between the experimentalists and the traditionalists. In the end it will come down to a single division between works that are interesting and those that are not, as Henry James wisely suggested in "The Art of Fiction." Carver states in his deceptively simple essay, "On Writing," that some writers with a "bunch of talent" find a "unique and exact way of looking at things" and end by creating marvelous worlds all their own. This is as true of Donald

Barthelme, he implies, as it is of Ernest Hemingway. Carver himself seems to be writing stories with as much freshness, if not originality, as a Barthelme, a Pynchon, or a Barth. To verify this, one might compare his "Cathedral" with D. J. Lawrence's "The Blind Man." The subjects and themes are remarkably similar and a subtle revelatory power is in each. Yet the effects produced by these stories are just as remarkably different. While each gives a wholly convincing impression of reality, the "marvels" of the American realist are not those of this British predecessor. They are surely his own.

It is, perhaps, Flannery O'Connor who proves that only one kind of story truly counts; for she is at once a traditional realist and an experimental writer, as indeed many authors like Vonnegut, Cheever, and Oates turn out to be. O'Connor called herself a "realist of distances," explaining that she produced the kind of realism in which the writer becomes a prophet, not by mirroring the modern world but by approximating it—that is, by showing us the grotesque, fantastic, often monstrously comic quality of modern life as it is lived by people without faith, without grace, and with only a world of physical appearances at which to look for meaning and significance.

The scope of this book is, in fact, defined and framed by Flannery O'Connor. We begin by presenting essays by Richard Giannone and John Darretta, whose studies provide us with the unique opportunity to examine differing views of O'Connor's "Judgement Day"—that which sees her character's ordeal as redemptive and that which sees it as retributive. To take full advantage of this opportunity, we invited Professors Giannone and Darretta to reply to each other's essays. They responded to our request with enthusiasm and graciousness, and their one-page responses represent a decided bonus for this book. We conclude the book with two studies of current writers who have been significantly influenced by Flannery O'Connor. Linda Adams Barnes traces the development of the grotesque from O'Connor to Bobbie Ann Mason, explaining how the freak has evolved and changed since O'Connor's time, and Barbara C. Lonnquist assesses the impact that O'Connor's artistic spirit has had on Raymond Carver.

We realize that experimental writers are not given full representation here, for the great bulk of submitted essays are on authors writing in the mainstream. However, Clarke Owens' essay on Donald Barthelme's stories as being, not existentialist philosophically, but existential "acts" of art, provides a glimpse of one of the most important experimental writers of our time. And John Cheever, whom many would consider a traditional writer, is examined by E. P. Walkiewicz as an experimental writer in his use of myths. Finally, Lance Olsen's essay on neorealism examines recent critical theory and places the new kind of story (though not so new as it was a decade ago) in cultural and political opposition to its more traditional brothers.

There are two well-established writers included here who, like Flannery O'Connor, might be considered to live somewhat in both worlds of traditional and experimental fiction. Eudora Welty's extensive use of mythology sets her apart from the traditional, yet she is not experimental in the strictest sense of the word. The same could be true of E. L. Doctorow and his use of history. What connects Welty and Doctorow, though, is that ultimately they are superb storytellers whose art transcends any convenient descriptive labels. Sally Wolff's essay allows us to pay tribute to Welty's uses of her own rich childhood, and Arthur M. Saltzman's study of Doctorow's *Lives of the Poets* provides essential insight into the intense narrative concerns of a writer who has emerged as a major force in recent American fiction.

The contributions of native American writers are examined by Helen Jaskoski, whose essay treats Louise Erdrich, Gerald Vizenor, and Leslie Silko. Recognition of Erdrich is important to us personally because our own *Mississippi Valley Review* published one of her early stories, ''The Red Convertible,'' in 1982. The native American writers combine with the Jewish and women writers to reveal that the contemporary American short story is greatly enriched by ethnic and minority writers. Jeanne Salladé Criswell's contrast between Grace Paley's modern, free vision of life and Cynthia Ozick's strong traditional Jewish bonds, and Joseph Lowin's explication of the relationship between a pair of Ozick's stories, demonstrates how two Jewish writers use materials from their ethnic experience. Stacey Olster, writing about another of the promising women writers, explains how Ann Beattie's fiction relies on the fantasies of photographs, fairy tales, movies, and TV to order experience.

One of the strengths of this collection of essays, we feel, is that it provides serious scholarly treatment of some new writers whose major works are perhaps yet to be written. If we have called attention to these writers and expanded our readers' awareness of them, then we have advanced the cause of the short story through the kind of encouragement which editors and teachers can provide. We do acknowledge that certain important writers are not represented here—Saul Bellow, John Updike, Bernard Malamud, Thomas Pynchon, and Joyce Carol Oates, to name only a few. We had an inquiry about an essay on Malamud and we encouraged the caller to submit the essay, but it never arrived. We felt that some treatment of Malamud's *The Magic Barrel,* especially, would have been important to our book. Also, we regret that we received only one or two essays devoted to Black short story writers. We were hoping to represent all major ethnic voices in the contemporary American short story.

We were fortunate in receiving many fine essays that contributed to our understanding of the contemporary American short story, and we wish that we could have used more of them than we were able to publish here. In many cases, there were multiple submissions on the same writers, and we had to seek the good advice of readers to assist us in choosing the ones we would include. The response to our call for papers was heartening. In itself, that response is a testimony to the vitality of interest in the contemporary American short story.

LL
CWM

Flannery O'Connor's Consecration of the End

RICHARD GIANNONE

> In suffering is concealed . . . the world's power of ascension.
> Pierre Teilhard de Chardin

Flannery O'Connor has a knack for imbedding self-disclosure in her appreciations of other writers. Lofty pronouncements about the artist's job revolt her, so her comments, whether made in spontaneous letters or prepared talks, are always informal and grounded in a problem that she is tackling in her own work at the moment. There is an unpublished lecture of 1956, tucked in an unmarked folder among her literary remains, that is more than usually revealing about O'Connor's practice. The pertinent section holds no new evidence of O'Connor's thinking, but it does crystallize her view of artistic integrity and intensify its implications for her own work by offering a way into her final effort.

The remarks concern Joyce. O'Connor makes them to illustrate to her audience that the artist must present the truth as she or he sees it first-hand in the concrete, human particulars. "At the end of 'Portrait of the Artist as a Young Man' Joyce has Stephen Dedalus say that he intends to go out and 'forge in the smithy of my soul the uncreated conscience of my race,' but in the next book," O'Connor observes, "that's not what we find him doing." Rather, "we find him meeting Mr. Leopold Bloom," she adds, "and instead of creating a new pattern, discovering a very ancient one."[1]

With hindsight we can see that O'Connor's sympathy for Stephen's backward progress derives from the lesson shaping her development. She too must submit pretension to experience. When she begins to write, Eliot's poetry hovers as her ideal of craft infused with knowledgeable witness to Christian faith. Early drafts of *Wise Blood* (1952), her first novel, depict a youthful yet depleted Southern Tiresias foresuffering all as he roams the Tennessee byways of the waste land. Again, "The Geranium" (*Accent*, 1946), as Sally Fitzgerald so well argues, uses "Gerontion" to portray the old hero's isolation.[2] But whatever fascinates O'Connor about the Southern conscience forged in the workshop of high modernism becomes quickly transformed by the act of writing hammered on the habit of feeling. Mr. Leopold Bloom, emissary of the everyday, takes the form of good American country people to check O'Connor-Dedalus' grand scheme.

We find O'Connor grappling with Hazel Motes, a nihilist Protestant saint, and with Francis Marion Tarwater, a teenage murderer called to be a prophet. Through the trials of these and many other footsore and violated wanderers, O'Connor, like Stephen, discovers an old pattern instead of making a new one. Their tracks through rural Tennessee and Georgia, in fact, chart an older route than does the quest of Homer's pilgrim. The more truthfully O'Connor as storyteller renders what she sees and not what she thinks she ought to see, the closer she approaches the most ancient pattern of all—the biblical cycle of guilt and transcendence.

"The Geranium" provides a shortcut to O'Connor's discovery of what the heart is and what it feels. It is her first published story and becomes the title-story of her Iowa M.F.A. thesis (1947); and since the publication of *The Complete Stories of Flannery O'Connor* (1971), readers have known that her first story is the basis of her last, entitled "Judgement Day," which concludes her posthumous volume *Everything That Rises Must Converge* (1965). The neat parallel between the beginning and the end of O'Connor's career has intermediate ties. One researcher has explained the relation of "Exile in the East," an uncollected story, to these pivotal stories.[3] There is a still finer link. Absorbed by the need to get this material just right, O'Connor revised "Exile in the East" before sending it as "Judgement Day" to her publisher within four weeks of her death. If we pause to consider the signal features of the three preliminary versions, and then examine the distinctive moral force of the last draft, we can appreciate the odyssey that O'Connor undertakes.

At the outset I should add a word about my approach to O'Connor's development. Though archival details can pinpoint changes, they of course cannot unravel the creative process effecting the transformation. Nor do I intend to reduce O'Connor's masterly late story to the harmless irrelevance of place in her canon. "Judgement Day" has a richness gained from a lifelong involvement with a single predicament, that of a dying man's trials. As O'Connor goes beyond influence and styles to feel through the romance and the anguish of his exclusion, she comes to perceive its possible contribution to the saving plan of God.

Only in the final retelling of the old man's plight does his hardship yield dignity, and that grace comes about through a reversal of our usual way of thinking about the pain of estrangement and the responsibility of the hostile world. Being cut off can bring one to know what one owes the world; and, in paying such an unexpected debt, the outcast can release the energy of love that raises the rejecting world. Within personal loss and recovery O'Connor finds a new order of creation. The pattern beneath all patterns for her turns out to be a death and a resurrection. In the mature unfolding of O'Connor's imagination, the duty to suffer amounts to the devoir to redemption. The mysterious power of guilt to mediate this conversion in "Judgement Day" is the subject of this essay.

II

The basic situation of all the versions of the story is simple. A disabled old man lives outside his native Georgia in New York City with his daughter and son-in-law. "The Geranium" names the displaced widower Old Dudley and finds him stuck sharing a bedroom with an indifferent sixteen-year-old grandson in a cramped walkup apartment on the sixth floor. The tenement and its altitude frighten the countryman. Concrete separates him from solid earth, and the dog run of a hallway looms as an extension of the cavernous subway that coils to platforms of perilous heights. But Old Dudley's acrophobia is geographical: up north he can topple to death, whereas down south he stands on safe ground. Memories gauge the distance between mortal danger and secure life. He recalls Coa County's slow, red river, which he fished with Rabie, his black friend, every Wednesday, and the quail and oppossum that they hunted together. The river and woods have shriveled into a grimy urban alley, which he can only fish and hunt from his sixth floor window with his eyes and regrets.

Old Dudley lives in New York by rural southern values. When a black man rents the adjacent apartment, the old Southerner assumes that the new neighbor will know a stream and a place where they can hunt. He trusts blacks but learns that northern blacks are as cold as northern whites. Though he expresses a dislike for "Yankee niggers" with their airs, Old Dudley comes to need the black neighbor to help him back to his daughter's flat when he becomes weak in the hall while playing hunter. He needs the black New Yorker just as back home he needed Rabie to help him feel that he was a vigorous outdoorsman.

O'Connor's treatment of the relations between white and black in "The Geranium" is not political. Her interest is spiritual. The old man's ambivalent view of blacks—affection mingled with condescension—results from a deeper ambiguity. He resents his infirmity, his aging, his dependency, and his confinement; and he fights against these inevitabilities by blaming the city and its inhabitants for his affliction. He once lived in a "good place," he rationalizes after the black man lends him a hand; and now he is stranded in a bad place where a black person can presume to call him "old-timer." Prejudice masks his fear of death. To deny the signs of old age, Old Dudley shifts the onus onto the black man.

Though "The Geranium" leaves no doubt in the reader's mind that O'Connor agrees with Old Dudley's disgust for the hellish New York, she is also careful to shade his anger with culpability. He chooses to come north. When the prospect of being sick and alone in Georgia frightens him, he sees the New York home of his daughter as a refuge. An endearing egoism supports his decision. New York, he reasons, is bigger than Atlanta and therefore the right size to welcome him. "It was an important place and it had room for him!"[4]

The idea that there is no place for him is intolerable. When New York betrays his expectation, he indicts the city and recognizes Coa County as home. As reproach for New York covers his fear of approaching death, so pride erases the memory that he decided to come and blinds him to whatever care his daughter provides. He also makes her responsible for his natural condition. She is at fault for being so taken up with filial duty that she coerced him to leave home.

O'Connor, as young as twenty-two, appreciates so well the attachment to roots that she grasps the emotional dodges expressing it. The lot of advanced years brings her to explore without sentimentality the last hope to belong and the dislocation of its fulfillment by death. Old Dudley wants power in his decrepitude and mistakes inner shambles for outer decay. The tenderness of his condition comes to us through the objective correlative of the potted geranium. Every day from his window the old man watches the pink flower (not the vivid kind that Georgia soil bears) which a neighbor puts out for air between 10:30 a.m. and 5:30 p.m. The plant reflects his crocked life in foreign soil. Framed by the window he composes a portrait of an infirm and all to human stray, stuck yet stuck-up. An old dud sits forlorn staring at a pink geranium that he does not think much of. Here is youthful O'Connor's first protagonist, an old man in a sterile place.

Old Dudley is the Nestor of O'Connor-Dedalus' adventure. He is neither Homer's retired warrior who enjoys tranquility in the bosom of his daughters' family nor Joyce's bigoted Mr. Deasy who dispenses sententious wisdom about the past—Old Dudley, in short, is neither the flower nor the daisy weed of old age. O'Connor's Nestor is an ordinary geranium, which manages to remain alive in the humus between epic romance and its parody. That subsoil is the province of guilt and yearning in which O'Connor enacts her spiritual comedies.

On the day of the story, Old Dudley waits tearfully for the geranium. The plant eventually appears to him in the alley below, shattered, its roots exposed to the killing air. Beneath the sympathy for her Nestor's loneliness, O'Connor uncovers the source of alienation that lies deeper than locale. We see in the human soulscape the roots of pride, the origin of estrangement to which all of O'Connor's subsequent fiction returns. Pride can be transcended, and there is a city of hope beyond the city of exile; but these possibilities lie in the future of O'Connor's search.

To find a way out of the old man's lostness, O'Connor first goes deeper into his deracination. The very title of the next version, "Exile in the East," indicates that the hero's banishment from home becomes the central issue. The plain sign of the geranium gives way to nuanced differences between the congenial ways in Georgia and the harshness of New York. To stress the dispiriting effect of the North, O'Connor adds several details to the hero's face. The red and purple spots on his face change into a sickly yellow with brown blotches. He has a new name, Franklyn R. T. Tanner, to go with his new aspect. And the daughter acquires a big square face (but not a name) to match the air of "righteous exhaustion" that comes with putting up with her father. Despite the importance of her care for Old Tanner, the daughter has no impact on the events of the story. She, with her duty-proud weariness, remains a function of the hero's sadness, a dejection which overshadows all of his connections except that with his recollected Georgia. "Exile in the East" adds a sociological dimension to the drama of "The Geranium" without altering the old man's destiny. Both end with the dying hero alone and alive at memory's gateway.

"Getting Home," the next version, does modify his fate. The common southern phrase that O'Connor uses for the title foretells her ease with the material and the hero's basis of comfort with life in the story. "Getting Home" makes the place of rest at the journey's end more prominent than exile. The hero longs for a home burial. Perhaps to suggest the ultimate propriety of what might seem a chauvinistic ranting to a Yankee daughter, O'Connor renames the hero F. T. Fairlee. Fairness requires that Old Fairlee be put to rest back home. Getting home is a spiritual urgency. If it means being cut up alive and thrown to the dogs, the price is worth paying for the peace of knowing that his body will be in native dirt. Rest means restoration; and getting home to rest is more than a manner of speaking, since the old hero dies in this version.

His death prompts O'Connor to develop the character of the hero's daughter. Getting the old man home acquires an importance for her too. In fact, from the manuscripts we can see that the hero's death opens a double drama in the story as the crisis of Old Fairlee's death becomes the crisis of his daughter's life. Her reluctance to bother with a trip south to bury her father is a given in her urbanized character; but as O'Connor works on the story, she approaches the daughter's resistance in different ways. We hear the daughter argue with her Yankee husband to defend the cranky old man's presence in their apartment; and in the course of taking his side, she manages to express a limited understanding of the old Georgian's desire to get home.

The typescript of "Getting Home" with the most extensive handwritten revisions in the O'Connor archives at Georgia College has two endings. Taken together, they epitomize the moral expansion that results from O'Connor's careful remodeling of her Nestor episode. Both endings shift the narrative focus from the earlier concern for the old man to a new interest in his daughter. The first ending is typed as part of the manuscript, and it shows the woman achieving a matter-of-fact victory over her insensitive husband. The final paragraph runs:

> She and her husband had an extended argument over the telephone about where he should be buried. He said here. She said at home. And she won. She wanted to rest at night, and if she didn't follow his instructions to the letter, he was just the kind, she said, who would haunt her the rest of her life.[5]

In seeing F. T. Fairlee to his Georgia grave in "Getting Home," O'Connor momentarily reflects on the way in which the end of his life marks a decisive turn in the life of a surviving relative.

The adjustment seems more to quicken O'Connor's mind than to satisfy the requirements of form. The new direction, once opened, widens the horizon of O'Connor's imagination. She deletes by hand the paragraph quoted above; and she writes in the following ending for "Getting Home":

> She buried him in N.Y.C. but after she had done it, she could not sleep at night, so she had him dug up and shipped the body to Corinth. And now she rests well at night, which at her time of life is essential.[6]

The changes are pure O'Connor. Ghosts are instructive for her, so she dispenses with the petty spat with the daughter's husband in favor of the fierce grappling with a revenging spirit. It does not matter that self-interest calls the daughter to undo the hasty burial. What counts is Old Fairlee's getting home. He gets home, and home gets the name Corinth, which is the right name for the Georgia place where things are set true with God. The daughter gets to sleep at night. O'Connor, for her part, gets her story: she lines out the title "Getting Home" and in the large rheumatic scrawl of her terminal illness writes the words "Judgement Day" across the top of the title page. And the reader gets a masterpiece.

III

O'Connor in the end writes about her displaced Southerner from an inwardness that unlocks his depths. She keeps the essential drama behind his brows by setting the story abstemiously. "Judgement Day" embraces no more of the physical world than a seriously impaired stroke victim can handle. The time is a winter morning in New York; the locale, the short distance from the old man's chair to the staircase where he dies. But a few hours are sufficient for the Day of the Lord to dawn in the life of T. C. Tanner, and several yards are expanse enough in O'Connor's austere world for him to reach his destiny. In making his way to the banister, Old Tanner gets home by forging his way to God.

The depth that O'Connor finds within the here and now lies in the meaning that ordinary things hold for the aged man. Without restricting her wisdom to his perception, and without imposing her understanding on his bafflement, O'Connor reveals the invisible through the interplay of the hero's consciousness and his circumstance. His failing vision, his failed health, the falling snow, his waiting for God are the restrictions that shape "Judgement Day." O'Connor seats Tanner at his window to look at the brick wall that sinks into a fetid alley, and she stirs his inner vision to gaze into the past that led him to the grim present and that also will lead him all the way back to the future in Corinth. Then she has him hobble to his death. Tanner's recollecting and stumbling constitute the last trial of his life.

The final act of Tanner's mind and body dramatizes the intense state of heart that his infirmity can barely make known. Above all, he feels that his life is in danger. The peril is neither dying nor death. Rather, he has a holy fear of being buried in a profane place. He wants to rest in earth set aside for the service of God. Corinth by name and personal history is consecrated to carry out the divine plan, whereas New York is ordained for the use of cats and garbage. A proper burial to him is more than a pious act. Consecrated ground is the necessary material provision for the world that Tanner believes will come, and he wants to be ready for it. His daughter's indifference to his burial instructions amounts to an opposition to the approaching reign of God and arouses a thundering warning from the frail old bear. "Bury me here and burn in hell!"[7] The fear and trembling of his body communicate the terrible judgment that his thin voice hardly enunciates.

The daughter may dismiss hell as "a lot of hardshell Baptist hooey" (p. 248), but Tanner sees damnation as a hard reality that the soft-minded may deny but will have to confront. The more she recommends the distractions of TV to mollify this morbid stuff" (p. 258) that grips her father's mind, the more vividly do death and hell and judgment preoccupy him. Her refusing to feel the dire changes that are apparent in her father's body and spirit makes him more defensive about the truths that he lives by. This Nestor speaks with apocalyptic conviction. " 'The Judgement is coming,' he muttered. 'The sheep'll be separated from the goats. Them that kept their promises from them that didn't' " (p. 258).

Fear of not being in God's favor is not a last-minute desire to make amends. It has been with Tanner from childhood. Over the years, the fear of God has humanized Tanner by checking his strong instinct to seize his gun or knife to settle accounts with those who threaten him. Fear of divine retribution weakens his violence by making him feel the responsibility incurred by his actions. During his final, exilic days in New York, fear becomes the basis for a more positive relation to God. Dread of never getting back to Corinth makes Tanner value home and hometown cronies as part of the divine scheme; and deprived of his cherished vitality and autonomy, he recognizes his utter dependence on God. Even his anxiety over his daughter's trustworthiness turns his heart to God. He realizes that the divine readiness to help those in need, as he now is, outbalances everything else. Fear of God, then, is negative in word only. Tanner's fear contains his confident love of God, who is recognized and loved because Tanner feels the total difference between his helplessness and guilt and God's absolute justice.

O'Connor's theology of fear underlies the old man's preparation for the end of the days. As his final reflections unfold, the combative old hero's lifelong fear of God transforms into a loving reverence for God. This subtle change of heart is the crowning variation on O'Connor's repeated inquiry into conversion. When young and prone to violence, Tanner obeys and loves God out of fear; when old and courageous, he fears God out of love.

Two waves of memory enact Tanner's conversion; both center upon his departure from Georgia and his friendship with Coleman, whom he left behind. After he overhears his daughter conceding to her husband's insistence that Tanner be buried in New York, Tanner puts up his emotional dukes to fight for his dignity and tries to deny that he wanted to come to New York in the first place. Only after the land on which he and Coleman squat is sold to the black Doctor Foley does Tanner agree to his daughter's demand that he come north. Foley's terms encroach on Tanner's self-esteem. To stay on the property, Tanner must run his still for Foley. Rather than work for the uppity black doctor, Tanner heads north. Racism props up his tottering honor. As pride drives him from Corinth, humiliation sends his thoughts back in contrition. Had he known that he would be stuck "in this no-place" because of his child's treachery, he "would have been a nigger's white nigger any day" (p. 257).

Tanner has another reason to stand grateful before a black person. For thirty years he shares a life with Coleman, a black man. Though they live as partners in poverty in a shack on the forsaken property, Tanner's pride requires him to believe that his wit gives him the upper hand with Coleman. After all, Tanner is "known to have a way with niggers" (p. 252). He does have a way with Coleman, but his talent has nothing to do with his keen mind or the very sharp penknife that he keeps. The two men need each other. Both are uprooted and settle on a land not their own; both have an instinct for violence that holds the other's brute force in respectful control. Because the penknife of each could easily be directed by some intruding intelligence into the other's gut, the threat keeps both vulnerable. Black and white bruiser can grin in a direct, even tender, recognition of the other's radical similarity. After thirty years Tanner can still not decipher his initial sensation on meeting Coleman. He has only a vague perception of seeing "a negative image of himself, as if clownishness and captivity had been their common lot" (p. 255). The dimness of Tanner's vision, however, is clear enough for the reader, who can see in the image a love born of respect and need and apprehension that both black and white live by in their exclusion.

Incarceration in strange New York sensitizes Tanner to feel what it is like to be marked to suffer the evil of others. Burial in New York means that Tanner, in the words that he would know from the famous fifty-third chapter of Isaiah, will be the one "who has borne our griefs and carried our sorrow" (53:4). By oppression "he was taken away" and "cut off out of the land of the living," and now Tanner must contemplate the ignominy of his daughter's making "his grave with the wicked" (Isaiah 53:8-9). Tanner bears at the end of his life the burden that Coleman shoulders from birth. By virtue of being black and regarded as disgraced, Coleman must endure the accumulated injustices of the whole community. The common lot of clown and captive is that of the scapegoat, which biblical reflection exalts to the calling of the suffering servant.

The approach of Judgment Day hallows their bond. When they first meet, Coleman needs Tanner for a job, but at the end Tanner needs Coleman for the gathering of the crosses. Coleman becomes the minister of the last days. Like a lost child, Tanner has a note pinned in his pocket to an anonymous messenger: "IF FOUND ·DEAD SHIP EXPRESS COLLECT TO COLEMAN PARRUM, CORINTH, GEORGIA" (p. 246). Coleman will pay for the body. Below this order Tanner writes his last will and testament.

COLEMAN SELL MY BELONGINGS AND PAY THE FREIGHT ON ME & THE UNDERTAKER. ANYTHING LEFT OVER YOU CAN KEEP. YOURS TRULY T. C. TANNER. P.S. STAY WHERE YOU ARE. DON'T LET THEM TALK YOU INTO COMING UP HERE. ITS NO KIND OF PLACE. (p. 246)

Tanner's advice to his fellow Corinthian acquires its full meaning in light of the hero's remembering a recent experience with another black person, this one an actor who rents the nextdoor apartment. Tanner tries to befriend the new neighbor. "Preacher" (p. 262), he calls the actor and then proceeds to ask if the man knows of a pond nearby. Tanner assumes that the black man fishes and that he witnesses for God, flattering assumptions that he does not make about his white son-in-law. The slick actor, however, misconstrues "Preacher" to be a racist slur; and he responds by cursing the old codger and slamming the "red-neck son-of-a-bitch peckerwood old bastard" (p. 263) through the apartment door. Before the actor attacks the old man, he blasphemes God. "I don't believe that crap. There ain't no Jesus and there ain't no God" (p. 263).

The black New Yorker's "unfathomable dead-cold rage" (p. 262) tells us that he is settling older scores than that of being addressed as a preacher. To get rid of his historical rage for being the object of oppression, the black man displaces his wrath onto Tanner. The tanning the old man receives far outweighs the affront of his country greeting. The injury is severe. Tanner's thick tongue, which stays frozen for days, would indicate that the battered man sustains a cerebral accident. The disparity between his offense and punishment is the spiritual portion of his trauma that pays for the abuses of the entire white race at the hand of the angry black man. Tanner's affliction reenacts the trouncing experienced by those whom Isaiah sees as "wounded for our transgressions" (53:5).

The actor's rough treatment also pummels Tanner's heart. Now more than ever he must make his daughter understand his need for Corinth. After wringing a promise from her that she will ship him home, "he slept peacefully" (p. 264). Rest brings a dream, and the dream buoys him up. An imagined voyage takes him from death-in-life in New York to life-in-death in Georgia. In the dream a pine box carries him home. The cold morning air of Corinth inspires him through the cracks in the coffin. He sees Coleman and hears Hooten, the stationmaster, grumble about the latest of Tanner's "tricks." When they are about to pry open the lid, the clown of captivity springs like Lazarus from the tomb. " 'Judgement Day! Judgement Day!' he cried. 'Don't you two fools know it's Judgement Day!' " (p. 265)

Folly is one way of reaching the End. The wise person discerns the ways of God with clarity and can meet judgment with confidence. The fool, however, who is usually hot-tempered (Proverbs 14:17) and quarrelsome (Proverbs 20:3), comes by a different route; and though wisdom surpasses folly, the fool has a chance. The fool learns the hard way. The rod of discipline (Proverbs 10:13) must force the fool into God's plan. Tanner's way is the fool's way. Tanner's impulse is to reject God's law and harm others, but a fear of hell keeps him obedient. "The fear of the Lord,"we read in Proverbs (1:7), "is the beginning of knowledge." In the end Tanner's godly fear brings him home where he belongs, and he arrives in the dream as the fool of the apocalypse who heralds the new day.

The simple movement of the dream holds the ancient pattern that O'Connor discovers in everyday life. Tanner travels down south and rises up to celebrate a reunion. Grief ends in joy. The twofold pattern holds a momentous design. Descent and reascent, dejection followed by sudden exaltation, provide a rough sketch of a death and resurrection.

The ending of "Judgement Day" actualizes the movement of falling and rising in both the body and spirit of Tanner. From the highpoint of the dream there is a steady letdown in the hero's confidence that he will get home. He senses the worthlessness of his daughter's promise and decides to get there on his own. This decision leads first to self-reproach and then to reconciliation. "He felt guilty" (p. 265) about leaving his daughter after being such a nuisance. "I'm sorry if I've give you a lot of trouble getting sick" (p. 266). Contrition speaks to gentleness. "I wouldn't have you any other place" (p. 266), the daughter confesses. Tender amends yield to dread when Tanner feels the difficulty of walking out so that he can get home. When his body betrays him, he sinks into helplessness. "A sensation of terror and defeat swept over him" (p. 267). He lumbers six feet beyond the apartment door before he collapses and is pitched upsidedown on the flight of dark steps.

Downcast as he is, Tanner must fall still further in order to get home. When the black actor finds the stricken man, he finishes the old man off by shoving his head and arms between the spokes of the banister. Tanner dies with his feet dangling over the stairwell like "a man in the stocks" (p. 269). With a ritual gesture of good riddance to an old plague, the black man contemptuously pulls Tanner's hat over his head. Tanner hangs from the spokes a cursed man. He must suffer not only the pangs of death but also the slings and arrows of the actor's massive, impersonal fury. The responsibility for the additional pain falls on the black man who incurs the very racist guilt that he tries to expel by heaping it on Tanner. The violence, however, serves the higher purpose that the old man tries to meet by getting home. Rebuke humbles the prideful old man. Tanner at the end becomes the man of sorrows who Isaiah says must bear "the sin of many" (53:12).

The suffering servant embodies O'Connor's fullest recognition of human worth as achieved through the ordinary pattern of falling and rising. The trials heaped on the servant, in both Scripture and O'Connor's art, plunge the servant into agony; but loving acceptance of the yoke exalts the servant. Surrender usually comes quietly, and that is how Tanner submits to divine providence. "The Lord is my shepherd," he mutters as he wobbles toward the sofa. "I shall not want" (p. 267). The twenty-third psalm gathers together the various references to service in a story to underscore their ultimate importance.

Moreover, the way in which Psalm 23 celebrates dependence and sacrifice parallels the technique of "Judgement Day." In the decline of life the psalmist looks back over the past to take heart in Yahweh's help through daily vicissitudes. That guidance assures the psalmist that Yahweh will be present for the final trials of the world. Two images portray divine help. Yahweh is a caring shepherd and a generous host. The shepherd leads the flock through an arid desert and a dark valley to find green pastures; and the host provides shelter at the journey's end, where he festively anoints the wanderer's head with oil. The frank confession of trust in Psalm 23 describes O'Connor's manner in "Judgement Day." A simple habit of mind—recollection transposed into anticipation—conveys the faith evolved from commonplace experience.

The arduous path through the valley of the shadow of death passes into the unlighted corridor of the New York building, through its alley, and down to Corinth. The steps on which Tanner stumbles in his effort to negotiate a precipitous turn in the path serve as a bridge, like Jacob's ladder, from one world to the next. Tanner can even feel a way opening up for him. Before the actor pushes him, Tanner lifts his hand, "as light as a breath," to beg for help and, perhaps, to wave good-bye. The neighbor's scorn does not dismay him. He does not want. Everything about the heavy man rises. He utters his last words "in his jauntiest voice." "I'm on my way home!" (p. 269)

The story does not end in otherworldly triumph or in melodramatic death. O'Connor is after a hard reality. She follows Tanner's passage after death to its thisworldly effect on his daughter, whose domestic preoccupations are the actuality in which she prepares for judgment. O'Connor lays down no rules, devises no theological categories for the task. Common duty sets the terms: the daughter is obliged to bury her father in Georgia. Her initial response is to dispose of his body to suit her convenience, but conscience makes her worry about her betrayal. When she disinters the body for reburial at home, she too makes a descent into guilt; and she reascends by doing right by her father. The last sentence of the story reads: "Now she rests well at night and her good looks have mostly returned." O'Connor allows the eschatological aura to arise out of the poetic representation of the pattern of fall and ascent. The daughter, who has been a generous hostess, becomes the caring shepherd.

The smooth ending makes "Judgement Day" an anomaly in O'Connor's work; but that singularity, arrived at over some twenty years of attention, indicates where the heart of the story and her total effort lies. Love and transcendence are O'Connor's true subject. The physical maiming and senseless killing and spiteful holocaust for which she is known are displays of how far humanity has strayed from God's will. The shock of violence in each story serves to remand the sinner back into the world of guilt and sorrow from which he or she tries to escape. All the deaths in O'Connor's fiction exhibit the positive dimensions of action and suffering. "Judgement Day" shows the benefit of acting to assuage suffering. With the return of the daughter's ability to sleep and good looks, the insoluble tangle of refusal and submission untangles. Harmony prevails, and peace is the gift of God that O'Connor gives as a foretaste of glory. The repose concluding "Judgement Day" corresponds to a special moment in O'Connor's letters. "That's the sweetest thing I ever heard, now ain't it," she reassures a friend about her resting comfortably seven weeks before her death. "Peaceful days & nights. My."[8]

"Judgement Day" does not pretend to dramatize the full mystery of redemptive peace. Rather it shows how the new dispensation comes to each of us personally when the divine act of dying and rising reaches us through small acts of love. The legacy of destitute Tanner is to bring his daughter out of her guilt to shepherd his transition from death to life. Getting home is arriving at the dwelling of the Lord (Psalm 23:6). The world of sin and death, which dominates O'Connor's art, leads to the order of resurrection, which "Judgement Day" announces.

O'Connor prepares her characters for the elevation to a richer life by bringing them to the bedrock of experience: the awareness of limitation. This state of want is a sign that the last days have begun. Such poverty has nothing to do with money. It has rather to do with mystery, and it is the central mystery of our position on earth as debtors to God in relation to one another. The poor in spirit can recognize their reliance on the divine and be amazed by the gracious result of their admission. With midwinter in his heart and shadows closing around him Tanner gives thanks.

O'Connor writes from a similar position. "I work from such a basis of poverty that everything I do is a miracle to me," she says.[9] The act of perceiving fulfillment in privation comes to the reader through the poetry of O'Connor's ideas about deliverance, of which the last story of her last book is the epitome. "Judgement Day" comprises her *Nunc Dimittis,* a gathering up of Flannery O'Connor's total experience of life with one final testament of acceptance.

NOTES

I am grateful to Nancy Davis and the staff of the Russell Library at Georgia College for their hospitality while I was working in The Flannery O'Connor Collection. A grant from the Mellon Faculty Development Fund at Fordham made the trip possible; and the unpublished material cited in the essay is quoted with the permission of Robert Giroux, Flannery O'Connor's literary executor. I thank the Mellon Foundation and Mr. Giroux for their generosity.

[1] From an unpublished lecture which O'Connor gave to the AAUW in Lansing, Michigan, in 1956. The passage is on page 6 of the manuscript, which is in an unmarked folder in the O'Connor Collection.

[2] Sally Fitzgerald, "The Owl and the Nightingale," *The Flannery O'Connor Bulletin,* 13 (Autumn 1984), 44-58.

[3] Jan Nordby Gretlund, "Flannery O'Connor's 'An Exile in the East': An Introduction," *The South Carolina Review,* 2 (November 1978), 3-11. The entire text of "Exile in the East" is published right after Mr. Gretlund's essay (12-21).

[4] *The Complete Stories* (New York: Farrar, Straus and Giroux, 1971), p. 4.

[5] From an unpublished manuscript in Folder 194d. of the O'Connor Collection, p. 27.

[6] Unpublished manuscript.

[7] *Everything That Rises Must Converge* (1965; New York: Farrar, Straus and Giroux—Noonday Press, 1968), p. 248. Hereafter pages are cited within the body of the text.

[8] Flannery O'Connor, *The Habit of Being,* ed. Sally Fitzgerald (New York: Farrar, Straus and Giroux, 1979), p. 583.

[9] *Ibid.,* p. 127.

From "The Geranium" to "Judgement Day": Retribution in the Fiction of Flannery O'Connor

JOHN L. DARRETTA

Flannery O'Connor's first story, "The Geranium," introduces the predominant concern of her life's work—the concept of retribution. Her final story, "Judgement Day," reveals that, within the twenty-year span of her writing career, O'Connor's idea of retribution had expanded. Her original rendering of the concept was a personal and familial one; her final concept shows an interest that is eschatological. Retribution expresses O'Connor's interest as a writer; it also defines the contour of her achievement as artist. The changes in the theme and form of retribution reveal just how O'Connor kept doing things over and over until they not only came out but came out right.

Both "The Geranium" and "Judgement Day" are narratives about proud old men who become alienated by alienating others. In "The Geranium," Old Dudley's retributive experience is a personal one. His desire to return to his Southern home and to escape from the stifling atmosphere of the East is never satisfied. Because Old Dudley refuses to be helped up the stairs by a black man, he abandons his attempt to retrieve a potted geranium that has fallen from the window ledge into the back alley. The uprooted geranium parallels the final isolation in which Dudley remains. In the reworking of the story—which becomes a new story—"Judgement Day," Tanner (the metamorphosis of Dudley) receives a harsher retribution. His desire to return "home" is not only a longing to return South but a movement toward what O'Connor has called the "true country."[1] In the end, Tanner, who is racked between the rungs of a banister like a captive slave, is violently dispatched from this world to the "eternal world." O'Connor's last story reveals that her concept of retribution has in fact been reinforced and deepened.

In her last collection of stories, *Everything That Rises Must Converge,* O'Connor's moral view seems steadily to rise from the familial and the personal to the eschatological. In rising, the perception cuts through the rural world of Southern manners that doubles for narrowness of egocentricity, to the edge of final mystery, a world beyond where the platitudes and selfishness by which man lives are corrected in love. From the idea of Teilhard de Chardin, that by sheer force of consciousness man will advance his own humanity, in Christ, O'Connor realized a theological poetry with which to extend her sense of retribution, of justice without revenge, of on-going love checking man's dark ways. That O'Connor's sense of retribution persists through the other changes in her work notifies the reader of its centrality.

I

Flannery O'Connor's "The Geranium" had its initial printing the summer of 1946 in *Accent*.[2] The theme of the story dramatizes a personal alienation. The central character, Old Dudley, has been uprooted from the earth of his Southern region and transplanted into the polluted environment of the big city, New York. His preoccupation lies in retrieving the fallen geranium: "It was at the bottom of the alley with its roots in the air" (p. 14). Dudley does not save the geranium which is reminiscent of the "geranium at home" and his own existential condition.

Those who know O'Connor's later work expect an eschatological dimension. "The Geranium" is important, because it denies such expectations. In this story, the sense of alienation is deeply personal but not eschatological. O'Connor's narrative is about the empty existence of a bitter old man. In fact, O'Connor's name for this character is significant: he is an "old dud," an empty failure, a valueless, worthless thinker. He is not worthless as a person, but he is worthless when he thinks.

The controlling symbol of the story is the geranium. The plant is closely related to the experience of Old Dudley himself. He feels that he has been removed from the idyllic past of Southern living where a man could fish and hunt and treat a black man like a "nigger." The geranium, which is potted rather than solidly rooted in the earth, images Old Dudley as *déraciné*. Placed in a precarious position on the window ledge, it is an unhealthy plant. To Old Dudley, the geranium is like "the Grisby boy at home who had polio and had to be wheeled out every morning and left in the sun to blink" (p. 3). In the rural South, the geranium would have been thriving "in the ground," and it would have been "worth looking at" (p. 3).

Old Dudley wishes that he had never been transplanted. He regrets the moment that he had given in and said that he had wanted to go to New York. In the city, Dudley finds himself trapped and isolated, like the geranium, in the brick apartment house where he lived with his daughter and her family:

> Inside you could go up and you could go down and there were just halls that reminded you of tape measures strung out with a door every inch. . . . he'd look out the door and there they stretched like dog runs. The streets were the same way. He wondered where he'd be if he walked to the end of one of them. One night he dreamed he did and ended at the end of the building—nowhere. (p. 6)

The tenants of the urban apartment house live by one rule: Mind your own business (p. 261). When Dudley makes a trip down the hallway, he is met with a cold reception:

> He looked over the banisters and saw it was a woman—a fat woman with an apron on. From the top she looked kind er like Mrs. Benson at home. He wondered if she would speak to him. When they were four steps from each other, he darted a glance at her but she wasn't looking at him. When there were no steps between them, his eyes fluttered up for an instant and she was looking at him cold in the face. Then she was past him. She hadn't said a word. He felt heavy in his stomach. (p. 10)

When Dudley looks across the alley to inquire about what has happened to the missing geranium, the man leaning on the opposite windowsill abruptly replies:

"I seen you before. . . . I seen you settin' in that old chair every day, starin' out the window, looking in my apartment. What I do in my apartment is my business, see? I don't like people looking at what I do." (p. 14)

None of the apartment dwellers is as submissive or respectful to Dudley as was Rabie, his black "friend" in the South.

Old Dudley pines to return to the South and to escape from what he sees as the strange, artificial reality of the big city. After a harrowing experience on the platform of an "El," his daughter tries to comfort him: " 'Come on,' she said, 'you'll feel better when we get home' " (p. 7). Dudley questions her concept of "home," when he replies, "Home?" To Dudley, home is the old, rural South:

The apartment was too tight. There was no place to be where there wasn't somebody else. The kitchen opened into the bathroom and the bathroom opened into everything else and you were always where you started from. At home there was upstairs and the basement and the river and downtown. . . . (p. 7)

The only neighbor who is remotely amicable and helpful to Dudley is a black man, but Dudley cannot accept his kindness. Whereas Dudley dominated the submissive "nigger," Rabie, the urban black man dominates Dudley. This reversal of roles is not tolerable to the old man. He tells his daughter:

"You ain't been raised to live tight with niggers that think they're just as good as you, and you think I'd go messin' around with one er that kind! If you think I want anything to do with them, you're crazy." . . . He knew Yankees let niggers in their front doors and let them set on their sofas but he didn't know his own daughter that was raised proper would stay next door to them—and then think he didn't have no more sense than to want to mix with them. Him! (p. 9)

On a trip down the stairs, Dudley relives an old hunting experience and points an imaginery gun. Unexpectedly, he is sighted by the black man, who, out of human concern, helps Old Dudley up the stairs. The man's actions humiliate Dudley. Ironically, when human connections become possible, Dudley intensifies his isolation by refusing to have anything to do with "niggers." This cold treatment of others is reflected on Dudley, who feels separated from his daughter, her family, the tenants of the apartment house and the population of the city. He does not realize that his own condition contains the same alienation that he perpetrates.

After the geranium has fallen from the window ledge to the alley below, Dudley abandons a trip back down the stairs to save the sickly plant. In order to avoid risking another meeting with the black man, he opts for minding his own business. He leaves the plant to die. To be assisted by a black man has proven too personally degrading for him:

The steps dropped down like a deep wound in the floor. They opened up through a gap like a cavern and went down and down. And he had gone up them a little behind the nigger. And the nigger had pulled him up on his feet and kept his arm in his and gone up the steps with him and said he hunted deer, "old-timer," and seen him holding a gun that wasn't there and sitting on the steps like a child. He had shiny tan shoes and he was trying not to laugh and the whole business was laughing. There'd probably be niggers with black flecks in their socks on every step, pulling down their mouths so as not to laugh. The steps dropped down and down. He wouldn't go down and have niggers pattin' him on the back. He went back to the room and the window and looked down at the geranium. (p. 14).

In this Dantesque vision, the retributive experience of having to exchange roles with a black man leaves Dudley in the arid atmosphere of his own making; he is left like the geranium with "it's roots in the air."

II

Flannery O'Connor reworked the material of "The Geranium," and instead of exhausting her vision she deepened it. Here are her words on how she works:

I'm afraid it is possible to exhaust your material. What you exhaust are those things that you are capable of bringing alive. I mean if you've done it once, you don't want to do the same thing over again. The longer you write the more conscious you are of what you can and cannot make live. What you have to do is try to deepen your pentration of those things.[3]

The result of such deepened penetration was "Judgement Day."

On August 3, 1964, Flannery O'Connor died. Her last work was the final revision of "The Geranium" into "Judgement Day." It appeared as the concluding story in *Everything That Rises Must Converge,* which was published posthumously in 1965. In a letter dated June 27, 1964, she had written:

Will you look at this one ["Judgement Day"] and say if you think it fitten for the collection or if you think it can be made so? It's a rewrite of a story that I have had around since 1946 and never been satisfied with, but I hope I have it now except for details maybe.[4]

In "Judgement Day" O'Connor's concerns are eschatological. The new title signals her shift in emphasis. At the time of *A Good Man is Hard to Find* (1955), she had written another version of "The Geranium," which was to be entitled "An Exile in the East."[5] O'Connor was insistent in rewriting her original story until she was satisfied: "I simply keep doing things the wrong way over and over until they suddenly come out right."[6] By the time of "Judgement Day," her vision had sharpened. She had found in the works of Teilhard de Chardin a "kindred intelligence." Her beliefs that the natural revealed the supernatural, that the ethical revealed the eschatological, were reinforced by the ideas of the French Jesuit. She found that the poet must "penetrate matter until spirit is revealed in it."[7]

A prime example of O'Connor's expanding vision is found in her last story. The symbolism of the "geranium" is omitted in "Judgement Day." The moral center of the story has been shifted to a theological center. Judgment takes the place of the geranium. In contrast to Old Dudley's personal alienation in the earlier story, Tanner's reaching for home, in the final story, is more pointedly spiritual: ". . . he would be home. Dead or alive. It was being there that mattered; the dead or alive did not."[8] At his moment of death, when the reader realizes that it is judgment day for Tanner, he is on his way towards his "true home": "Hep me up, Preacher, I'm on my way home!" (p. 269)

In "Judgement Day," Tanner's retribution is harsh. He is not left suspended as Dudley is, nor does he gloriously return home, as he thought he would, freeing himself from the confines of his coffin, announcing to his friends: "Judgement Day! Judgement Day! . . . Don't you two fools know it's Judgement Day?" (p. 265) Instead, an outraged black man, a professional actor, who was not as docile as Tanner thought he should be, violently delivers the old man's punishment. Tanner's behavior, which is prejudiced by his thinking that all black men are subservient shells of docility like his old "friend," Coleman, offends the actor:

> He [Tanner] was known to have a way with niggers. There was an art to handling them. The secret of handling a nigger was to show him his brains didn't have a chance against yours; then he would jump on your back and know he had a good thing there for life. He had had Coleman on his back for thirty years. (p. 252)

Tanner's first encounter with the black actor begins his process of retribution. After Tanner has approached the man as though he were a weak-minded, mill-worker, the actor slams him against a wall. Once he has been dominated by a black man, Tanner approaches a state of realization; his tongue is "frozen in his mouth" and one eye is "crossed" (p. 264). Typically for the proud in O'Connor's fiction, his vision becomes unbalanced; his voice is stilled.

At the final encounter, Tanner's retribution is complete. The old man has collapsed in the hallway. Dreaming that he has been shipped home in his coffin, he calls for "Coleman." The black man, believing that Tanner is taunting him with racial slurs by calling him a "coal man," becomes furious. At this point, O'Connor's aesthetic choice of changing the character's name from the original "Dudley" to "Tanner" is a significant detail in her demonstration of personal retribution. Tanner (more tan in skin tones) becomes Coleman (coal man); they are literary doubles in O'Connor's equalizing vision. Earlier in "Judgement Day," she had suggested it:

> The Negro [Coleman] reached for the glasses. He attached the bows carefully behind his ears and looked forth. He peered this way and that with exaggerated solemnity. And then he looked directly at Tanner and grinned, or grimaced, Tanner could not tell which, but he had an instant's sensation of seeing before him a negative image of himself, as if clownishness and captivity had been their common lot. The vision failed him before he could decipher it. (p. 255)

O'Connor artfully denigrates Tanner. His retributive experience turns him into "nigger." In another technical twist, the black actor, with his "horn-rimmed spectacles," doubles for Coleman. The treatment that Tanner had visited on Coleman is reflected on himself; he creates his own judgment. The black man witnesses Tanner's passage into the "true country."

In death, the braggart master, Tanner, becomes the submissive slave: "His hat had been pulled down over his face and his head and arms thrust between the spokes of the banister; his feet dangled over the stairwell like those of a man in the stocks" (p. 269). On his judgment day, Tanner's faults have been balanced. At the end of the story, O'Connor reveals to the reader that Tanner's personal vision of his judgment and resurrection is false. He gets what he wants, but not as he expected. Tanner is not jokingly resurrected out of his coffin shouting "Judgement Day" to his Southern cronies. His daughter has him buried in New York City. Later, however, she relents and has his body "dug up" and shipped to Corinth, Georgia—a silent testimony to the mortal desires of the proud.

Tanner's retribution in "Judgement Day" is not the same as Old Dudley's in "The Geranium." Dudley's black man (the instrument of revelation in both stories) is not violent. The black man even says that he "Never was much at killing anything!" (p. 12) He is not as docile and submissive as Rabie (the prototype of Tanner's Coleman), but he is pleasant and helpful:

> "You better be careful," the Negro said. "You could easily hurt yourself on these steps." And he held out his hand for Old Dudley to pull up on. . . . Old Dudley's hands hung between his knees. The nigger took him by the arm and pulled up. "Whew!" he gasped, "you're heavy. Give a little help here." Old Dudley's knees unbended and he staggered up. The nigger had him by the arm. "I'm going up anyway," he said. "I'll help you." Old Dudley looked frantically around. The steps behind him seemed to close up. He was walking with the nigger up the stairs. The nigger was waiting for him on each step. "So you hunt?" the nigger was saying. "Well, let's see. I went deer hunting once." (p. 12)

In "The Geranium" Old Dudley's retribution was not as emphatically presented nor as violently experienced as Tanner's in "Judgement Day." In the end, Dudley is given a warning that he should heed. The angry owner of the geranium, like a reprimanding voice of justice, shouts to the old man: "I only tell people once" (p. 14). Dudley is warned, but he is not dispatched into eternity. He is left isolated at the window ledge like a sickly, trapped geranium. By the end of *Everything That Rises Must Converge,* O'Connor's sense of retribution is comprehensive; it is nothing less than apocalyptic. A just balance *must* be effected to offset the downgrading faults of the transgressor. "Judgement Day" ends with a violent death, as Tanner is assaulted and racked between the posts of the banister. While O'Connor's vision of man's divine origin grew, so did her concept of retribution against those who would thwart his spiritual progress.

III

"The Geranium" and "Judgement Day," O'Connor's first and last works, reveal a great deal about her growth as artist and moralist. The understanding of this growth is important. Although her career was brief, and the volume of her work small, there are still important stages of growth that determine her aesthetic choices. One could say that her vision was prophetic: "In the novelist's case, it is a matter of seeing near things with their extensions of meaning and thus of seeing far things close up."[9] She believes that the ethical concerns of the natural world point toward the eschatological mysteries of the supernatural world.

A study of retribution in O'Connor's fiction reveals the foundation of her theological thinking: one is paid back for the evil one does or for the failure to do good. Christ's redemptive death balances, for eternity, all of man's evil. In the present, man slowly participates in that redemption, and his individual faults are balanced by a personal retributive experience.

The concept of retribution is an ancient one. Compensation for transgressions has always been one of man's primary moral and theological concerns. The Book of Proverbs reveals that a man is punished according to the manner of his sins:

> . . . they must eat fruits of their own courses, and choke themselves with their own scheming.
> For the errors of the ignorant lead to their death, and the complacency of fools works their own ruin. . . . (I.31-32)

The evil that man does bends back and revisits him; for, as St. Augustine says, "every sin harms him who commits it more than the one against whom it is committed."[10] And in the *Commedia*, Dante presents this concept of retribution in the form of *contrapasso:* one is punished in a manner representative of the punishment he has inflicted on others. Chaucer adapts the Dantesque idea and translates it into his tales as *countrepeisen,* a force of equilibrium. His "Parson's Tale" illustrates that every fault has a balancing element: the remedy for pride is humility.

Flannery O'Connor's concept of retribution is traditional, and it is derived from her theological background and its literary heritage. She believes, like Dante, that "the penalty of sin is to dwell in it. Man is punished *by* his sins rather than *for* them. Hell is to live in the evil character one has made for himself."[11] In O'Connor's world, justice is imposed from the outside; it comes in the form of violence from an insolent individual, or from a brutalizing event, or from an unexpected situation, which forces the character toward the brink of a revelation that is to expose to him his own malignant faults. Although justice derives from divine intervention, the characters present the condition and consequences of retribution; therefore, they participate in their own judgments. O'Connor's characters undergo the experience of retribution. The voice of the "stranger" in *The Violent Bear It Away* attempts to convey this concept of retribution to Tarwater, and to O'Connor's readers: "Don't everything you do, everything you have ever done, work itself out right or wrong before your eye and usually before the sun has set? Have you ever got by with anything?"[12]

From Old Dudley in "The Geranium" to Hazel Motes in *Wise Blood* to the displaced persons of *A Good Man is Hard to Find* to Tarwater in *The*

Violent Bear It Away to the alienated souls of *Everything That Rises Must Converge,* which concludes with Tanner in "Judgement Day," Flannery O'Connor expanded her vision of man as a stranger in a strange land, immersed in pride, and brought to the edge of spiritual awareness through the balancing force of divine retribution. A total view of her work reveals a moral growth from the personal, the familial and the social, toward the eschatological. While her vision was expanding so was her concept of retribution. In idea and image it operates through all of O'Connor's fictions.

NOTES

[1] The "true country" for O'Connor is what "the writer with Christian convictions will consider to be what is eternal and absolute." See Flannery O'Connor, "The Fiction Writer and His Country," in *Mystery and Manners,* eds. Sally and Robert Fitzgerald (New York: Farrar, Straus and Giroux, 1969), p. 27.

[2] This story has been reprinted in *Flannery O'Connor: The Complete Stories,* Intro. Robert Giroux (New York: Farrar, Straus and Giroux, 1971), pp. 3-14. All further references to this work appear in the text. Giroux notes that "The Geranium" is the opening story (pp. 1-21) in the typescript of O'Connor's master's thesis, *The Geranium: A Collection of Short Stories,* submitted for the degree of Master of Fine Arts, in the Department of English, in the Graduate College of the University of Iowa. It is dated June, 1947. See Intro. to *The Complete Stories,* p. vii, and Notes, p. 551.

[3] Quoted by C. Ross Mullins in "Flannery O'Connor, An Interview," *Jubilee,* June 1963, p. 35.

[4] "To Catherine Carver," 27 June 1964, *The Habit of Being: Letters of Flannery O'Connor,* ed. Sally Fitzgerald (New York: Farrar, Straus and Giroux, 1979), p. 588.

[5] Robert Giroux, Intro., *The Complete Stories,* p. xvi. See also the letter "To Elizabeth McKee," 13 January 1955, *the Habit of Being,* pp. 74-75.

[6] Quoted by Robert Donner in "She Writes Powerful Fiction," *Sign,* March 1961, p. 48.

[7] Flannery O'Connor, "Review of *The Phenomenon of Man,*" *American Scholar,* 30 (1961), 618.

[8] Flannery O'Connor, "Judgement Day," in *Everything That Rises Must Converge* (New York: Farrar, Straus and Giroux, 1965), p. 246. All further references to this work appear in the text.

[9] Flannery O'Connor, "The Role of the Catholic Novelist," *Greyfriar,* 7 (1964), 9.

[10] *Enchiridion de Fide, Spe et Caritate,* trans. Louis A. Arand, Ancient Christian Writers Series (Washington, D.C.: Catholic University Press, 1947), p. 25.

[11] Charles Allen Dinsmore, *The Teaching of Dante* (New York: Houghton, Mifflin, 1902), p. 94.

[12] Flannery O'Connor, *The Violent Bear It Away* (New York: Farrar, Straus and Giroux, 1960), p. 46.

Commentary by
Darretta and Giannone

EDITOR'S NOTE: Because the authors of the previous essays, Richard Giannone and John Darretta, separately submitted manuscripts on Flannery O'Connor's first and last stories, the editors decided to ask each to comment on the other's essay. Their responses follow.

JOHN DARRETTA'S RESPONSE

Richard Giannone's essay carefully traces the growth of Flannery O'Connor's perspective on man's death and resurrection. In doing so, it reflects her dual vision of *this* country and the "true country," that which is now and present in relation to that which O'Connor has defined in "The Fiction Writer and His Country" as "eternal and absolute." Giannone also underscores the dichotomies present in the various revisions of "Judgement Day": city/county, black/white, exile/home, death/life.

Focusing on the concept of divine retribution that O'Connor inherited from the Bible, Dante, and Chaucer, my intentions were to analyze that part of her vision which looks at reality from the vantage point of the "true country." In taking a "thisworldly" view, Giannone's essay is an appropriate and perspective counterbalance to that perspective. He offers keen observations in his analysis of "Judgement Day" and opens the story further by emphasizing the importance of judgment for Tanner's daughter and the black actor and not just for Tanner alone. However, I am not as optimistic as Giannone is about the story's ending.

Structurally, "Judgement Day" balances the collection's first and title story "Everything That Rises Must Converge." Both narratives have parallels: obvious character doubles, familial concerns, psychological and spiritual alienation, and comeuppances delivered by irate black persons. In each case, a self-righteous character, delivered of a lesson and punished for inordinate pride, ends by oafishly teetering on the brink of revelation. Mrs. Chestny is knocked off balance by the outraged black woman. Her eyes distorted, she calls for "Home" and dies, while her son wanders silently into a "tide of darkness . . . postponing from moment to moment his entry into the world of guilt and sorrow." This ending is similar, in kind if not degree, to that of "Judgement Day." The black actor slams Tanner against a wall. The old man's eyes distorted, he becomes disoriented and dies trying to make his way "home." Tanner's dream of getting home and rising on a self-created Judgement Day is comic parody, a botched resurrection. Similarly, the story's last line—since Tanner's daughter, like Mrs. Chestny's son, reaches no conscious realizations about the spiritual state of her soul—can be seen as facetious irony: "Now she rests well at night and her good looks have mostly returned." Her worldly benefits may be the results of abated fear and guilt, but they are of no consequence in the "true country."

In Flannery O'Connor's fiction judgment is rendered through mysteries that reside outside the purview of the human mind or volition of the individual character. Fear and guilt initiate from within, from psychological realities. Unlike Giannone's reading, I find that, in "Judgement Day," it is not so much those human feelings that bring Tanner home as it is the enigmatic movements of divine retribution. Nonetheless, I am happy that his analysis introduces a warmer and more optimistic side of O'Connor's vision, wherein mercy and love offset the hard objectivity and impersonality of divine justice. Together, our interpretations can explain what O'Connor meant in "The Nature and Aim of Fiction," that understanding good fiction rests with the "mind that is willing to have its sense of mystery deepened by contact with reality, and its sense of reality deepened by contact with mystery."

RICHARD GIANNONE'S RESPONSE

John Darretta's essay is true and necessary. It identifies retribution as a shaping theme in Flannery O'Connor's work; and then, after showing the suitability of punishment to sin in "The Geranium" and "Judgement Day," his analysis concludes that these, O'Connor's first and last tales of aged southern émigrés, bracket the evolution of her entire career.

I have two responses to Darretta's argument. First, a caution. The contrast between Old Dudley's emotional comeuppance at the end of "The Geranium" and the otherworldly aura surrounding Tanner's brutal death in "Judgement Day" is so striking that we might be tempted to end our consideration with this difference, and that would be a mistake. There is a crucial lesson to learn from their dissimilar fates. The transition comes about through O'Connor's gradual recognition that within Old Dudley's exile and anguish lies the raising power that brings Tanner in the final book into convergence with God's saving power.

When answering queries about "The Artificial Nigger," O'Connor said that her interest was in "the redemptive quality" of suffering (Letters 78). As I see O'Connor's growth, the shift that Darretta finds accomplished in "Judgement Day" derives from a theology of suffering that comes to inform her art. Her recognition that agony—especially Tanner's undeserved chastisement—can redeem the victim changes everything. Lacking the sense of atonement, "The Geranium" presents an old man defeated in estrangement; but Tanner goes beyond geographical exile to gain a victorious homecoming.

This emphasis on the transcendent aspect of suffering and guilt leads to my second response, and here I take issue with Darretta's reading. "Judgement Day" for me celebrates love. Tanner's humility before Coleman (his black double) and his professed dependence on "my shepherd" overcome Tanner's prideful deceit as well as the vicious assault by the black actor. By turning contritely to God, the old codger becomes free from his wrath and is able to picture himself returning to Corinth. If imagination carries Tanner home, as Darretta argues, then it is because a dying man's dream speaks to eschatological vision. Also, those curious two final paragraphs about the message of the night coming to Tanner's daughter, usually ignored by critics, remind us that the story moves toward the activity of love in a woman who does what she is supposed to do and buries the dead. "Judgement Day," the epitomizing story of O'Connor's consummate collection, brings to a joyous end a volume of characters who through violence learn not to be afraid of love.

Always it is like this with Flannery O'Connor: one cannot consider seriously the persistent trials of blood and dread without seeing that she transforms them by restating them in terms of grace and love. Even the guilt of a mass murderer on the side of a dirt road is recorded as a sign of grace discarded, fulfillment missed, tenderness rejected. Taking an overview of O'Connor's fiction, we can see that an old man's loneliness in the New York desert holds the promise of an exile's return to his ultimate home. O'Connor resolves her drama of the two locales through nuances of retribution. Thanks to John Darretta we have before us the span of O'Connor's strategy. I am also grateful that Darretta stops where he does so that there is room for my complementary perspective on a writer who, brave in her life, is still braver in her fiction, avowing that the love she believed in consecrates human life to the end.

Cheever's "Metamorphoses": Myth and Postmodern Short Fiction

E. P. WALKIEWICZ

In throwing off his well-known and inordinately influential comments on Joyce's use of the *Odyssey,* T. S. Eliot, of course, was primarily concerned with adumbrating a structural method. Joyce's manipulation of a "continuous parallel between contemporaneity and antiquity," Eliot asserted in "*Ulysses,* Order, and Myth," should be seen as "simply a way of giving a shape and a significance to the immense panorama of futility and anarchy which is contemporary history." But as the title of his essay suggests, perhaps only unintentionally, if Eliot saw Joyce as an artist-hero employing "the mythical method" to complete a *nostos,* he defined that method not only as a way of "making the modern world possible for art" but also as a "step toward" creating "form," a return to "classicism." If Joyce poses as "Noman," it is not to make a statement about ontology, to proffer "an invitation to chaos," but to effect a stratagem that may permit him to make "order" out of "anarchy." Concealing his personality, the artist builds a "foundation," shaping "the material at hand," including "the emotions and feelings of the writer himself."[1] Behind or beyond the wandering hero, Eliot implies, stands a Dedalian craftsman whose portrait bears some similarity to that of Stephen's "God of creation," remaining "invisible, refined out of existence, indifferent, paring his fingernails."[2]

While Ezra Pound read *Ulysses* as primarily the product of a Flaubertian naturalism that verges on Rabelasian satire, he believed the mythic method of the book to be a much more arbitrary adventure in ordering. The Homeric "correspondences" were for him chiefly Joyce's "own affair," a manifestation of his "mediaevalism." Serving as "a scaffold, a means of construction," they are "justified" only because they constitute a "triumph in form, in balance, a main schema, with continuous interweaving and arabesque."[3] In *The Cantos,* after all, Pound too was developing an Odyssean persona, a man with a mind like a god's who would not only sail after knowledge but, like Amphion, raise up by his craft the stones of the eternal city.

Whether or not Joyce conceived his role in such terms remains a matter for conjecture, although the prevalence of metamorphosis and displays of ventriloquism in the later chapters of *Ulysses* and in *Finnegans Wake* indicates, possibly, a more than slightly different conception of form and fathering. What I am proposing, merely, is that there was a tendency among some of the major modernists to portray the artist-hero as an Odysseus or Dedalus, returning to reestablish an order, laboring to invent a labyrinth, a tendency that seems to be associated with a fear of flux. Indeed, even in a work such as *The Sun Also Rises,* Hemingway has constructed a series of Homeric parallels that may define the plot of the novel as a demonic parody of the epic but that thereby also, at least by implication, refer us to that need to give significance to the contemporary futility of which Eliot speaks, a need that may be fulfilled in the careful craftsmanship of Hemingway's controlled prose.

Together with the "mythical method," narrowly defined by Eliot as an ordering device, this modernist manner of mythologizing the writer is something, I would argue further, that is countered or transformed by certain American postmodernists who are more apt to employ metamorphosis than metaphor, more likely to refer to a mythological prefiguration[4] that foregrounds the protean nature of word and world. John Barth, for instance, implies in "The Literature of Replenishment" that one of the things he envisions postmodernist fiction "synthesizing" or "transcending" is "the modernists' insistence, borrowed from their romantic forebears, on the special, usually alienated role of the artist in his society, or outside it: James Joyce's priestly, self-exiled artist-hero; Thomas Mann's artist as charlatan, or mountebank; Franz Kafka's artist as anorexic or bug." Elsewhere, Barth offers an alternative type, that of "Menelaus on the beach at Pharos," a genuinely "baroque" hero who "is *lost,* in the larger labyrinth of the world, and has got to hold fast while the Old Man of the Sea exhausts reality's frightening guises so that he may extort direction from him when Proteus returns to his 'true' self."[5]

As Charles Caramello convincingly argues, at the same time that Barth wishes to subscribe "to a conception of authorial mastery" he also finds it necessary to voice an "apparent rejection of the Dedalian analogy" (32-33) that "leads him toward characterizing imagination, toward characterizing artistic creation, as intertextualism," and his work, like much postmodern fiction, "sustains the collapse of ontologically distinct authorial selves," remaining, therefore, "in a state of profound ambivalence."[6] It is this altered or alternate myth of the ontological predicament of the artist as Everyman that Barth, fairly obviously, plays with in "Life-Story" and "Lost in the Funhouse," this protean figure or its avatars that he disembodies in "Menelaiad," "Echo," and "Bellerophoniad." Interestingly enough, though, one may find examples of a similar use of mythological materials, as well as the at-least-implicit expression of a similar attitude toward experience and creation, in the short fiction of John Cheever, a writer not included in Caramello's study and one not usually thought of as being quite as exemplary a "postmodernist."

Cheever, certainly, may have early on in his career earned a reputation as an exemplary realist, an astute and accurate "chronicler" of contemporary mores, but, as critics such as Robert M. Slabey have noticed, in "his later work the discernible progress is into more innovative techniques and a bleaker vision. He has moved deeper into the darkness of the American funhouse." We find narrators and narratives that are more "self-conscious, reflexive, metafictional," and discover that Cheever has responded to a typically "postmodernist" urge to give "new twists to the perennial conflict between ideal and real and to the 'modern' concern with illusion," often adopting "Reality itself" as his primary theme.[7]

Particularly apparent in the short stories he published from the late 1950's onward,[8] Cheever's use of self-conscious and reflexive narration to evolve variations on this theme takes the form of a questioning of not only the Dedalian model but the principles of Jamesian realism. In an opening statement that resonates throughout Cheever's later work, the narrator of "The Death of Justina," for instance, tells us:

> Fiction is art and art is the triumph over chaos (no less) and we can accomplish this only by the most vigilant exercise of choice, but in a world that changes more swiftly than we can perceive there is always the danger that our powers of selection will be mistaken and that the vision we serve will come to nothing. We admire decency and we despise death but even the mountains seem to shift in the space of a night and perhaps the exhibitionist at the corner of Chestnut and Elm streets is more significant than the lovely woman with a bar of sunlight in her hair, putting a fresh piece of cuttlebone in the nightingale's cage. Just let me give you one example of chaos and if you disbelieve me look honestly into your own past and see if you can't find a comparable experience . . . .[9]

The Jamesian historian faithfully rendering the surface of things to arrive at their essences, the Odyssean voyager after knowledge and order, would seem to have been succeeded by a character more akin to Barth's Menelaus, a figure desperately hoping to hold on to a world that threatens to unravel into anarchy.

Even though he gave the title proper to but one medley of short pieces incorporated in *The Brigadier and the Golf Widow* (1964), for more reasons than the fact that many of the stories embrace change in this and other ways, it may be appropriate to call Cheever's later short fiction as a whole his "Metamorphoses." For one thing, we may find in a number of places in his third through sixth volumes a fairly forceful emphasis on "artistic creation as intertextuality." Unlike Ovid's poem, Cheever's collections, certainly, are not intended to function as a completely inclusive storehouse of all the myths of classical antiquity, but they do retell several of them while also weaving together numerous references to mythological types. Searching through the stories for "allusions to classical myth," Father George W. Hunt has found references to such figures as Venus, "an Aphrodite-like chimera," satyrs, Artemis, Hecate, Actaeon, Orpheus, Hermes, "and many more." He argues, moreover, that "The Country Husband" and "The Swimmer" constitute attempts to rewrite the *Aeneid* and *Odyssey,* the former story bearing throughout classical allusions that "give it the contour of an abbreviated comic epic," the latter taking the shape of "a surrealistic epic, deftly shortened."[10]

Cheever's efforts to change Homer's corpus into new forms,[11] however, involve more than the simple development of a "continuous parallel." Responding to an interviewer's question about his use of "resonances from myth," he once stated that "The easiest way to parse the world is through mythology. There have been thousands of papers written along those lines—Leander is Poseidon and somebody is Ceres, and so forth. It seems to be a superficial parsing. But it makes a passable paper."[12] By using the term "parallel" to describe his understanding of Yeats's and Joyce's "mythical method," Eliot suggests that he is concerning himself with a kind of allegorization involving the extended development of 1:1 correspondences,[13] while Cheever, it would seem, found such a "parsing" of both work and world a bit too limited. In fact, in "The Swimmer" the "parallels" become multiple, the correspondences proliferating perhaps to the point of meaninglessness. If Cheever wields mythological references in that story to inscribe a "scaffold," the structure he alludes to is in Barth's and Borges' sense of the word a "baroque" one, one that implies the possible exhaustion of its own possibilities.

The Homeric correspondences in *Ulysses* may be the most obvious, but Joyce's development of them is neither straightforward nor precise, and Bloom-Odysseus, like Stephen-Telemachus also comes under Proteus' sway, anticipating the performances of the all-encompassing HCE of *Finnegans Wake* by playing a variety of other roles from the Wandering Jew to Don Juan. Similarly, in attempting to complete his own journey home, Cheever's Neddy Merrill seems to take on a number of guises. Most critics have noticed the Homeric parallel, but this is sketched in a manner even less explicit or exact than it is in Joyce's novel, and as Slabey, for one, has perceptively pointed out, the story alludes to more than one mythological or heroic prefiguration, connecting Neddy's *nostos* to the journeys of Rip Van Winkle, Columbus, and Bunyan's pilgrim, mixing the waters of his "Lucinda River" with those of the "Hudson, Concord, Mississippi, Thames, Nile, and Ganges."[14]

Reading "The Swimmer," then, may become a process not of drawing a series of comparisons between the "contemporary" events and relationships and a single prefigurative pattern but rather of attempting to conceive as contemporaneous the "present" events and a number of myths and legends, and discovering the entire complex gradually taking the shape of a more archetypal design. This, of course, is the game Joyce challenges the reader to participate in in *Finnegans Wake,* the one Barth plays with him in several of the pieces of *Lost in the Funhouse,* in *chimera,* and, exhaustively, in *Giles Goat-Boy.* Approaching the quest archetype, glimpsing something like the emerging outlines of a "monomyth," the reader may suppose that, by lending his "powers of selection" to the effort, he has contributed to art's "triumph over chaos," although, to return to Eliot's terms, one may wonder whether "significance" as well as "shape" has been imparted, as the "truths" associated with the pattern threaten to dissolve into cliches ("Life is a journey;" "Things happen in cycles"). Concentrating on the proliferation of types, however, the reader may have his attention drawn to change itself, may sense that both sides of Eliot's equation are variable, that both the mythic model and contemporary experience are characterized by flux, that "to look honestly into" the "past" may lead to the realization that "in a world that changes more swiftly than we can perceive there is always the danger . . . that the vision we serve will come to nothing."

This latter sense of the story, the impression that the reader has glimpsed chaos instead of or while helping make cosmos, is reinforced by Neddy Merrill's failure to make something of his vision "of himself as a legendary figure" (pp. 603-04). One of the reasons, perhaps, that some critics have labelled "The Swimmer" "metafictional" is that in undertaking "a long swim" to "enlarge and celebrate" the "beauty" of his "day"

(p. 604), Neddy himself in a semi-conscious way tries to apply something like the "mythical method" to experience, to forge a "continuous parallel between contemporaneity and antiquity" that will permit him to see himself as "a pilgrim, an explorer, a man with a destiny" (p. 604), to discover structure in his surroundings, envision his neighbors' scattered swimming pools as a "chain of water" (p. 606), a continuous "quasi-subterranean stream" (p. 603) leading back by a route "remembered or imaginary" to "clemency" and "beneficence" (p. 604).

Merrill's attempt, however, to create a scenario in which he swims toward an archetype of heroism is denied by the fictional actuality. Neddy, after all, does not soar above or glide over the fluid stuff but imbibes and immerses himself in it, and unlike Odysseus' triumphal reestablishment of rule in home and kingdom, or even Leopold Bloom's more dubious restoration, his homecoming is an arrival at a terminus. Whereas Odysseus and Joyce's "Ulysses" both by craft gain entry to their homes and physically reclaim their marriage beds, Cheever's wanderer is left outside a locked and deserted house, and while Bloom's return and future course are ambiguous enough to have allowed some readers to view the Homeric correspondence as "ennobling" the modern character,[15] Neddy's inability to complete the pattern makes it difficult to suppose that he has ever risen above the level of pathos. Feeling "cold, tired, and bewildered," "so stupified with exhaustion that his triumph" seems "vague," he finds himself shut out from the past, thrust into the present, and confronted by evidence of transformation and entropy: "He tried the garage doors to see what cars were in but the doors were locked and rust came off the handles onto his hands. Going toward the house, he saw that the force of the thunderstorm had knocked one of the rain gutters loose" (p. 612). If we can place Cheever "in the line of fabulist and mythopoeic writers, participating in the chief business of American fiction, the creation of American Reality," then, Slabey proposes, what we learn from works such as "The Swimmer" is that "America—and Reality—are composed of change, flux, chaos, contradiction."[16]

For the reader, this perception of increasing entropy is further intensified by his efforts to recognize and reconcile the multiple temporal contexts of the story. Reading *Ulysses,* John M. Warner has argued, we are constantly made aware "of how Joyce tries in the novel to approximate the seemingly contradictory voices of the historian and the myth-maker," attempts to integrate the "diachronic" and the "synchronic."[17] Likewise, pursuing Neddy on his "quest" requires the reader to follow concurrently several streams: that of the protagonist's consciousness, ordered by his inner sense of time; that of external "historical" events, seeping at times into Merrill's awareness; and that of natural, cyclical time, hinting, through its associations with the romance and the "monomyth," at the possibility of synchronic experience, of stasis and timelessness. Bloom's journeying ends with the descent of his thought into the period that concludes the "Ithaca" chapter of Joyce's book, a sign that has been taken as both marking the stopping of time and connoting the archetypal womb-tomb, emblem of the recurrent and eternal. Cheever's story, in some contrast, collapses about or into its final word—"empty" (p. 612), and for the reader cognizant of Neddy's failure to deny dissolution by maintaining an equivalence between subjective time and mythic time, at that point the multiple currents of the work merge into the historical, into "the more tenuous and inconclusive behavior of particular individuals who live in the shapelessness of temporal sequence."[18]

If and when that collapse takes place, the allusions in the tale to the succession of the seasons, promising potential renewal when read in a mythic context, retroactively become what they are in the "Time Passes" section of Virginia Woolf's To the Lighthouse, references to the inevitability of loss and decay. Ned Merrill "might" once "have been compared to a summer's day, particularly the last hours of one" (p. 603). By the time, however, that he seems "to see Andromeda, Cepheus, and Cassiopeia" (p. 611), it has become clear to the reader, if not to him, that no eternizing conceit will be forthcoming. Having "been immersed too long" (p. 612), he has fallen into "That time of year" when he and we behold nought but "Bare ruined choirs, where late the sweet birds sang."

Neddy's descent into the flux of the real is a replica of an Icarian pattern Beatrice Greene has discerned in the Wapshot novels:

> Cheever's downward movement is from fable to floor, and ultimately the floor itself is gone and we find ourselves falling still in the glare of the mythic element indigenous to Cheever's work and latent beneath the surface of all his characters and events. In Cheever's Wapshot novels myth and fable are a constant charged energy whose playing lightning not only reveals to us the heights of the dream but searches out in the grey bones of normality the skeleton of nightmare.

Citing "The Death of Justina" and "The Country Husband" in addition to The Wapshot Chronicle and The Wapshot Scandal, Greene traces an "anatomy of decline" generated by the "pervasive play of myth and mundane," and manifested in structure, incident, characterization, imagery, and even diction. Time and again, she proposes, Cheever with Dedalian skill uses "the language and imagery of classical myth and fable" while also drawing on "national heritage and tradition" to invoke a "succession of scaffoldings," only to evoke in the reader feelings of "disequilibrium," "deflation," "disbalance."[19]

In that Cheever in both the Wapshot novels and "The Swimmer" employs mythological materials to suggest a movement from the everyday to the "heights of the dream," he follows to an extent the method Eliot outlined, and therefore begins by taking an approach that Barth in a frequently cited and reiterated statement, adjudged to be backward:

> I always felt that it was a bad idea on the face of it, though there are some beautiful counter-examples, to write a more or less realistic piece of fiction, one dimension of which keeps pointing to the classical myths—like John Updike's Centaur, or Joyce's Ulysses, or Malamud's The Natural. Much as one may admire those novels in other respects, their authors have hold of the wrong end of the mythopoeic stick. The myths themselves are produced by the collective narrative imagination (or whatever), partly to point down at our daily reality; and so to write about our daily experiences in order to point up to the

myths seems to me mythopoeically retrograde. I think it's a more interesting thing to do, if you find yourself preoccupied with mythic archetypes or what have you, to address them directly.[20]

No matter what one thinks of the validity of these remarks,[21] one must conclude that Barth's objections do not really apply to the works of Cheever we have been examining, for, again in terms of gross anatomy, if Cheever manipulates references to classical myths to begin to build a superstructure that might lend shape and direction to the anarchic panorama of contemporary history, he dismantles that creation as he erects it. If he "points up," he, afterwards or at the same time, also "points down," and if the reader has sensed himself being tugged out of the everyday, more often than not, his final impression is of a precipitous return to the now. Moreover, in the sequence that actually bears the title "Metamorphoses," Cheever manages to convey the shapelessness of the quotidian while adopting a mythic method closer to the one Barth espouses in the quotation and actually toys with in "Echo," "Menelaiad," and *Chimera.*

Coming to treat not necessarily the "mythic archetypes" but individual myths "more directly" than does "The Swimmer," the four fairly short short stories that make up "Metamorphoses" also embody an assertive emphasis on the "intertextualism" of both fiction and the self. Incorporated first in the same collection that contains not only Neddy's story but also two tales of possibly supernatural transformation ("The Angel of the Bridge," "The Music Teacher"), the sequence opens with a description that may be read as both a standard, if quite clichéd, attempt to establish verisimilitude and character by means of conveying physical details, and a "self-conscious" allusion to the strategy employed by the fiction's creator: "Larry Actaeon was built along classical lines: curly hair, a triangulated nose, and a large and supple body, and he had what might be described as a Periclean interest in innovation" (p. 536). Cheever may be identified as the godlike artist who drafted Larry's form, but his lines are based on those of Ovid, who himself drew on older blueprints, and from the very beginning Cheever's work refers to itself as not an original but a copy of a copy, a retelling of a retelling.

Larry's story, a version of the Actaeon-Diana episode recounted in Book III of the *Metamorphoses,* seems on a first reading to establish a principle of translation that will be evident throughout the series of four Ovidean tales: following the Joycean precedent, physical metamorphoses in the "original" will be replaced by abstract or psychological equivalents in order to "modernize" the classical myths and encourage the modern reader to continue to willingly suspend his disbelief. Thus, unlike that of his namesake, Larry's voyeurism leads not to his transformation into a stag but to a loss of identity and status. Motivated by "pure enthusiasm" (enthousí[a], possession by a deity), he looks on "the formidable and immaculate beauty" of one of his business partners, Mrs. Vuiton, realizing that "underlying all his fancies of good and evil, merits and rewards, was the stubborn and painful nature of things" and knowing "that he had seen something that it was not his destiny to see" (pp. 536-37). Joining those who "watch the afternoon go down," he has a premonition of "nameless doom" (p. 537) that is realized when, following his descent to "a kind of infernal region, crowded with heaped ash cans" (p. 538), he becomes a true "Noman," nearly, like Kafka's Gregor Samsa, a nonentity.

Larry had been an inventor and organizer and had attempted to create a new breed of dogs, but after his "boisterousness" leads him to intrude, so do disaster and disorder. As he descends the social ladder, not only is the investment banker mistaken for first a deliveryman and then a waiter, but he also loses authority and audience, finds he is no longer capable of "commanding attention" (p. 539). As things wind down, the headlights of his car fade "to nothing," its battery gives "up the ghost," and Actaeon's vision literally fails as he falls, to end up, presumably, both dismembered and dis-remembered (p. 540). Cheever, here, may be "updating" Ovid, but the transition is not necessarily an easy one,[22] since the reader, in a sense, drops with Actaeon from the classical version of the myth, in which the young man's "error" (Metamorphoses, III. 142) is obscurely related to the fate of Cadmus and the mysterious machinations of the gods, through Pound's modernist version, in which his crime is emblematic of irreverence toward nature, to Cheever's, in which all concepts of order and comprehensibility, all systems of "merits and rewards" may be revealed by chance to be but "fancies" mistakenly produced by "our powers of selection."

Larry's descent into isolation, Actaeon's loss of voice have their ironic analogues in the second tale in "Metamorphoses," a retelling of the Orpheus and Eurydice myth in which the former has been transformed into one Orville Betman, a singer whose voice is "distinguished not by its range and beauty but by its persuasiveness" (p. 541). The translation of "Orpheus" as "Orville" can be seen again as merely part of an effort to "update," or to maintain verisimilitude, but the narrator comes close at times to punching out of the realistic dimensions of the fiction, and Cheever does not seem to be particularly interested in concealing the mythological model in order to involve the reader in a guessing game. Rather, the more likely effect of Cheever's playing with names, naming, and etymologies and indulging in other kinds of wordplay here and throughout the series is to draw the reader's attention to the protean nature of language itself, its dubious power and referentiality. Indeed, by the time he has completed Cheever's adaptation of the Orpheus myth, he may feel that this perception has been promoted to a theme.

Although "the element of persuasiveness" in Betman's voice is "infallible," the truth he sings of is a materialistic one, the things he praises, "shoe polish, toothpaste, floor wax" (p. 541). Winning the woman "life meant him to have" only to lose her to her perpetually dying father, he travels to a place that has taken on for him "legendary proportions" in hope of regaining her (p. 542). There, at "that instant where death enters the terrain of love," he is moved to song not by "the bare facts of life but its ancient and invisible storms" (pp. 544-45). Yet even at this point, the closest we come perhaps in "Metamorphoses" to rising to an orphic state, to contracting that "playing lightning" that might "reveal the heights of the dream,'' what Orville gives voice to is not his own Vision but simply a rendition of ''Handel's air and words.'' The effect upon his audience, moreover, remains a mystery; ''to courteous perhaps to interrupt or moved perhaps'' by the music, the ''elderly maid'' who guards the threshold of the old man's ''preposterous abode'' says ''nothing'' (pp. 543-44). Finally, having reclaimed his Eurydice, he ''of course'' loses her again ''because he loved her too well,'' maintaining his persuasiveness but incapable of communicating even his loss to a public that trades archetypes for appliances: ''You can still hear him singing about table polish, bleaches, and vacuum cleaners. He always sings of inessentials, never about the universality of suffering and love, but thousands of men and women go off to the stores as if he had, as if this was his song'' (p. 544).

After presenting the reader with two tales that tell, among other things, of the recalcitrance of the beautiful, its power to overwhelm, to resist efforts to possess it, Cheever includes a piece in which a woman attempts to create it by fiat. Mrs. Peranger is a socialite who has lost her husband, her son, and her looks and therefore seeks to shape the only material that remains to her, ''her only daughter, the nymphlike Nerissa'' (p. 545). Blind to or ignoring the knowledge that the ''thin and wasted spinster of thirty'' is ''plainly one of those'' who are ''burdened with the graceless facts of the world,'' Mrs. Pranger habitually proclaims that ''Everyone *loves* Nerissa. Everyone adores her. She is *too* attractive for *words*'' (p. 545). But the Nereids were the offspring of a shape-shifter, and Nerissa repeatedly ruffles ''the still waters of her mother's creation,'' demonstrating that it ''is her nearly sacred call to restate the pathos and clumsiness of mankind'' (p. 546). When she expresses her desire to marry a veterinary, her ''imperious'' parent seizes control of the situation and has the man destroyed, causing Nerissa to pine away and die. True to form, Mrs. Peranger essays verbally to reshape the past: ''She was *so* attractive—she was so *frightfully* attractive'' (p. 547). What she comes to hear in response, however, is not an echo but the sound of water saying *''Mother, Mother, I've found the man I want to marry.''* ''Her only daughter,'' the narrator informs us, ''had been turned into a swimming pool'' (pp. 548-49).

In telling Betman's story, the narrator employs several techniques and formulae, including the use of ''of course,'' to break out of a predominantly realistic mode and remind the reader of the ways in which Orville's tale is to be identified with that of Orpheus. By the time he reaches the final line of the third piece in the series, the self-conscious reader finds that he is not quite so certain about which end of the mythopoeic stick his attention is focused on, perhaps begins even to question the principle of translation he deduced earlier. Part of the burden of maintaining verisimilitude has been shifted to him, for what the narrator says at the end of the tale he delivers as literal truth. This evolution of the reader's role continues through the fourth, final, and possibly most humorous, of Cheever's Ovidean episodes, one that demands that the reader function much as he does in following ''The Swimmer.''

''Metamorphoses'' concludes with a surrealistic narrative that is about nothing so much as the principle of metamorphosis itself. ''Mr. Bradish wanted a change," it begins, a change in "his scenery, his pace, and his environment" (p. 549), and from that point forward the reader must pay close attention to every modification of perspective, every "seemed" and "actually" in order to interpret as hallucination the "manifestly absurd" (p. 549) transformations Bradish observes. Believing that the "quality of discipline shines through a man's life and all his works, giving them a probity and a fineness that preclude disorder" (p. 550), Bradish decides to prove both the principle and himself by giving up smoking. In attempting to remake himself, however, he not only fails to preclude, but actually promotes, "disorder," in several senses of the word. As his "customary point of view" alters, he feels "himself to be gaining some understanding of the poetry of the force of change in life" (p. 551), but that force overwhelms him until there is "some definite injury" to his vision, "damage" to his "equilibrium" (p. 552).

Maintaining for a time enough self-awareness to realize that he has become "unlike himself" (p. 552), Bradish must admit to himself that "he had changed, and so had his world" (p. 553). As he begins to see such things as "a young woman wearing" a "tube-shaped dress, her long hair the color of Virginia tobacco" (p. 552), he no longer is capable of even this degree of detachment. Discovering that everything around him is in flux, that the entire "population of the city" is being transformed before his eyes into a collection of "Winstons, Chesterfields, Marlboros," Bradish, ultimately, loses control and merges with this protean reality as both he and it unravel:

> It was a young woman—really a child—whom he mistook for a Lucky Strike that was his undoing. She screamed when he attacked her, and two strangers knocked him down, striking and kicking him with just moral indignation. A crowd gathered. There was pandemonium, and presently the sirens of the police car that took him away. (p. 553).

When Bradish's world collapses with him into discord, the reader has the impression that the narration has, for the most part, become "realistic," that, as may happen in reading "The Swimmer," subjective, surrealistic, and mythic contexts have submerged themselves in the historical, "the shapelessness of temporal sequence." This is not to say, however, that the narration has been "disciplined," made uniform. Reminiscent of Bradish's own "self-righteousness" (p. 552), the "just moral indignation" with which the strangers attack him is, for instance, mildly suggestive of a momentary shift in to a more subjective perspective, while, echoing the third verse of Genesis, the narrator's evocation of "pandemonium" may remind the reader of the opening lines of the series, taking him "out" to the narrative level on which the fiction self-consciously refers to its own evolution. If this is the case, then he may also discover that whereas Ovid begins his *Metamorphoses* with a description of the emergence of cosmos out of chaos and ends it with the founding of a lasting social order and a vision of his own ascension and immortality, Cheever begins his "Metamorphoses" with allusions to creation and classical conceptions of order and ends it with an allusion to an infernal realm, with a fiat that evokes not cosmos but chaos.

In an early study fostered by the hermeneutic climate created by Eliot et al., Sister M. Bernetta Quinn argues that an examination of both the art and critical writings of several of the major modernists reveals that they "selected ancient metamorphoses" and employed the "metamorphic principle" not only "as descriptive of the natural world and the way in which that world is known" or "as verbal equivalents for contemporary emotional situations" but also in order to dramatize "the search for an absolute," to treat change in its "highest form," the "transcension of the limits" of the "senses, the boundaries of matter," and to arrive at a "means of unifying their longer works, even to the extent of creating . . . new myths." Interpreting the works, thus, almost entirely within the context of "Ulysses, Order, and Myth," she clearly adopts the Odyssean or Dedalian concept of the artist-hero, suggesting that many modernists adapted the "metamorphic principle" as a stratagem for shaping or eliciting a shape from the inchoate. Viewed as such a maker, Ezra Pound, for example, becomes a poet committed to a process of "reforming" that will bring "order out of confusion" in a manner that "parallels" the genesis of "cosmos out of chaos with which Ovid begins his Metamorphoses," while T. S. Eliot is seen, "like Pound," as an "absolutist in his insistence upon perfection underlying the imperfections of ordinary life, and capable of being summoned forth at the bidding of the greatest masters."[23]

Whether or not contemporary readers still discern a congruence between Sister Quinn's model of modernism and their own, what seems clear is that Cheever, like certain other postmodern fiction writers, came to express a different attitude toward making, developed in his later short stories a different treatment of Ovid, order, and myth. As John Vickery has noted, in John Updike's The Centaur what evolves is not a "continuous parallel between contemporaneity and antiquity" but "a complete fusion of ancient event and contemporary character . . . of scientific fact and mythic tale"; and "the protean elision of characters," the "surealistic metamorphosis of settings and events," the "startling shifts in point of view," all "call attention to the narrative act itself," affirming, finally, "the total freedom of the story-teller" who has sacrificed "his own verbal identity."[24] In "Memelaiad," Barth's hero is "lost on the beach at Pharos," having become the protean voice that tells his tale, whereas in "Bellerophoniad," a pseudo-Bellerophon falls after becoming a perfect imitation of a hero by modeling his life on the archetypal pattern, surviving only as "bellerophonic letters afloat between two worlds, forever betraying, in combinations and recombinations, the man they forever represent."[25] And, in the first two of his "Metamorphoses" Cheever translates a pair of episodes from Ovid in which men who glimpse or attempt to possess beauty end up dismembered after losing the power of speech, following these up with two tales in which the desire to invoke perfection or to impose discipline results only in the realization of loss, the fostering of disorder, and the reduction of language to hallucination or a siren's wail.

If the reader discovers in "Metamorphoses" a strand of self-conscious narrative, then he may also notice that that story begins with the building of a form along classical lines and ends with a collapse into pandemonium, presenting him along the way with an artist-hero who is figured not, or not only, as a Dedalus or an Amphion raising the walls of Thebes but as an Icarus or an Orpheus among the Ciconian women. The "old analogy between Author and God . . . can no longer be employed unless deliberately as a false analogy," the protagonist of Barth's "Life-Story" presupposes.[26] Likewise, in response to an interviewer's question about the act of creation, Cheever once equated the "power of control" with "a sense of ecstasy," stating that he had "never felt godlike."[27] It is perhaps because of this that his later short fiction is informed by the strategy of synthesizing or transcending "modernist and premodernist modes of writing" and fusing "straightforwardness and artifice, realism and magic and myth," making him, by Barth's definition at least,[28] "an exemplary postmodernist and a master of the story-teller's art."

NOTES

[1] T. S. Eliot, "Ulysses, Order, and Myth," The Dial, Nov. 1923; rpt. in Selected Essays of T. S. Eliot, ed. Frank Kermode (New York: Harcourt Brace Jovanovich, 1975), pp. 176-79.

[2] James Joyce, A Portrait of the Artist as a Young Man (New York: Viking, 1964), p. 215.

[3] Ezra Pound, "Ulysses," The Dial, June 1922; rpt. in Literary Essays of Ezra Pound, ed. T. S. Eliot (New York: New Directions, 1968), p. 406.

[4] In using the term "prefiguration" to refer to the antecedent myth or archetype pointed to by the modern fiction, I am following the approach taken by John J. White. See, for example, his "Mythological Fiction and the Reading Process," in Literary Criticism and Myth, Yearbook of Comparative Criticism 9, ed. Joseph P. Strelka (University Park: Pennsylvania State Univ. Press, 1980), pp. 72-92, and Mythology in the Novel: A Study of Prefigurative Techniques (Princeton: Princeton Univ. Press, 1971).

[5] John Barth, "The Literature of Replenishment: Postmodernist Fiction" The Atlantic, 245, No. 1 (1980), 68; "The Literature of Exhaustion," The Atlantic, 220, No. 2 (1967), 34.

[6] Charles Caramello, Silverless Mirrors: Book, Self & Postmodern American Fiction (Tallahassee: Univ. Presses of Florida, 1983), pp. 32-33, 30.

[7] Robert M. Slabey, "John Cheever: The 'Swimming' of America," in Critical Essays on John Cheever, ed. R. G. Collins (Boston: G. K. Hall, 1982), p. 189.

[8] For similar estimations of Cheever's career, see not only Slabey, pp. 188-90, but also Frederick Bracher, "John Cheever's Vision of the World," in Critical Essays on John Cheever, ed. Collins, pp. 168-80. Bracher sees Cheever evolving greatly after the publication of The Housebreaker of Shady Hill (1958), but I see some of the characteristics of the later work in at least a few of the stories in that collection.

[9] "The Death of Justina," in The Stories of John Cheever (New York: Knopf, 1978), p. 429. All excerpts of Cheever's fiction are taken from this collection.

[10] George W. Hunt, S. J., John Cheever: The Hobgoblin Company of Love (Grand Rapids: William B. Eerdmans, 1983), pp. 273-80. Although Father Hunt's observations are quite useful, he comes very close on occasion to making what White calls "the most common mistake" in myth criticism, "the substitution of a particular myth for an archetype" (Mythology in the Modern Novel, p. 45). Throughout this essay I have tried to avoid the same pitfall by imitating White in using "myth" to refer to a specific myth, such as the story of Actaeon, and "archetype" to refer to the more general pattern or model.

[11] "In nova fert animus mutatas dicere formas/ corpora;" (Ovid, Metamorphoses, I. 1-2).

[12] Annette Grant, "John Cheever: The Art of Fiction LXII," in Writers at Work, The

Paris Review Interviews, Fifth Series, ed. George Plimpton (New York: Viking-Penguin, 1981); rpt. in *Critical Essays on John Cheever,* ed. Collins, p. 97.

[13] In asserting that Eliot had a kind of allegory in mind, I am following Haskell M. Block. See his essay, "The Myth of the Artist," in *Literary Criticism and Myth,* ed. Strelka, pp. 18-19.

[14] Slabey, pp. 182-85.

[15] See White, *Mythology in the Modern Novel,* p. 88, on the history of this kind of reading.

[16] Slabey, p. 190.

[17] John M. Warner, "Myth and History in Joyce's 'Nausicaa' Episode," *James Joyce Quarterly,* 24 (1986), 19-31, esp. 22-23.

[18] Warner, 23.

[19] Beatrice Greene, "Icarus at St. Botolphs: A Descent to 'Unwonted Otherness,' " *Style,* 5 (1971), 119-37; rpt. in *Critical Essays on John Cheever,* ed. Collins, pp. 154-59.

[20] Joe David Bellamy, ed., *The New Fiction: Interviews with Innovative American Writers* (Urbana: Univ. of Illinois Press, 1974), pp. 8-9.

[21] White, for one, believes that "as long as Barth's skeptical argument is confined to particular novels, rather than working from premises that are assumed to be axiomatic, it makes good sense." To "decide from the outset," however, that there is "a single 'mythopoeic stick,' which can be grasped in only one way," strikes him as "methodologically less prudent" than remaining cautious about such relationships. ("Mythological Fiction and the Reading Process," in Strelka, p. 73.)

[22] According to Clinton S. Burhans, Jr., "In 'Metamorphoses,'" Cheever updates Ovid, and the ease with which Actaeon and Orpheus wear modern dress illustrates Cheever's sense of the past and of the permanence of the human condition." See his "John Cheever and the Grave of Social Coherence," *Twentieth Century Literature,* 14 (1969), 187-98; rpt. in *Critical Essays on John Cheever,* ed. Collins, p. 110. Richard H. Rupp provides some helpful hints about Cheever's adaptation of details but like Burhans sees the work as simply expressing "an Ovidian mood." See "Of That Time, of Those Places: The Short Stories of John Cheever," in *Critical Essays on John Cheever,* pp. 236-37.

[23] Sister M. Bernetta Quinn, *The Metamorphic Tradition in Modern Poetry* (New Brunswick, NJ: Rutgers Univ. Press, 1955), esp. pp. 5-13, 28-29, 147. Working and reading in a later, altered hermeneutic climate, Charles Tomlinson treats many of the same works differently, focusing, for instance, on the metamorphosing of meaningful language into noise in *The Waste Land* and on the connections between patterns of metamorphosis and loss of voice or the projection onto nature of the fragmentation of the self. See his lectures reprinted as: *Poetry and Metamorphosis* (Cambridge, Eng.: Cambridge Univ. Press, 1983).

[24] John B. Vickery, "*The Centaur:* Myth, History, and Narrative," *Modern Fiction Studies,* 20 (1974), 39, 41-43.

[25] John Barth, "Menelaiad," in *Lost in the Funhouse* (New York: Doubleday, 1968), p. 167; "Bellerophoniad," in *Chimera* (New York: Fawcett, 1973), pp. 145-46.

[26] John Barth, "Life-Story," in *Lost in the Funhouse,* p. 128.

[27] Grant, p. 100.

[28] Barth, "The Literature of Replenishment," 70, 71; in defining his program for postmodernist fiction, Barth does not include Cheever among his exemplars, citing instead Gabriel García Márquez and Italo Calvino.

Eudora Welty's Nostalgic Imagination

SALLY WOLFF

The nostalgia for childhood runs deep in Eudora Welty's fiction and essays. Her early stories and novels are alive with complex physical and psychological scenes of growing up. In later works, *The Optimist's Daughter* (1969) and *One Writer's Beginnings* (1984), Welty explores even more carefully and perceptively the joys and confusions of childhood, the transition into adulthood, and the dawning of artistic sensibility. She portrays childhood as a time of innocence, protected from mischance by love and family. Out of the shelter of home, Welty's child ventures curiously forth to encounter a world of mystery. But the uninitiated youth must wait, as Clement Musgrove says in *The Robber Bridegroom,* for the "time of cunning" to come. And some mysteries may never be penetrated, fostering what Welty calls "an abiding respect for the unknown in a human lifetime."[1] Only fullness of time and depth of experience can engender the deep comprehension that usually accompanies maturity. Self-knowledge and respect for human truths are the distinguishing marks of Welty's wisest characters. "Comprehension," she writes, "is more important to me than healing."[2]

"I am a writer who came from a sheltered life," Welty boldly admits in *One Writer's Beginnings* (p. 104), suggesting the condition of both her personal and artistic origins. Welty's fictional and autobiographical renderings of childhood show it to be enclosed, often within an aura of fairy-tale-like enchantment. It is a time of perceiving the secrets of the world but not the clues to them. The children in her stories make awkward guesses about the truths of adult life, and they suffer to know secrets only vaguely apparent. Although they watch and listen closely, children hear stories they cannot quite understand. "Family stories," Welty writes, "are where you get your first notions of profound feelings, mysterious feelings that you might not understand till you grow into them. But you know they exist and that they have power."[3] Hardly able to formulate the appropriate questions to ask of life, these characters nevertheless make daring if awkward attempts to discover the mysteries they perceive around them.

Welty shapes characters with ever deepening comprehension of the beauty and treachery of life. Mysteries unfold, stories are told and finally understood, secrets are fully revealed. Growing up for Welty means achieving a full understanding of the elemental inevitabilities of life. Her stories often depict characters coming to the awareness of sex and death or experiencing the pleasure as well as the sorrow of life. Either the introduction to sex or the devastation of grief usually initiates Welty's children into adulthood.

"Sheltered" also describes the circumstances which fostered Welty's artistic origins. In her writings, emerging physically from protected childhood to the adult world correlates with artistic growth. The processes are virtually inseparable. Wondering, waiting, listening, watching, and anticipating eventually lead the curious child to discovery, comprehension, deep feeling, and self-knowledge. Growing up resembles storytelling in its progression through observation, expectation, and suspense to the revelation of truth. "Time as we know it subjectively," she explains, "is often the chronology that stories and novels follow: it is the continuous thread of revelation" (p. 69). In *One Writer's Beginnings*—at once a memoir and a treatise on writing—Welty reminisces about what life has taught her about becoming an artist—learning to listen, learning to see, and finding a voice.

In her early essay "The Little Store," Welty reconstructs the narrow circumference of the child's perspective. Taking the worn path to the corner store on a "Princess" bicycle, she focuses upon the ground, within the child's close scope of vision, and evokes the daring and invulnerability of the youthful spirit.

> The sidewalk here was old brick, which the roots of a giant chinaberry tree had humped up and tilted this way and that. On skates, you took it fast, in a series of skittering hops, trying not to touch ground anywhere. If the chinaberries had fallen and rolled in the cracks, it was like skating through a whole shooting match of marbles. . . . Setting out in this world, a child feels so indelible.[4]

Despite the regularity of her past trips there, the store itself is yet again a wondrous surprise, with an enchanting array of clay bubble pipes, kite-string, sparklers, peppermints, gum drops, Baby Ruths, and briny pickles. "I believed the Little Store to be a center of the outside world, and hence of happiness—as I believed what I found in the Cracker Jack box to be a genuine prize, which was as simply as I believed in the Golden Fleece."[5] Parents only reinforce the sheltering: "Of course it's easy to see why they both overprotected me," she writes of their caring ways. "Why my father, before I could wear a new pair of shoes for the first time, made me wait while he took out his thin silver pocket knife and with the point of the blade scored the polished soles all over, in a diamond pattern, to prevent me from sliding on the polished floor when I can (pp. 18-19). Childhood for Welty is a pristine world where Cracker Jack prizes and the Golden Fleece are realities—a world yet untouched by peril or sorrow.

Being read to and then reading to another has first a nurturing and then a rehabilitative property in several works which focus upon the security of childhood. In *The Optimist's Daughter,* for example, Laurel recollects heartwarming moments when her parents read to one another. Helped by memory, the attentive child within the grown woman still feels a profound and continuing love:

> In the lateness of the night, their two voices reading to each other where she could hear them, never letting a silence divide or interrupt them, combined into one unceasing voice and wrapped her around as she listened, as still as if she were asleep. She was sent to sleep under a velvety cloak of words, richly patterned and stitched with gold, straight out of a fairy tale, while they went reading on into her dreams.[6]

The act of listening in Welty's essay "Listening" (1984) again brings the child close to her parents' world. Their voices wrap the child in a "richly patterned" "cloak" of sound:

> When I was young enough to still spend a long time buttoning my shoes in the morning, I'd listen toward the hall: Daddy upstairs was shaving in the bathroom and mother downstairs was frying the bacon. They would begin whistling back and forth to each other up and down the stairwell. My father would whistle his phrase, my mother would try to whistle, then hum hers back. It was their duet. I drew my buttonhook in and out and listened to it—I knew it was "The Merry Widow." The difference was, their song almost floated with laughter; how different from the record, which growled from the beginning, as if the Victrola were only slowly being wound up. They kept it running between them, up and down the stairs where I was now just about ready to run clattering down and show them my shoes. (Epigraph to *One Writer's Beginnings*)

Welty also associates the chiming of clocks with a happy childhood. The listening child is comforted by the familiarity of the clocks' sounds, which answer one another like the morning duet:

> we grew up to the striking of clocks. There was a mission-style oak grandfather clock standing in the hall, which sent its gong-like strokes through the living-room, diningroom, kitchen, and pantry, and up the sounding board of the stairwell. Through the night, it could find its way into our ears; sometimes, even on the sleeping porch, midnight could wake us up. My parents' bedroom had a smaller striking clock that answered it. (p. 3)

Listening to reading and to the rhythm of clocks provide the ultimate childhood happiness in her mother's arms: "My mother read to me. She'd read to me in the big bedroom in the mornings, when we were in her rocker together, which ticked in rhythm as we rocked, as though we had a cricket accompanying the story. She'd read to me in the diningroom on winter afternoons in front of the coal fire, with our cuckoo clock ending the story with 'Cuckoo,' and at night when I'd got in my own bed" (p. 5).

Reading and listening to stories read thus become part of Welty's "sensory education" as an artist:

> My love of the alphabet, which endures, grew out of reciting it, but before that, out of seeing the letter on the page. . . the word's beauty and holiness that had been there from the start. . . .
>
> Learning stamps you with its moments. Childhood's learning is made up of moments. . . .
>
> In my sensory education I include my physical awareness of the *word*. (pp. 9-10)

Curiosity complicates these blissful and naive scenes of early life. Both in her fiction and in her autobiographical essays, she depicts children who have strong intimations of profound mysteries. In *Delta Wedding*, for instance, Laura feels the magnetic force of life in the days preceding her sister's wedding, although she cannot quite fathom its meaning: "All these things held the purest enchantment for her; once, last year, she threw her arms around the pickle barrel, and seemed to feel then a heavy, briny response in its nature, unbudging though it was."[7]

But of course, the child longs for an end to the waiting, like Josie in

"The Winds," sheltered in the house of her parents and physically protected at first by her father's embrace: "she looked steadily up at the moon. The moon looked down at her, full with all the lonely time to go."[8] She finds a love note in the street which articulates what she cannot: "O my darling, I have waited so long, when are you coming for me? Never a day goes by that I do not ask When? When? When?"[9] Later in *Delta Wedding* Laura also hopes for an answer:

> She imagined that one day—maybe the next, in the Fairchild house—she would know the answer to the heart's pull, just as it would come to her in school why the apple was pulled down on Newton's head, and that it was the way for girls in the world that they should be put off, put off, put off—and told a little later; but told, surely.[10]

The awareness of mystery often signals the awakening of sexual feelings in Welty's stories. Like Laura, who has intuitions about the force of life when she embraces the pickle barrel, Loch Morrison in *The Golden Apples* (1947) dreams of the "sweet golden juice to come" from the fig tree outside his window. He senses that "Something was coming very close to him, there was something he had better keep track of. . . . he might give a yell, like 'Coming, ready or not!' "[11] Another of the adolescent children in *The Golden Apples,* Nina likens fulfillment to ripening fruit:

> To all fruits, and especially to those fine pears, something happened—the process was so swift, you were never in time for them. It's not the flowers that are fleeting, Nina thought, it's the fruit—it's the time when things are ready that they don't stay. She even went through the rhyme, 'Pear tree by the garden gate, How much longer must I wait?'—thinking it was the pears that asked it, not the picker.[12]

Again Welty's fiction closely reflects her own curiosity about the world:

> From the first I was clamorous to learn—I wanted to know and begged to be told not so much what, or how, or why, or where, as when. How soon?
> > *Pear tree by the garden gate,*
> > *How much longer must I wait?*
> This rhyme from one of my nursery books was the one that spoke for me. But I lived not at all unhappily in this craving, for my wild curiosity was in large part suspense, which carries its own secret pleasure. (p. 22)

The curious child, India, in *Delta Wedding* (1945), one of the youngest and most eager girls in the novel, rises onto her toes during her sister's wedding celebration "to see if she could tell yet what there was about a kiss."[13] Even an older daughter, Dabney, the bride-to-be, expresses India's desire to know the answer to the mysteries which lie before her:

> She wondered if she would ever know. . . . What could she know now? . . . The cotton like the rolling breath of sleep overflowed the fields. Out into it, if she were married, she would walk now—her bare foot touch at the night's hour, firmly too, a woman's serious foot. . . . Draw me in, she whispered, draw me in—open the window like my window, I am still only looking in where it is dark.[14]

The craving to know and curiosity about secrets surface many times in Welty's accounts of growing up. Gossip and stories provide fascinating secrets of other people, and Fannie the loquacious sewing woman epitomizes the teller of fabulous tales:

> This old black sewing woman, along with her speed and dexterity, brought along a great provision of up-to-the-minute news. . . . nothing could stop her. My mother would try, while I stood being pinned up. :'Fannie, I'd rather Eudora didn't hear that.' 'That' would be just what I was longing to hear, whatever it was. 'I don't want her exposed to gossip'—as if gossip were measles and I could catch it. I did catch some of it but not enough. 'Mrs. O'Neil's oldest daughter she had her wedding dress *tried on,* and all her fine underclothes featherstitched and ribbon run in and then—' 'I think that will do, Fannie,' said my mother. It was tantalizing never to be exposed long enough to hear the end. (p. 14)

For children, the stories must remain incomplete, the secrets kept, the answers withheld. The child must simply wait and continue to listen:

> Long before I wrote stories, I listened for stories. Listening *for* them is something more acute than listening *to* them. I suppose it's an early form of participation in what goes on. Listening children know stories are *there.* When their elders sit and begin, children are just waiting and hoping for one to come out, like a mouse from its hole. (p. 14)

But while listening may seem a passive activity like waiting, Welty adds that it led her to storytelling: "The *scene* was full of hints, pointers, suggestions, and promises of things to find out and know about human beings" (p. 15).

The secrets of sexuality "electrify" the young Welty as they do her characters. She begs her mother to reveal them, and yet like Shelley Fairchild, is shy and unprepared to accept the facts:

> It was when my mother came out onto the sleeping porch to tell me goodnight that her trial came. . . . I in the single bed at my end of the porch would be lying electrified, waiting for this to be the night when she'd tell me what she'd promised for so long. Just as she bent to kiss me I grabbed her and asked "Where do babies come from?" . . . She'd told me that the mother and the father had to both *want* the baby. This couldn't be enough. . . . I could not help but know she was not really *telling* me. And more than that, I was afraid of what I was going to hear next. This was partly because she wanted to tell me in the dark. I thought that *she* might be afraid. . . . On the night we came the closest to having it over with, she started to tell me without being asked, and I ruined it by yelling, "Mother, look at the lightning bugs!" . . . I had missed my chance. The fact is she never did tell me. (pp. 15-16).

In another example, listening to her parents' private talk makes her aware of powerful, if indefinable feelings:

> They sat talking. . . . I don't remember that any secrets were revealed to me . . . perhaps I was too young to know what to listen for. But I was present in the room with the chief secret there was—the two of them, father and mother, sitting there as one. I was conscious of this secret and of my fast-beating heart in step together. . . . (pp. 20-21)

With revelation, knowledge, and understanding come the often harsh facts about life and death. Almost by accident Welty's mother revealed to her that she had a baby who died in infancy. "She'd told me the wrong secret—not how babies could come but how they could die, how they could be forgotten about" (p. 17). Also, when Welty's characters feel love and grief, their long initiation into adulthood finally draws to a close. Robbie Fairchild is maturing in *Delta Wedding* during her marriage to George, learning not only about compromise in relationships but also about pleasure and an end to waiting: "She breathed the night in beside him, away off from dreams and time and her own thoughts awake—the companion of his weight and warmth. Then she was glad there was nothing at all, no existence in the world, beyond George asleep, this real and forgetful and exacting body."[15] When Snowdie marries and conceives the children of King MacLain in "Shower of Gold," she looks "like a shower of something had struck her, like she'd been caught out in something bright."[16] A more complex initiate than Snowdie, Virgie Rainey in "The Wanderers" is "full of the air of wildness," "exciting as a gypsy" in her independent spirit. She has an affair with a sailor, plays Beethoven passionately, and drinks vanilla "out of the bottle . . . and it didn't burn her a bit."[17] Of Virgie, Welty writes, "she knows to the last that there is a world that remains out there, a world living and mysterious, and that she is of it. . . . Virgie, at her moments, might have always been my subject" (p. 102).

Welty's own "plunge" into life is not headlong like Virgie's, however:

> I have always been shy physically. This in part tended to keep me from rushing into things, including relationships, headlong. Not rushing headlong, though I may have wanted to, but beginning to write stories about people, I drew near slowly; noting and guessing, apprehending, hoping, drawing my eventual conclusions out of my own heart, I *did* venture closer to where I wanted to go. As time and my imagination led me on, I did plunge. (pp. 21-22)

The fact of death is finally inescapable. How well Welty characters adapt to it is a measurement of sanity and maturity. In "The Little Store," tragedy strikes the owners of the candy store:

> There was some act of violence. The shock to the neighborhood travelled to the children, of course; but I couldn't find out from my parents what had happened. They held it back from me, as they'd held back many things, "until the time comes for you to know." . . . We weren't being sent to the neighborhood grocery for facts of life, or death. But of course those are what we were on the track of, anyway. With the loaf of bread and the Cracker Jack prize, I was bringing home the intimations of pride and disgrace, rumors and early news of people coming to hurt one another, while others practiced for joy—storing up a portion for myself of the human mystery.[18]

Loss and grief afflict many Welty characters and change them irrevocably. Mrs. Larkin's overwhelming and unrelieved despair drives her to ask existential questions about the nature of living and dying: "Life and death, she thought, gripping the heavy hoe, life and death, which now meant nothing to her but which she was compelled continually to wield with both hands, ceaselessly asking, Was it not possible to compensate? to punish? to protest?"[19] Others know different losses. Jennie in "At the Landing," repeatedly raped by men at a fishing camp, confronts the reality of loneliness, disillusionment about love, and the uncertain future. "No Place for You My Love" from *The Bride of the Innisfallen* (1955) presents a failing relationship in excruciating detail.

But in the mortality of a parent or spouse Welty creates her most brutal stories of psychological and emotional maturity. This ultimate mystery is the most difficult for her characters to comprehend. The fragile but secure world of the child vanishes in "The Wide Net" when the young Grady remembers his father, who was drowned in the river: "Grady's inflamed eyes rested on the brown water. Without warning he saw something . . . perhaps the image in the river seemed to be his father, the drowned man— with arms open, eyes open, mouth open . . . . Grady stared."[20]

Welty's most rivetting and uncompromising depictions of grief come with the death of parent and spouse in *The Optimist's Daughter* and the similar passages in *One Writer's Beginnings*. The healing balm of reading voices in Laurel's memory now transforms into the sounds of a daughter's desperate attempt to help her dying father:

> He'd loved being read to, once. With good hopes, she brought in a stack of paperbacks and began on the newest of his favorite detective novelist. He listened but without much comment. She went back to one of the old ones they'd both admired, and he listened with greater quiet. Pity stabbed her. Did they *move too fast* for him now? . . . Here was his daughter, come to help him and yet wrenched into idleness; she could not help him. . . . "I'm not asleep," said her father. "Please don't stop reading."[21]

The once comforting sounds of chiming clocks also become silent and still. After the death of Judge McKelva, what Laurel "listened for tonight was the striking of the mantel clock downstairs in the parlor. It never came."[22] Standing at her father's coffin, she looks at the mantel clock and knows why:

> And she saw that the clock had stopped; it had not been wound, she supposed, since the last time her father had done duty by it, and its hands pointed to some remote three o'clock, as motionless as the time in the Chinese prints. . . . She felt as though in death her father had been asked to bear the weight of that raised lid himself, and hold it up by lying there, the same way he'd lain on the hospital bed and counted the minutes and the hours to make his life go by. She stood by the coffin as she had sat by his bed, waiting it out with him. Unable to hear the ticking of the clock, she listened to the gritting and the hissing of the fire.[23]

For this acute listener, the contrast in sound from the quiet chimes of her girlhood to the "gritting and hissing" is a grim reminder of all that is lost to death.

Describing the clock tower her own father had designed for his work building in downtown Jackson, now overshadowed by taller buildings, Welty again uses the masking and silencing of the clock to symbolize death and irrevocable loss: "The Lamar Life tower is overshadowed now, and you can no longer read the time on its clocktower from all over town, as he'd wanted to be possible always (p. 83).

Welty's images of death reach their most unsparing clarity in *The*

Optimist's Daughter. The deathbed scenes of the Judge, Becky, and Becky's father are all frightening, and the children who witness their parents' deaths are thrust violently into the reality of human frailty and helplessness. Welty recounts her grandfather's death with similar ruthlessness:

> It was in the quilted bed in the front of this house where he lay in so much pain . . . that he once told Mother, a little girl, to bring the knife and plunge it into his side; she, hypnotized, almost believed she must obey. It was from that door that later she went with him on the frozen winter night . . . to a hospital. . . . Mother had to return by herself from Baltimore, her father's body in a coffin on the same train (pp. 50-51).

Even more shocking still is Welty's portrayal of Laurel's dead husband, Phil. Like Grady's drowned father in "The Wide Net," the visage of Phil emerges horribly—mouth gaping in the remembered pain of the death of fire and water he endured. "Now, by her own hands, the past had been raised up, and *he* looked at her, Phil himself—here waiting, all the time, Lazarus. He looked at her out of eyes wild with the craving for his unlived life, with mouth open like a funnel's."[24] Phil's specter is the most evocative of the dread of death—both by those who die and those who survive. "The fantasies of dying could be no stranger than the fantasies of living. Surviving is perhaps the strangest fantasy of them all."[25]

Only in reaching an understanding of love and death can Laurel Hand eventually find solace. Welty's own comment is applicable to Laurel: "Comprehension is more important to me than healing."[26] Love can no longer be "sheltering": protection from peril or pain is untenable. Until her marriage to Phil, Laurel thinks of love "as shelter; her arms went out as a naive offer of safety. He had showed her that this need not be so. Protection, like self-protection, fell away from her like all one garment, some anachronism foolishly saved from childhood." Laurel learns to take emotional risks—to plunge into relationships. She then can find relief from her grief by embracing it bravely and openly, as when her dead grandmother speaks to her in a letter written long before: "A flood of feeling descended on Laurel. She let the papers slide from her hands and the books from her knees, and put her head down on the open lid of the desk and wept in grief for love and for the dead."[27] Near the end Laurel achieves what Welty means by "comprehension" when she finds words to tell the uncomprehending Fay that her mother's breadboard, which Fay has carelessly scarred, represents "The whole solid past."[28] Welty names this moment as Laurel's revelation: "it was a focusing and bringing together and revelation—self-revelation—when everything cleared for her. She realizes a great many complicated things at once about herself and her parents, and about Fay, all together."[29]

Memory is the final pathway leading Laurel to comprehension of the most difficult of human truths. "It is memory that is the somnambulist. It will come back in its wounds from across the world, like Phil, calling us by our names and demanding its rightful tears. It will never be impervious. The memory can be hurt, time and again—but in that may lie its final mercy. As long as it's vulnerable to the living moment, it lives for us, and while it lives, and while we are able, we can give it up its due.''[30]

Welty's mature artistry has drawn from and grown beyond the sheltered life of her childhood. "A sheltered life can be a daring life as well," she says, "for all serious daring starts from within" (p. 104). She has fashioned in her canon these stories of growing up with all its changing perspectives— from the electrifying wonder of discovering secrets, and the search for answers to the heart's pull, to the revelations of adulthood. Yet in these tales Welty always maintains her abiding respect for mystery, for that which is "unknown in a human lifetime," and cannot be revealed even in the wisdom of age.

NOTES

[1] Eudora Welty, *One Writer's Beginnings* (Cambridge, MA: Harvard Univ. Press), p. 90. All subsequent references to this volume are within parentheses in my text.

[2] *Conversations with Eudora Welty,* ed. Peggy Whitman Prenshaw (Jackson: Univ. Press of Mississippi, 1984), p. 116.

[3] Ibid., p. 212.

[4] Eudora Welty, *The Eye of the Story: Selected Essays and Reviews* (New York: Random House-Vintage, 1979), pp. 328-29.

[5] Ibid., p. 332.

[6] Eudora Welty, *The Optimist's Daughter* (New York: Random House, 1969), pp. 57-58.

[7] Eudora Welty, *Delta Wedding* (New York: Harcourt, Brace, 1945), p. 137.

[8] Eudora Welty, *A Curtain of Green* (New York: Doubleday, 1941), p. 133.

[9] Ibid., p. 140.

[10] *Delta Wedding,* p. 76.

[11] Eudora Welty, *The Golden Apples* (New York: Harcourt, Brace, 1947), p. 23.

[12] Ibid., p. 116.

[13] *Delta Wedding,* p. 189.

[14] Ibid., p. 90.

[15] Ibid., p. 148.

[16] *The Golden Apples,* p. 6.

[17] Ibid., p. 39.

[18] *The Eye of the Story,* pp. 334-35.

[19] *A Curtain of Green,* pp. 216-17.

[20] Eudora Welty, *The Wide Net and Other Stories* (New York: Harcourt, Brace, 1943), p. 57.

[21] *The Optimist's Daughter,* pp. 19, 24.

[22] Ibid., p. 58.

[23] Ibid., p. 73.

[24] Ibid., p. 154.

[25] Ibid., pp. 161-62.

[26] *Conversations with Eudora Welty,* p. 116.

[27] *The Optimist's Daughter,* pp. 161, 154.

[28] Ibid., p. 178.

[29] *Conversations with Eudora Welty,* p. 237.

[30] *The Optimist's Daughter,* p. 179.

From the Time Immemorial: Native American Traditions in Contemporary Short Fiction

HELEN JASKOSKI

Contemporary Native American fiction concerns itself with a kind of cultural borderland, where lines between ethnic groups are drawn, denied, defied, and proudly distinguished. Sometimes the lines are territorial, involving geographic boundaries. More often they are psychological, economic, and linguistic: distinguished by separateness and often misunderstanding of custom and world view.

In discussions of these texts, a generalized set of categories—"Indian" and "white"—emerges, as suggested in the subtitle of one of the works considered in this paper: "Indians and Whites in the New Fur Trade." More often, however, the characters' affiliations are specified: Norwegian-American, French-Canadian, Spanish-American, or Mexican, for instance, on the one hand; Navajo, Laguna, Chippewa, Kiowa, Ute, on the other. The subject is complex, and the writers discussed in this essay have used innovative and experimental forms to meet the complexity of their subject.

This essay discusses short fiction by three writers who identify themselves as American Indian or Native American: Louise Erdrich, Gerald Vizenor, and Leslie Marmon Silko. Each author uses traditional American Indian material in a unique manner, each plays variations on the short story genre, and each has published a work which, as a single text, is built on the short story form but which, in its final shape, is more unified than simply a "collection" of short stories. Erdrich's *Love Medicine,* Vizenor's *Wordarrows,* and Silko's *Storyteller* contain short fiction forms, yet the "short stories" in them can only be understood in the context of each book as an integrated whole.[1]

I

Among the works discussed here only *Love Medicine* does not incorporate explicitly autobiographical material. Erdrich's stories do, however, make references to Chippewa lore and culture. A case in point is the Nanapush family name. Variously spelled as Wenebojo, Nanabush, Nanabozho, the name belongs to the great creator/trickster/culture hero at the center of Algonkian mythology. Other Chippewa lore is embedded within the gossipy accounts of the on-going exaltations and tribulations of the Kashpaw, Nanapush, and Lamartine families. Careful reading of Erdrich's stories reveals an intermingling of Chippewa and European motifs and symbols.

A close look at a single story shows Erdrich's use of Chippewa traditions in contrast and parallel with European materials. "Saint Marie," the second story in *Love Medicine,* epitomizes the complex relations between Indians and non-Indians throughout the book. The story's protagonist, tough, intelligent and willful Marie Lazarre, embodies what Paula Gunn Allen describes as "cultural conflict . . . in the psychological and social being" of the individual of mixed heritage.[2] The nuns at the Convent of the Sacred Heart look down on Marie as "Indian," whereas her future husband, Nector Kashpaw, regards her as merely a "skinny white girl" (p. 59) from "a family of horse-thieving drunks" (p. 58).

"Saint Marie" can be read as a ritual tale incorporating both Chippewa and European elements. In the story Erdrich fuses elements of Chippewa *Windigo* stories with European romance and fairy tale motifs and allusions to Christian practice and iconography. Marie Lazarre's great vision, at the center of her story, is related both to European and to Native American traditions.

The central conflict in "Saint Marie" resembles a legendary joust: a demented nun, Sister Leopolda sees herself as fighting the devil for control of Marie's soul and insurance of her salvation, while Marie can only regard such control as fatal. The contest is imaged in parodies of chivalric legend: Leopolda hurls her lance at the devil in the schoolroom coat closet, and later engages in hand-to-hand fencing with poker and fork. Marie's battle with Sister Leopolda also plays out the larger cultural conflict between European/Christian and Native ways of life, the contradictory aims of Christian colonizers having been to maintain power over colonized peoples while at the same time claiming to elevate them as "brothers in Christ."

In doing battle with Leopolda, Marie actually wars against herself, aiming at the contradictory ends of victory and acceptance. Like the heroines of "Cinderella" and "Hansel and Gretel" and other stories of ritual initiation, Marie Lazarre is searching for a "true" parent. Seeking a better home than her own impoverished family's, she enters the convent as the slave-like protege of Sister Leopolda, with all the contradictory love/hate motives that belong to her condition of alienation: "I wanted Sister Leopolda's heart. And here was the thing: sometimes I wanted her heart in love and admiration. Sometimes. And sometimes I wanted her heart to roast on a black stick" (p. 45). But, as in the fairy tales, Leopolda turns out to be a wicked stepmother. Like Cinderella, Marie must dress poorly, sleep behind the stove, and eat meager and coarse food. Like the heroine of "Hansel and Gretel," Marie attempts to thrust her tormentor into the oven. Eventually (but not in this story), she marries a "prince," though that triumph is ambiguous, and she does not, like Gretel, succeed in cremating her tormentor. Rather than the warrior's physical victory, Marie gains the trickster's triumph of cleverness—and, in her special case, moral insight.

Marie Lazarre's ceremony of initiation and maturity also incorporates references to Christian religious traditions. The Christian elements, however, consistently reflect the inversion of putative Christian values in historical relations between Indians and white colonizers.

Sister Leopolda's hooks, first on the long oak window-opening pole and then on the poker, recollect two biblical hooks: the shepherd's crook adopted as a symbol of bishops' guidance and authority, and fishhooks, reminiscent of the New Testament passage in which the apostles are to become "fishers of men" and "catch" souls for heaven. Marie compares herself in her naive faith to a fish that has taken bait, and at the end of the story squirms like a gaffed fish in her recognition of Sister Leopolda's pathetic hunger for love. Yet in retrospect, Marie has been the one fishing, commenting that "maybe Jesus did not take my bait, but them Sisters tried to cram me right down whole," following this recollection with the pungent comparison of herself to a lure that a walleye has swallowed (p. 41).

The gulping fish is one of many references to food and eating throughout the story (and the whole novel). Further paralleling the comparison of fish's bait to the "lure" of faith is Marie's allusion to Indians who had eaten the smallpox-infected hat of a Jesuit; instead of receiving healing power they consumed infection. There are many traditional accounts of the white man's "gift" of smallpox; in some, trade goods are infected,[3] and in one version Smallpox is personified as a missionary himself.[4] In "Saint Marie" the image is a central metaphor for relations between the Christian Sister Leopolda and the powerless children she teaches. In a parody of the sacrament of communion, which to believers imparts life and healing, the Indians swallow disease; Leopolda fasts herself gaunt but is consumed by madness, possessed by the dark power that Marie understands as the Christian's Satan or the Chippewa's *Windigo.*

While Marie's and Leopolda's job in the convent is baking bread— "God's labor" (p. 47) according to Leopolda—Marie does not eat bread in any communion with the nuns; rather, Leopolda feeds the girl first the priest's goat cheese—"that heaven stuff" (p. 47) Marie calls it—and then cold mush. Marie's initiation into the Christian life of the convent also includes a blasphemous "baptism," as Sister Leopolda first pours scalding water over the girl and then rubs her back with salve, parodying the use of anointing oils in several Christian rites. Finally, Marie's eventual triumph also begins with an image of eating, when she envisions Leopolda following her and swallowing the glass she walks through.

In addition to allusions to the sacraments, traditional Christian iconography and familiar superstitious practices appear in the story. When Leopolda places her foot on Marie's neck she is imitating a popular representation of the virgin Mary in which the madonna is shown to be standing with her foot on the neck of a serpent representing Satan. Related to this powerful madonna is the woman clothed with the sun described in the book of Revelation, which pious art frequently identifies with the virgin Mary, and which resembles Marie's vision of herself as transfigured in gold and diamonds. Finally there is the stigmata: the belief that the bodies of certain holy individuals spontaneously reproduce the wounds of Christ. Marie, seeing that Sister Leopolda has used the appearance of stigmata to avoid having to admit that she stabbed the girl's hand, ironically colludes with Leopolda in deceiving the naive nuns and humbling Leopolda.

In finally turning the tables on Leopolda, Marie plays a trickster's part, using her enemy's own weapon against her and accomplishing through apparent acceptance and submission ("swallowing" the stigmata story) the triumph that had eluded direct confrontation and violence. The whole complex of Christian allusions, however, builds to subvert the moral claims of Christianity: the unholy "sacraments," the perversions of images of sanctity and glorification, all tend to underscore the corruption of Sister Leopolda's and the whole missionary enterprise.

Less explicit, but essentially to the story's significance as a tale of the quest for identity, are the suggestions of traditional Chippewa *windigo* stories, and allusions to the ritual of "crying for pity." "*Windigo* story" actually refers to two kinds of stories: traditional tales of the cannibal giant of myth and legend, and reports of real persons afflicted with "*windigo* psychosis."[5] In the traditional tales *Windigo* is a giant, a skeleton of ice, the embodiment of winter starvation, a cannibal who can devour whole villages. *Windigo* sickness occurs when this dangerous spirit takes possession of a human soul, causing an irresistible desire to consume human flesh. Individuals subject to such possession show signs of their vulnerability in greedy gluttony, especially an insatiable appetite for fat and grease. In the legends, the *windigo* monster is usually clubbed to death or killed in fighting; the body is often subsequently burned. Cure for the psychosis, however, often involves pouring boiling water or tallow on or into the afflicted one or even death by fire.

In many stories the *windigo* meets defeat at the hands of a child, sometimes a little girl. Often, such a hero must become a *windigo* herself in order to defeat the monster. Sometimes the monster itself is not killed but returns to natural human life after being relieved of its icy carapace; in the same way, a person afflicted with *windigo* psychosis might return to normal after melting or losing the heart of ice. A second, sometimes related, complex of Chippewa stories involves one person using magic or spell to "possess" another; the possessed one, often a younger relative, then defeats the worker of evil.

"Saint Marie" contains several elements of such *windigo* and possession stories. Marie apparently recognizes Leopolda's nemesis, Satan, as the *windigo*, for she says that the nun "knew as much about him as my grandma, who called him by other names and was not afraid" (p. 42). The earliest known written reference to *windigo*, in the missionary Paul le Jeune's *Relation* of 1636, associates *windigo* cannibalism with demonic possession, and the first reference in English, in James Isham's *Observations and Notes: 1743-1749* offers the definition "the Devil" for the term "*Whit te co.*"[6]

Marie describes herself as a potential candidate for intimacy with *windigo:* "Before sleep sometimes he came and whispered conversation in the old language of the bush. I listened. He told me things he never told anyone but Indians. I was privy to both worlds of his knowledge" (p. 43). She has the appetite for fat attributed to the incipient *windigo:* "It was the cheese that got to me. When I saw it my stomach hollowed. My tongue dripped. I loved that goat-milk cheese better than anything I'd ever ate. I stared at it. The rich curve in the buttery cloth" (p. 47).

The whole boiling water episode parallels several *windigo* tales in which the monster perishes after having boiling water or tallow poured on it, or in which the possessed person is cured by being made to drink boiling tallow. In a number of tales moving kettles foreshadow the appearance of the *windigo*,[7] and in "Saint Marie" the prostrate Marie hears the kettle moving on the stove and takes it as an ill omen. Moreover, the girl's rigid coldness calls to mind the *Windigo*'s heart of ice. Marie recalls herself as clothed in "veils of hate petrified by longing" (p. 42). Leopolda refers several times to the girl's coldness, and before pouring boiling water on her in that depraved baptismal rite, the nun intones, "You're cold. There is a wicked ice forming in your blood," then threatens to "boil [the "evil one"] from your mind if you make a peep . . . by filling up your ear" (p. 49).

But it is the skeletal, starving, spiritually cannibalistic Leopolda who is truly possessed by the *windigo,* who tries to possess Marie, and who must be defeated. Leopolda's physical gauntness hints at the anorexia often associated with *windigo* sickness,[8] just as her spiritual cannibalism manifests itself in her mania for total control of the children she teaches. She has "snared in her black intelligence" (p. 42) the lonely child, Marie, first through fear, by locking the irreverent girl in a coat closet, then through promise of love: "He *wants* you," Leopolda tells the girl, "That's the difference, I give you love" (p. 44). But like the dangerous, domineering uncles, aunts, and strangers in the folk tales, Leopolda offers only sick possession, not the nurturing love the young woman seeks. She must be defeated.

Besides traditional Chippewa tales of *windigo* and of magical possession, "Saint Marie" also alludes to an important ritual complex among many plains peoples: the youth's ordeal of "crying for pity" from the powers of the spirit world in search of a guiding vision.[9] In Chippewa tradition both girls and boys alike sought visionary power through fasting and isolated meditation. Boys were encouraged to fast as children in preparation for the great vision quest associated with puberty, and girls sequestered themselves to receive a vision at menarche. Marie Lazarre, in "near age fourteen" (p. 40) at the time of the story, has come to the time for her vision quest.

It is characteristic of the irony throughout Erdrich's story that while Sister Leopolda continually fasts, it is Marie who has the vision. Marie's own ordeal of boiling water and piercing fork resembles tests of physical endurance and mutilation practiced by prairie tribes such as the Crow, more than it reflects traditional Chippewa practice.[10] Certainly, though unwillingly, Marie cries out, both in the coat closet and in the kitchen under the scalding water: "God's face. Even that did not disrupt my continued praise. Words came. Words came from nowhere and flooded my mind. Now I could pray much better than any one of them. Than all of them full force" (p. 49).

In the depths of her ordeal Marie undergoes the "loss of self" that precedes the enabling, integrating vision: "I despaired. I felt I had no inside voice, nothing to direct me, no darkness, no Marie" (p. 50). Immediately she decides to throw out her food—an act of metaphorical fasting—and then receives her magnificent power vision. The vision is a turning point in the story. Afterwards, Marie can confront Leopolda with the hard truth that both are engaged with the power of darkness: " 'He was always in you,' I said. 'Even more than in me' " (p. 52), and she recognizes for the first time a vulnerability in the nun: "But for the first time I had gotten through some chink she'd left in her darkness. Touched some doubt" (p. 52).

This knowledge of their mutual humanity culminates in Marie's eventual, reluctant understanding of Leopolda's own pathetic need for love, a recognition that destroys the savor of her hard-won, duplicitous triumph. While Marie Lazarre, the stubbornly ambitious, love-starved girl has been crying for pity from the powers of the universe, Saint Marie, the trickster heroine and emblem of virtue, succumbs to unwilling pity for her tormenter: "I pitied her. Pity twisted in my stomach like that hook-pole was driven through me. I was caught" (p. 56). Here again we catch a sense of those *windigo* stories in which, when the ice is chipped away from the monster, "in the center, there was a regular man";[11] so Marie sees Leopolda "kneeling within the shambles of her love" (p. 56), a "regular human" underneath it all. In her pity for poor old Leopolda, Marie also reaches the "regular human" within the stony defenses of the tough, ambitious little girl.

I have focused in this discussion on "Saint Marie" as an autonomous short story. But the story is more, an integral part of "a novel, a solid, nailed down, compassionate and coherent narrative."[12] The structure of *Love Medicine* is a complex series of such tales, interlocking through recurrence of character and event and through variation of point of view. There is some parallel to those series of episodes that make up the great sequences of traditional Native American myth, and certainly other traditional themes (like motifs from the Nanabozho stories, and the more recent Chippewa adaptations of the Cinderella tale) must be examined to savor the full richness of the work. The nearest parallel in narrative organization, however, is probably the works of William Faulkner. Erdrich shares with Faulkner above all a down-to-earth comic vision. Beyond this, *Love Medicine,* like the sagas of the Compsons and Snopeses, aims at a complex rendering of the intricate and far-reaching minglings and conflicts and interlocking fates among people of differing races and culture groups, all of whom feel a deep sense of their ties to the land and to their history upon it.

II

Scholar, journalist, editor and activist as well as author of fiction, Gerald Vizenor explains the subtitle of *Wordarrows* as "Cultural Word Wars Between Whites and Indians in the New Fur Trade." The fact that in its final publication the book has a different subtitle suggests something about the outcome of such wars when one side is tribal and the other is industrial. Vizenor allows legitimacy to such generalized conceptualizations as "white" and "Indian," but rejects the term "Indian" as a EuroAmerican construct— "the idea of the invented Indian"[13]—in favor of the term "tribal." As he explains in his Preface to *Earthdivers,*

> The word *Indian,* of course, is an invention which has rendered extinct thousands of individual and distinct tribal cultures. . . . There are limitations to the use of the word *tribal,* because the word suggests a colonial and political derogation of oral traditional and communal cultures. Notwithstanding the colonial usage, the author intends the word *tribal* to be a celebration of communal values which connect the *tribal celebrants* to the earth.[14]

Most preferable, however, are specific tribal designations; in the introduction to *anishinabe adisokan* Vizenor explains why he rejects the designation Chippewa (or Ojibwa): "The name *anishinabe* has been consistently used in this book rather than *chippewa* or *ojibway indians* which are all invented names . . . . The word *anishinabe* [also anishinaabe] means *the people* in the language of the *anishinabe* people."[15] All of Vizenor's works, but *Wordarrows* in particular, reflect an ongoing concern with naming, and with the nature and power of language.

In many of his writings Gerald Vizenor has identified himself with the Native American figure of the trickster. The Native American trickster, as described by Paul Radin in the classical work on the subject, is a character of many guises: creator, destroyer, culture hero, fool, shapeshifter, amoral gluttonizer, and bringer of rules for correct behavior.[16] Vizenor envisions the trickster as shapeshifter, con man, magician, and—above all—a manipulator of and creator with language. The non-European trickster offers a crucial corrective to western-tradition ethnocentrism and cultural and power-greedy myopia; in considering the trickster's function as showing the essential relativity and flux and finitude of any world-view, Vizenor finds common ground with the thinking of some post-structuralist philosophers. Vizenor's unique contribution to the character, however, is his conceptualization of the compassionate trickster: a figure who ultimately bring comfort and paradoxical wisdom to tribal people beleaguered in the contemporary "urban reservation."[17] *Wordarrows* offers layers of verbal trickery and shapeshifting, mixing fiction and history in vignettes of modern, urban life for people at the "cultural edge."

Vizenor himself appears in the stories collected in *Wordarrows,* at times as an anonymous "tribal advocate," occasionally in his own person, and sometimes under the name of Clement Beaulieu. In appropriate trickster fashion, he has it both ways: he puts on a disguise in the stories, but lets the reader in on the trick in his Introduction. Although he has not commented directly on it, the metaphorical significance of the name cannot have escaped Vizenor: Clement (merciful) and Beaulieu (beautiful place). The last name especially suggests the deep and nurturing ties of tribal peoples to their land (and foreshadows the debilitating consequences of removal, especially to the sterile urban environment). The fictional character of Clement Beaulieu is a compassionate yet skeptical social worker, a tribal advocate, harried by the bureaucracy above and the intractable and overwhelming problems around him, but maintaining above all a sense of humor in the face of historical and existential absurdity.

There is more to the pseudonym "Clement Beaulieu," however, as Vizenor explains in his preface to *Wordarrows.* "Clement is the first name of my father, who was born on the White Earth Reservation, and the first name of several distant relatives. Beaulieu, from Alice Beaulieu Vizenor, is the last name, the birth name, of my paternal grandmother from the White Earth Reservation" (p. x). In another collection of narratives, *The People Named the Chippewa,* Vizenor prints the testimony of one Clement Beaulieu before a Senator in an inquiry on the closing of a newspaper published by Theodore Beaulieu, who was Vizenor's great-uncle.[18]

Hence, Gerald Vizenor identifies his fictional persona with an earlier fighter in the "word wars" between the Anishinabeg and the surrounding white world. The issue in the earlier Beaulieu case was the right of the people to write about their problems in their own way, to define themselves and their reality in their own terms; opposition came from a BIA functionary who insisted that only the dominant culture's version and vision of reality was to be articulated.

The Beaulieu link with journalism and reporting is also significant (Vizenor himself has worked as a journalist, publishing two collections of his articles). Vizenor's mix of fact and fiction is an admission of journalism into the elevated world of "high art," and another weapon in the word wars. By intermingling fiction with fact—with the plain description of everyday reality—Vizenor seeks to undercut the euphemism, romanticism, and ignorance of the dominant culture's prevailing myth of "the Indian." In the contemporary critical idiom, Vizenor's project is the self-conscious demythologizing and deconstructing of the EuroAmerican invention of "the Indian"; it is meant to be an enabling activity that will further the re-construction of creative, generative tribal ways of thinking and feeling.

The issue of whose reality will prevail receives explicit focus in the story in *Wordarrows* titled "Marleen American Horse." The overwhelming concern in this story is language as determinant of reality, and the "cultural word wars" are fought over whose terminology is to prevail.

The plot of "Marleen American Horse" is deceptively simple, as befits a trickster story. In this tale the tribal advocate remains anonymous. Marleen, a young Oglala woman born on the Fort Berthold Reservation in North Dakota, who has lost everything, talks to the tribal advocate in Minneapolis about her problems: her loss of home, children and clothes, her alcoholism, her sense of helplessness. After a wild goose chase through various social services referral systems she leaves his office with two dimes and a promise to call him if she needs to.

A great deal of the dialogue between the two characters, and a major part of the story, is taken up with the tribal advocate's attempt to show Marleen how an alien language has shaped reality for her. Since, as she says, she is not white, he wants to know why she has a white problem: "Drunken Indian" (p. 43). He dilates at length on the way

> "We are treated like children in a new school on the first morning of classes, words are like prisons then, new controls, learning the definitions of tribute to the teachers. And we are taught to praise those who detain and define us in simple words, disagreement is defined as being a loser, and when we speak our own language, not tribal languages now, but the languages of our hearts and our experiences, the tongue of our hearts, we are shunned or punished for speaking without manners.
>
> "But you are not a child, you are not made out of white words." (p. 42)

All that the white world has to offer Marleen, he says, are word cures, definitions of a problem which only fit a non-tribal mentality, and solutions that are correspondingly inadequate: "These are dependencies. Word cures are like eating menus for dinner and wondering why our children still hunger" (pp. 43-44). Her sickness, in short, which she has contracted from the alien world surrounding her, is nominalism: separation of signifier from signified, and acceptance of empty language as substitute for gritty substance.

The tribal advocate's speech suggests an inundation of language, a torrent of words that effectually drowns the substance and soul of the tribal person, the one who is "other." Two elements in the story reinforce the sense of inundation and connect it with the creative uses of language.

The first allusion to drowning with language lies in the story's title and the name of its protagonist. Part of Vizenor's shapeshifting as a writer is nameshifting, not only in his own various guises as anonymous "tribal advocate" and pseudonymous Clement Beaulieu, but in treatment of characters as well. Naming is a crucial aspect of what Vizenor calls tribal thinking, and custom and ceremony in many tribes surround such events as naming a child, receiving a sacred name or speaking the name of the dead.[19]

Marleen American Horse bears the name of a nineteenth-century Oglala orator and leader who, in negotiations over the treaty at Pine Ridge, carried on one of the great filibusters of American history. American Horse spoke almost without interruption for three days. He talked not only about the treaty under discussion but also about "rations, boundaries, former treaties, agents, traders, schools, the past, the present, and the future."[20] In the end, he failed to persuade his people to adopt the course he felt was in their best interests. By the standards of history and the "real world," American Horse was a failure, as is his fictional namesake, Marleen. Nevertheless, in the paradoxical view of the trickster, it is his art—not its outcome—that matters.

In Vizenor's story, the tribal advocate actually acts the part of the historical American Horse, trying through a trickster's seemingly backward advice to persuade the puzzled and helpless Marleen to be, in the psychological jargon, less "other-directed" and more "inner-directed." "If you must drink," he tells her, "then drink in good humor, drink with the courage of a warrior and feel good, but never drink as a problem" (p. 44).

Another kind of inundation is important as well. The omniscient narrator opens this brief and rather intimate tale of an encounter between two individuals with a brief account of a historical event: "The United States Army Corps of Engineers contracted for the construction of the Garrison Dam to hold back the Missouri River in North Dakota. Elbowoods, a small tribal village, the home and birthplace of Marleen American Horse, fell beneath the new flood, the federal creation of Lake Sakakawea, on the Fort Berthold Reservation" (p. 38). The terminology here has echoes of Genesis, with the "new flood" and "the federal creation," and suggests the Faustian hubris associated with the historical American project of "settling" an "empty" continent. Parallel with the later references to the prevailing desire for success and corollary fear of failure, this passage suggests worship of the great god Progress, for whom, presumably, Elbowoods and its inhabitants, including Marleen, simply did not exist. Marleen left the home of her birth to escape the progress that promised to bring a "flood of white men and their pleasure boats" (p. 38), just as the original American Horse had seen a flood of white settlers come upon his land.

The *old* flood implied in the story's opening passage is the primeval inundation that covered the original, mythic world. According to the ancient traditions, in that time immemorial, the water being had caused a great flood after stealing the nephew that hunted for Nanabush. Muskrat, weakest of animals, dove beneath the flood and returned with bits of earth in his mouth and hands and around his genitals; then Nanabush the trickster and creator breathed on the drowned Muskrat, restoring him to life and beginning the creation of the present-day world from bits of the salvaged dirt. Marleen American Horse, whose "weaknesses were shunned on the street" and who "wanted nothing more than to be loved in a cold and insensitive world" (p. 40), plays the part of Muskrat to the tribal advocate's Nanabush. He tries, through his breath—which produces speech—to enable her to perform within herself the elemental creative act, "reaching deep down inside yourself" as a Cree commentator explained, "to find a tiny grain of sand. . . . To create meaning one must reach down inside and transform through the breath of creativity."[21]

The significance of diving within, and of revivifying through breathing and speech, connects the ancient tribal wisdom and the advocate's application of behaviorist and self-actualization therapeutic cliches. "Close your eyes while you listen and let your stomach go" (p. 42) he tells Marleen, and later, "Care for yourself" (p. 44), urging her to forget external definitions and reach within. The emphasis on inner vision also links Marleen's story to its epigraph from Carlos Castaneda, which asserts that we "make ourselves," either miserable or strong. (Castaneda himself was also a kind of trickster, cashing in on "self-realization" trends of the 1960s.) "We are living an impossible dream as winners and failures" (p. 42), contends the advocate, repudiating the prevailing American dream of success. It is the inner journey that counts, in which one dives deep down to "remake" the self.

One other manipulation of language bears on the theme of meaningless words versus felt reality. After presenting Marleen in all her helplessness and degradation, Vizenor inserts a poem into his text, introducing it with a qualification of Marleen's sorry state: "But she would not give up her translated tribal name" (p. 39). The poem begins with facts about language: "she learned english/ without a winter coat/ in a cold place for sacred names" (p. 39). The disjunction english/sacred names echoes the dichotomy of menus/food as a cure for starving children. In the poem, Marleen stands for a whole stereotyped image of tribal women, "squaw for the soldiers . . . she was down/ in a civilization she never understood" (p. 39). Nevertheless, "she raised the sacred flag of her people/ lifting with the eagles/ dreaming/ her children were coming home" (p. 39).

The opposition of Marleen's "dreaming" to the stereotype of the drunken "squaw" again parallels for Vizenor the dichotomy between "sacred names," that is, meaningful, creative, potent language, and "english," the medium for sterile word cures. In its verbal construction of reality the western-industrial world scorns dreams as unreal, in phrases like "living in a dream world" or "only a dream." Tribal people, according to Vizenor (and countless anthropologists), on the other hand, regard dreams as the source of significant knowledge—sometimes of all knowledge. Dreams are beyond words, only to be alluded to in sacred or ceremonial language. So, the tribal advocate assures Marleen that "ceremonies are cures" (p. 43), and ceremonies traditionally begin in visionary experience.

Like the folks who move in and out of Louise Erdrich's stories, Vizenor's characters tend to appear and reappear in different works. Vizenor begins an essay on alcoholism titled "Firewater Labels and Methodologies" with an account of one Plain Johnson, born Samuel American Horse, who "refused to reveal his tribal name in public"[22] and who intends to call himself Plain until he locates his mother Marleen and reunites his family. The fictional Plain is a metaphor, first of all, a personification of the Results of Alcohol in one sense, and of inexplicable survival and independence in another. His youth in a series of foster homes is also reminiscent, however, of Vizenor's own childhood,[23] and he represents yet another metamorphosis of the rebellious, compassionate trickster. Trickery, shapeshifting, and verbal survival endeavors carry on.

Gerald Vizenor's philosophical and artistic vision sees the medium of language as creating a single coherent reality that connects personal, family, tribal, historical, and mythic realities. Language is powerful and sacred, and its sacred function lies in ceremonialism and in storytelling. The essence of reality, then, is story. Culture-making, history-making, reality-making, all are really a function of story-telling. Bureaucratic, institutional verbiage, on the other hand, is a corruption of language: it is language that constructs lists, forms and questionnaires rather than stories, and it is divorced from the realities of individual human lives. A corrective to this unfortunate degradation of language is a kind of storytelling that subverts normal categories and expectations, that challenges the comfortable boundaries between "fiction" and "fact."[24] The interpenetration of fictional and factual realities, as seen in tribal points of view, produces a new kind of history, a counter-story to the official history of progress and success. "The real worlds are not unlike imagined mythic worlds. Differences in realities are never clear because the distances between tribal dreams, earthdiver myths, comedies and metaphors, and familiar places float free from time in some conversations."[25]

III

Fascinated, like Vizenor, with traditional reverence for the power of language, Leslie Silko also includes personal and historical material in *Storyteller*. In its form, Silko's book resembles a scrapbook: drawings, photographs, and traditional tales and poems mingle with personal reminiscence and conventional short stories, and the book is bound on the narrow side of the pages, further suggesting scrapbook form. While Vizenor uses the trickster's gambits of disguise and transformation to achieve an interpenetration of "fictional" and "factual" realities, Silko, in contrast, juxtaposes various elements against each other while maintaining the stubborn integrity of form in each individual piece.

Parallels to *Storyteller* in the visual arts would be the collage and the patchwork quilt. Silko places uncaptioned photographs (identified in a list at the end), traditional tales rendered in free verse, personal reminiscences, poems, and prose short stories next to each other without explanation or editorial comment, thus constraining the reader to make the connections between disparate visual and verbal elements—to "complete" the book through active participation in constructing connections and meaning. (The photographs also provide a necessary sense of visual milieu for non-Indian readers, most of whom having vague or no ideas of what Indians and the landscape of New Mexico pueblos really look like.)

Thematic connections emerge between visual and verbal elements. One example is a photograph of Silko's elderly Aunt Susie standing with a child three or four years old (the author?) in a windswept field next to a barbed-wire fence. This family picture captures several important themes in *Storyteller:* the continuity of tradition through generations in the shaping of reality through memory and storytelling, human connections to land and landscape, and the boundaries—sometimes barbed—that separate individuals of the same family from each other, and in the contemporary stories, divide groups of people into differing cultural, linguistic or racial categories. The photograph is placed within a passage of reminiscence about Aunt Susie, her concern for history and scholarship, and her care to transmit her knowledge to younger generations.

Two of the short stories in *Storyteller,* "Yellow Woman" and "Tony's Story," exemplify emphasis on the continuity of tradition. In "Yellow Woman" a young mother, living a placid if boring existence with her family, meets and elopes in a brief idyll with a handsome, masterful stranger. The narrator experiences the fulfillment of wishes familiar to readers of romantic novels, playing out in a semi-dreamlike state the fantasy of an exciting, anonymous encounter unburdened by guilt or consequences. The model the young woman turns to is the traditional Keres figure of Yellow Woman,[26] and the protagonist sees herself as becoming part of the tradition that lives in the stories: "I was sorry that old Grandpa wasn't alive to hear my story because it was the Yellow Woman stories he liked to tell best" (p. 62). The story, that is, will vindicate her experience, validate her reality.

"Yellow Woman" is contemporary in setting, placed within the pastoral environment of the reservation. Indeed, much of the narrator's winsomeness derives from her absolute confidence in the nurturing, supportive community of which she is a part. Yet even within this peaceable kingdom encounters between inhabitants of different cultural realities are full of misunderstanding. The seducer, Silva, describes his relations with Mexican ranchers as "I steal from them" (p. 58), and when the lovers encounter a white rancher looking for the cattle Silva has butchered "the white man got angry when he heard Silva speak in a language he couldn't understand" (p. 61).

Silko prefaces "Yellow Woman" with a fragment from a traditional Yellow Woman story, the words of Whirlwind Man, and follows it with retellings of two traditional Yellow Woman legends in "COTTONWOOD Part One: Story of Sun House" and "Part Two: Buffalo Story." Later, in a poem titled "Storytelling," she elaborates in yet another way her perception of how the past and its stories construct the story of the present. The issue is a recurring one with Silko, as indicated in an early interview, where she explained that "these kinds of things that I was doing when I was fifteen are exactly the kinds of things out of which stories like the Yellow Woman story [come]. I finally put the two together: the adolescent longings and the old stories, that plus the stories around Laguna at the time about people who did . . . use the river as a meeting place."[27] Stories, gossip, legends, dreams: these weave the fabric of the close-knit community life, constantly inventing and reinventing Yellow Woman and her world.

"Tony's Story" portrays the persistence of tradition in a context of ignorance, misunderstanding and violent injustice. The contemporary short story shares with another of the traditional tales in *Storyteller* an emphasis on witchcraft as accounting for irrational and evil behavior. In the traditional tale, "Estoy-eh-muut and the Kunideeyahs," a young wife deserts her husband for a witch-lover. After several adventures, her husband tries to return to the village to "warn the people about her" (p. 152), but is given a commission by Spider Woman to destroy her.

In the contemporary story, the assimilated Leon, who has been in the army and who accepts "white" concepts of law and due process, has no resources to explain or to cope with the unrestrained viciousness of the unnamed policeman. Tony, on the other hand, knows that the officer is in reality a witch, and seeks a violent and final answer to this trouble. Though his analysis of the problem is traditional, Tony's solution—a private revenge—is not.[28] Silko's vision in "Tony's Story" and in other of the tales in *Storyteller* offers a bleak picture of life "at the friction point between cultures."[29] Ignorance and misunderstanding are the rule, bearing out George Copway's observation more than a hundred years ago that, in direct contact on the (cultural or geographical) frontier, it is generally the least noble and most depraved whites with whom Indians must deal.[30]

One of Silko's most poignant presentations of this theme of mutual misunderstandings is in "Lullaby." The mode of "Lullaby" is essentially lyrical rather than dramatic. There is only one sentence of direct discourse, and the story's movement follows the protagonist's consciousness through association of images as she moves forward in a journey to find her husband, while drifting back in thought to earlier days.

Like elegiac poems, "Lullaby" depicts the process of coming to terms with death and loss. The protagonist, an elderly Navajo woman named Ayah, has much to grieve for: the death of her eldest son, Jimmy, in an incomprehensible and distant war; the deaths in infancy of other children; the forced removal and then deliberate alienation of her two remaining offspring; a long estrangement from her husband, Chato. Finally, as the story ends, she confronts and accepts her own death.

Intertwined with these human deaths is the more abstract but no less felt loss of heritage, culture, and way of life. There will be no children and grandchildren to teach and nurture in the way Ayah had been educated and cared for by her mother and grandmother. Art, religion, language, natural history—all is being lost. Even the sacred compact with the earth seems broken in the persistent drought. Once the land had produced all that the people needed—wool and bright dyes for strong, waterproof blankets, leather for leggings and shoes, meat hung on the rafters to dry. Now Ayah and Chato find themselves reduced to a drab Army blanket, boots with holes in them, and a meager welfare check that only buys dead flour and tinned peaches.

The harshness and emptiness of present life correspond to the coldness of the alien society that surrounds the Navajo world. After Jimmy dies the government can offer his parents nothing for their grief but his corpse. Clinical efficiency rather than feeling or tradition rules in the white world into which the younger children, Danny and Ella, disappear. Fear and hostility likewise characterize the bartender and his patrons, who tolerate Chato only insofar as he is like them—speaking their language. His former employer keeps Chato on only so long as the man can be exploited; when Chato can no longer work he is discarded like a broken machine. Efficiency, cost-effectiveness, and arrogance in the white world clash with Ayah's traditional reverence for the natural world, family ties, and continuing life.

Ayah makes her peace with loss by removing, so far as possible, from the white world of hostile strangers, and by returning to the old life. Living in the house of her mother and grandmother, with her husband to tend her flocks, she carries on the Navajo matrilineal tradition, which will end with her. The story takes her through her last day as, on her snowy search for Chato, she makes a spiritual journey back in memory and relives each of her earlier losses.

The story portrays Ayah as realizing stages of grief recognized by psychologists: denial, anger, despair, and finally reconciliation and peace.[31] She remembers the sense of unreality and disbelief that accompanied the death of her eldest: "It wasn't like Jimmie died. He just never came back" (p. 44). Then there had been anger, at herself and at Chato, because she had been duped into betraying herself and her younger children, when she signed the papers allowing Danny and Ella to be taken from her. Despair followed, in long years of numbing depression, and estrangement from Chato and the lost children. On this day, however, each recollection carries with it a sense of understanding and—finally—of peace.

Ayah's final sense of reconciliation with the past also brings a renewed spiritual union with the natural world. The snow recalls the weaving and dying she watched as a child, and then draws her to remembrances of childbirth. By the end of the story the recollections of her early life reawaken her aching love for her children, and bring to her mind the words of a traditional lullaby. The song, which has been sung by Ayah's mother and grandmother, unites the child with the universe and her family, telling her that she is related as a child and sister to the entire natural world: "The earth is your mother . . . The sky is your father . . . Rainbow is your sister . . . The winds are your brothers" (p. 51).

The imagery in "Lullaby" relates directly to Navajo traditions and culture.[32] At the opening of the story, Ayah hears the wind sing a *Yeibichei* song. *Yeibichei* are Holy People, spirits who inhabit sacred mountains, springs and other holy sites, and who are called upon in ceremonies, especially rituals for healing the sick or injured. A *Yeibichei* song is a sacred song, part of such a healing ritual, and when Ayah hears the wind singing such a song it signifies that her story may be understood as a healing ritual. The lullaby at the end of the story echoes the form of many healing songs in its structure of verse and repetition as well as in its imagery of earth mother and sky father, rainbow sister and wind brother. These are frequent figures in the sand paintings that form part of the great healing rituals: they always appear in pairs of doubles and represent a centering of the individual within a harmonious universe.

"Lullaby" as elegy concludes with a return to the ancient healing song and a reconciliation on many levels. Concepts of return and circularity also recur in Navajo thought and iconography. The hogan, the traditional Navajo home, is a roughly circular dwelling constructed as a deliberate microcosm of the round earth, and the quartered circle figures in many sandpainting designs as a symbol of harmony in the universe. Pathways and motion are also important. The ideal life is conceived as a journey along the correct, fruitful, beautiful road, often pictured as a rainbow, which will take the individual back to the original—that is, the perfect—harmonious balance with the universe. Though Ayah's day-long journey appears outwardly rambling and dreary, inwardly it is leading her to a "sacred place" in which she will experience healing.

As she follows her path in search of Chato, to bring the two of them back to their earliest and final home, Ayah twice makes inward observations about Chato's boots on her own, first comparing her worn rubbers to the beautiful elk and buckskin leggings and moccasins the people formerly had, then chuckling inwardly at Chato's worn and sock-stuffed boots "like little animals up to their ears in snow" (p. 50). Animals also figure significantly in Navajo thought and iconography. Life with animals—sheep, goats, horses, cattle—sustained the traditional way of life, and animals were a special kind of people, powerful and wise, in a universe in which all creatures were related as family. The comparison of Ayah to a spider is ironic, and points up the irreconcilability in this story of Navajo and alien points of view. The men at the bar feel contempt for the creature, but the spider, often portrayed as Grandmother Spider, is a revered figure of wisdom for all the peoples of the southwest. A weaver like Ayah, Spider Woman frequently helped her children out of dangerous situations by giving them good advice, as she is represented doing in "Estoy-eh-muut and the Kunideeyahs."

Traditional thought, however, is not a sentimental romanticizing of nature. The natural world can be as harsh as the human one: the hawk circling over Ayah and her children as they hide parallels the government authorities who will return inexorably to take the children away. Animals, like the *Yeibechei,* are neither good nor evil but terrible in their power. At the end of the story, Ayah sees the clouds as horses in the sky, figures of tremendous beauty and power, bringing strength and death at once. These horses call to mind the great horses that Sun and Moon ride across the sky. The horse is the special gift of Sun to his hero child, who then brings the first horse to the Navajo people. The horses in Ayah's musings suggest that she, too, is on a hero's journey.

The pathos of "Lullaby" should also be seen against the photograph in *Storyteller* of Silko's grandmother, Marie Anaya Marmon (Grandma A'mooh) reading from a picture book to two little girls, the author's sisters (p. 33). The photo images the continuity of grandmother to grandchild, contrasting with Ayah's remembrance of the old continuity of lullabies at the end of "Lullaby"—a continuance now broken and ended. Another parallel is suggested in a second photograph of Grandma A'mooh (p. 211): the elderly woman regards the reader with patience and serenity as she pauses in her crocheting of fine lace. The picture calls to mind thoughts of Spider Woman, spinner of wisdom and stories.

Storyteller in its physical layout echoes the thematic concern in individual stories with the clash between differing ways of looking at the world. Whereas Erdrich fuses her European and traditional Native American materials in a sophisticated and ironic blending of multiple texts and subtexts, the Vizenor uses shapeshifting transformations and disguises in a comic dance between the several worlds of tribal and white, fiction and fact, Silko allows no compromise in either form or theme. Just as the various elements of the book—pictorial and verbal—"bump against" each other with no explanatory bridges, so individuals from disparate traditions "bump against" each other with, all too often, few or no bridges of understanding, compassion or tolerance.

The three authors discussed here are all "wordspinners." Each works within traditional European short story forms, yet integrates the short story into experimental and coherent larger forms. All are fascinated with the boundaries between things: Indian and white, spiritual and physical, pagan and Christian, mythical and historical, fiction and fact. Their stories and the books of which they are a part challenge those boundaries in tales of defiance, conflict, trickery, transformation, shapeshifting, and disguise. In "The Storyteller's Escape" Silko's storyteller has the last word: "With these stories of ours/ we can escape almost anything/ with these stories we will survive" (p. 247).

NOTES

[1] Louise Erdrich, *Love Medicine* (New York: Holt, Rinehart and Winston, 1984); Leslie Silko, *Storyteller* (New York: Seaver, 1981); Gerald Vizenor, *Wordarrows: Indians and Whites in the New Fur Trade* (Minneapolis: Univ. of Minnesota Press, 1984). Subsequent refrences are identified by page number in the text.

[2] *The Sacred Hoop: Recovering the Feminine in American Indian Traditions* (Boston: Beacon, 1986), p. 81.

[3] Andrew J. Blackbird (Chief Mack-e-te-be-nessy), *History of the Ottawa and Chippewa Indians of Michigan; A Grammar of Their Language, and Personal and Family History of the Author* (Ypsilanti, MI, 1877; rpt. Petoskey, MI: Little Traverse Regional Historial Society, 1977), pp. 9-10.

[4] Frank Givens, "Saynday and Smallpox," *American Indian Mythology,* ed. Alice Marriott and Carol K. Rachlin (New York: New American Library, 1968), pp. 173-77.

[5] Material on the *windigo* complex comes from these sources: Victor Barnouw, *Wisconsin Chippewa Myths and Tales And Their Relation to Chippewa Life* (Madison: Univ. of Wisconsin, 1977); Sister Bernard Coleman, Ellen Frogner and Estelle Eich, *Ojibwa Myths And Legends* (Minneapolis: Ross and Haines, 1962); John Robert Colombo, ed., *Windigo: An Anthology of Fact and Fantastic Fiction* (Saskatoon: Western Producer Prairie Books, 1982); Ruth Landes, *The Ojibwa Woman* (New York: Columbia Univ. Press, 1938); Robert E. Ritzenthaler and Pat Ritzenthaler, *The Woodland Indians* (Garden City, NY: Natural History Press, 1970); Morton Teicher; *Windigo Psychosis: Proceedings of the 1960 Annual Spring Meeting of the American Ethnological Society,* ed. Verne F. Ray (Seattle: American Ethnological Society, 1960); Olivia Vlahos, *New World Beginnings: Indian Cultures in the Americas* (New York: Viking, 1970).

[6] Colombo, pp. 7-9.

[7] Barnouw, pp. 120, 122.

[8] Teicher, p. 6.

[9] Material on the Chippewa vision quest comes from these sources: George Copway (Kah-ge-ga-gah-bowh), *Indian Life and Indian History* (Boston: Albert Colby, 1860); Landes; Christopher Vecsey, *Traditional Ojibwa Religion and Its Historical Changes* (Philadelphia: The American Philosophical Society, 1983).

[10] Robert H. Lowie, *Indians of the Plains* (Garden City, NY: The Natural History Press, 1954), p. 170.

[11] Barnouw, p. 122.

[12] Kathleen Sands, rev. of *Love Medicine, Studies in American Indian Literatures,* 9 (1985): 12-24, 12.

[13] Neal Bowers and Charles L. P. Silet, "An Interview with Gerald Vizenor," *MELUS,* 8.1 (1981), 41-49.

[14] Gerald Vizenor, *Earthdivers: Tribal Narratives on Mixed Descent* (Minneapolis: Univ. of Minnesota Press, 1981), p. xxi.

[15] Gerald Vizenor, *anishinabe adisokan* (Minneapolis: The Nodin Press, 1970) n p.

[16] *The Trickster: A Study in American Indian Mythology* (New York: Schocken, 1972).

[17] Several critics have discussed Vizenor's adaptation of the trickster archetype and his fusing of it with traditional Native American and contemporary European/American theories of language; see, for instance, Franchot Ballinger, "Sacred Reversals: Trickster in Gerald Vizenor's *Earthdivers,*" *SAIL,* 8 (1984), 44-49; Elaine Jahner, "Allies in the World Wars: Vizenor's Use of Contemporary Critical Theory," *SAIL,* 9 (1985), 64-69; A. LaVonne Brown Ruoff, "Gerald Vizenor: Compassionate Trickster," *SAIL,* 9 (1985), 52-63; Bo Scholer, "Trickster and Storyteller: The Sacred Memories and True Tales of Gerald Vizenor," *Coyote Was Here: Essays on Contemporary Native American Literary and Political Mobilization* (Aarhus, Denmark: SEKLOS, 1984), pp. 134-46.

[18] Gerald Vizenor, *The People Named the Chippewa: Narrative Histories* (Minneapolis: Univ. of Minnesota, 1984), pp. 78-87.

[19] *The People Named the Chippewa,* pp. 13-14; N. Scott Momaday, *The Way To Rainy Mountain* (Albuquerque: Univ. of New Mexico, 1969), p. 33.

[20] James C. Olson, *Red Cloud and the Sioux Problem* (Lincoln: Univ. of Nebraska Press, 1965), pp. 316-17.

[21] Kim Echlin, "Ojibway Creation," *SAIL,* 8 (1984), 29-35, 30.

[22] *The People Named the Chippewa,* pp. 113-14.

[23] "Interview with Gerald Vizenor," pp. 41, 45; Ruoff, "Compassionate Trickster," pp. 62-63; Gerald Vizenor, "I Know What You Mean, Erdupps macChurbb," *Growing Up in Minnesota: Ten Writers Remember Their Childhoods,* ed. Chester Anderson (Minneapolis: Univ. of Minnesota Press, 1976), pp. 79-111.

[24] "Interview with Gerald Vizenor," p. 45.

[25] *Earthdivers,* p. xviii.

[26] Silko's use of traditional Laguna material, especially in "Yellow Woman," has been discussed by A. LaVonne Brown Ruoff, "Ritual and Renewal: Keres Traditions in the Short Fiction of Leslie Silko," *MELUS,* 5 (1978), 1-17.

27 "A Conversation with Leslie Marmon Silko," *Sun Tracks,* 3 (1976), 28-33.

28 Lawrence J. Evers analyzes "Tony's Story" in light of newspaper accounts and court records of the incident on which it is based in "The Killing of a New Mexico State Trooper: Ways of Telling an Historical Event," *Critical Essays on Native American Literature,* ed. Andrew Wiget (Boston: G. K. Hall, 1985), pp. 246-61.

29 Evers, p. 259. Kate Shanley Vangen uses discourse theory to analyze such friction points in the book's title story in "The Devil's Domain: Leslie Silko's 'Storyteller'," *Coyote Was Here,* pp. 116-23.

30 *Indian Life,* pp. 241-42.

31 Elisabeth Kubler-Ross, *Questions and Answers on Death and Dying* (New York: Macmillan, 1974); Bernard Schoenberg, Arthur C. Carr, David Peretz, and Austin H. Kutscher, *Loss and Grief: Psychological Management in Medical Practice* (New York: Columbia Univ. Press, 1970).

32 Material on Najavo myth, symbolism, and iconography comes from these sources: LaVerne Harell Clark, *They Sang for Horses: The Impact of the Horse on Navajo and Apache Folklore* (Tucson: Univ. of Arizona Press, 1966); "Seasons of a Navajo," Peace River Films for KAET, Phoenix, AZ, 1985, broadcast KCET (Los Angeles) 6 April 1985; Gladys A. Reichard, *Navajo Religion: A Study of Symbolism* (Princeton: Princeton Univ. Press, 1974); Donald Sandner, *Navajo Symbols of Healing* (New York: Harcourt, Brace, Jovanovich, 1979); Leland Wyman and Berard Haile, O.F.M., *Blessingway* (Tucson: Univ. of Arizona Press, 1970).

Donald Barthelme's Existential Acts of Art

CLARKE OWENS

What makes Donald Barthelme's fiction both experimental and "postmodern" (in an aesthetic sense) is, I believe, the existential act of reordering our notions of reality by reordering our notions of what fiction is and of how it works. I call this act "existential" because it attempts to be totally free, to create meaningful experience through fiction, rather than to pass meaning along by means of fiction. Perhaps it is only the self-consciousness of this act that makes it existential, and perhaps the best art has always done something like this, but self-consciousness is a part of Donald Barthelme's fiction, just as existentialism was an important part of the intellectual milieu that helped to shape his work when it came to prominence in the sixties.

I should not like to be misunderstood as saying that Donald Barthelme "is an existentialist," if by the word we mean an existentialist *philosopher*— someone like Sartre or Camus, who has articulated a philosophy, and who, if s/he also happens to be a writer of fictive forms, tends in those forms to create existential heroes to embody that philosophy, heroes such as Orestes in *The Flies,* Hoederer in *Dirty Hands,* or Mersault in *The Stranger.* Donald Barthelme does not create heroes to embody philosophies. He offers instead dreams which attempt to engage our full attention, not just that part of it concerned with rationally comprehensible and expressable truth. The distinction is between existentialist philosophy and existential acts of art.

William V. Spanos, not so hesitant as I about what can or cannot be called existential*ism,* has described that intellectual movement as "a kind of poetry of the philosophical imagination, defying rational systematization." "Both humanistic and theistic existentialists," Spanos writes, "recognize the threat of anonymity posed by the development of a mass technological society. They see the ultimate source of this threat, however, in man's real, if unconscious, obsession with order, which in the modern world has driven him into constructing rationally derived systems to replace the discredited Christian cosmology." Scientific rationalism is the counterpart of the technological society, for both "locate reality in the objective realm of measurable matter, and value in the production and utilization of objects. In so doing, they subordinate man to the tool, consciousness to efficiency, and the individual to the social and productive organizations (including educational institutions). By the inescapable logic of this system of valuation, the individual becomes dehumanized."[1]

Spanos' description of the existentialist is appealing in the era of the super-rational literary critic who arms himself with technocratic terms in order to please his limited public. But even those who, like Kierkegaard and St. Paul, imagine that the truth is revealed only to a single person, must pause to realize that one of the most important rationally derived systems replacing the Christian cosmology in our time (and ever since the Industrial Revolution) has been fiction, the art, the precious primary source. I believe Donald Barthelme's fiction implies an awareness of this fact.

Barthelme's awareness of fiction as a rational system is implied by his engagement of the possibilities of a non-rational non-system. It is not a case, as one of his critics has seemed to suggest, of their being scarcely any sense at all to be made of his stories, of his "shunning . . . any particular informing idea or attitude."[2] Rather, it is a case of what Sarte called being and nothingness: of their being a *negatite* for every *l'en soi*, a lack for every existing *it* or a desideratum for every existing negation of that desideratum. I continue to use the language of appallingly canonized existentialism because Barthelme himself, in his work and in his comments on it, is very conscious of that language and that thought. As everyone knows, existentialism-the-vogue (dig it now at your favorite university!) was omnipresent in intellectual life in the fifties and sixties—and an awareness of existentialism is highly illuminating when reading Barthelme. The point here, however, is that it is not so much reason and system that are the existentialist's enemies, but unswerving reason and fixed system. The fiction writer, especially the fiction writer with existential sensibilities, must avoid both jibberish and formulization if he wants his work to live. I used the word "appallingly" a moment ago in reference to Sartre, for the minute we begin to fix Barthelme's fiction as a phenomenon of the sixties we begin to kill it. Barthelme himself, like any artist worth his salt, would be the first to recognize this. By the end of this essay, I believe this uneasiness will have been dispelled. For now, let us say that we have to kill the living mystery a little in order to make the art live because, perhaps, art is a kind of *negatité* of life.

What, then, does it mean to say that Barthelme's fiction engages the possibilities of a non-rational non-system? I deny that it implies chaos. What it does imply is the *negatité* of the existing rational system. It means that one existential response to traditional fiction is non-traditional fiction, or experimentalism. In that sense, Barthelme's fiction is a response to fiction as well as (as much as?) to life, which may be what people mean when they use the word "metafiction" to talk about it. I am uncomfortable with the word "metafiction" because it sounds like a technocrat word, and I am not sure what it means. For me, nearly all of Barthelme's short fiction has to do with the relationship of "life" (all experience, or at least all human experience) to the imagination (all mental experience). One aspect of Barthelme's *negatité* of traditional fiction is his apparent perception of the synthetic nature of this relationship. He has said, for example, that "I am writing realistic fiction. . . . Every writer is offering a true account of the activities of the mind"[3]—signifying that even the fantastic is "realistic" in the sense that it is a real component of the mind, that the mind is real. Mental experience is a part of human experience; and how is it that we divide fantasy from realism in works of fiction so much more efficiently, it often seems, than we can separate our dreams and fantasies from the events of our daily lives? Imagination and "life" are not separate.

In a Donald Barthelme story, you do not have "the events" happening to "the characters" who then reveal to us, either through a narrator or through some device of an "implied author," "the meaning."[4] An event is not necessarily something that happens; it may be something that is thought. It may be, as it is in "Me and Miss Mandible," a "misconception":[5]

> Miss Mandible wants to make love to me but she hesitates because I am officially a child; I am, according to the records, according to the gradebook on her desk, according to the card index in the principal's office, eleven years old. There is a misconception here, one that I haven't quite managed to get cleared up yet. I am in fact thirty-five, I've been in the Army, I am six feet one, I have hair in the appropriate places, my voice is a baritone, I know very well what to do with Miss Mandible if she ever makes up her mind.

Now what is the event in this opening paragraph? Or what is the circumstance, if you prefer? Is it that a thirty-five year old man has somehow inadvertently been mistaken for an eleven year old by all the authorities (with the curiously uncertain exception of Miss Mandible), and that none of the children in his classroom seem much to notice or care? Or is it that an eleven year old boy mistakes himself for an adult with an adult history, or perhaps *wishes* he were an adult? Was I right a moment ago to say that the "misconception" is the event?

Before you answer that last question, imagine that I had not put quotation marks around the word "misconception." Had I not done so, you would have no way to prove whose misconception I meant. But because there *are* quotation marks around it, you know that the misconception is the one referred to by the narrator, by Joseph the boy/man; it is the mistake the authorities have made and that the children go along with, and that even the narrator submits to, on the surface. I have referred to the same "misconception" that Joseph has referred to, and therefore that misconception must exist; the authorities must be wrong. Correct?

Now read the rest of the story and decide what the facts are, whether Joseph is a man or a boy. I am not here concerned with the metaphor of the classroom, or the theme of the story, neither of which is hard to decipher, but with the story's un-traditionality. If this were a traditional story (I do not mean a realistic story) the narrator would be either one or the other, man or boy. Even in fantasies, we are given clues to the precise ontological nature of our fictional world. Kafka was innovative to attach fantastic premises to realistic development in "The Metamorphosis" and in other stories, but even in "The Metamorphosis" we know that Gregor *is* a dung beetle. And if Kafka had wished to expunge his story's fantastic premise, he could easily have done so by having Gregor awake from a *dream* of being a dung beetle. If, on the other hand, we read "Me and Miss Mandible" with an even-handed attention to its details, we will see that the answer to the question of *what Joseph is* is never clear, that it almost seems at times to be an irrelevant issue—except, at certain times, to *me and Miss Mandible*. "Of course," you will say, "that is the title of the story. The resolution of the sexual tension is the, er, climax of the piece, and Joseph finally bids farewell to the classroom, so he is obviously asserting his adulthood." Granted. But his assertion of adulthood—by no means an absolute one—is not the only assertion that carries weight in the story. In the world that Barthelme has created, the authorities remain "as dense as ever," believing that the boy has been the victim of child molestation, and *there is no one to contradict them.* No one, that is, except Joseph himself, who wants to qualify his contradiction, and who is not understood in any case. Nor can we be entirely sure how he views himself. He says that he is "only a minor in a very special sense"—but what does he mean by "special"? Does he mean "specific, limited"? Or does he mean "unique and important"? In his 14 November journal entry, he decided that the "distinction between children and adults, while probably useful for some purposes, is at bottom a specious one, I feel. There are only individual egos, crazy for love." Love, remember, (or at least sex) is the key to Joseph's adulthood on December 9 (the date of the final entry), but on 14 November it is the key to his double state. The children in this story are sexual beings (this part of the story is realistic) and so is the Joseph who is either a man or a boy, or who is physically a man (in his own and Miss Mandible's eyes) and intellectually a combination. We can only assert with any confidence at the story's end that Joseph is an adult *in a sense.* It is the existential sense: Joseph defines himself as what he is by his own action, in defiance of (but not exactly in opposition to) the authorities who previously defined him and thus imposed their reality on him.[6] That much is clear enough.

But is this story really, as I have suggested, the *negatité* of a rational system, rather than just a fantasy like other fantasies? I say it is, because the ontological framework is not one that reveals either reality or unreality as we commonly perceive them—and even fantasies normally do this, commonly by being allegorical—but rather, the ontological framework reveals a dynamic of being and nothingness: a series of givens and their competing desiderata. Joseph is either a boy or a man, not in fact, but depending on whom you ask. Each possibility is the desideratum resulting from or implied by the other. Joseph himself is not sure how to classify himself and neither is Miss Mandible. (They each *contain* being and nothingness.) Again, Joseph is in love with a girl and a woman, the woman being, in one sense, Sue Ann, in another sense, Miss Mandible; and vice versa. And love of the one is rejection of the other. Again, a more complicated *l'en soi:* the authorities are in possession of the "facts," or at least the records and the power to assign roles, and it is by no means certain that they have been defeated at the end, for where is Joseph off to—a destination of his own choosing, or some place of protection and treatment for child molestation victims? The *negatité* of authoritarian fact is Joseph's own subjectivity, which we and he naturally want to believe is "fact," although we are told that the truth "does no good" against the authorities. There is never any absolute distinction between possibility and reality, between the lack and the in-itself. The rational system that this existential world opposes is the system of rationa*list* ontology—in the words of Spanos, "[the] philosophy of essences, defining nature—including human nature—and imposing abstract structures upon it."[7] The authorities in "Me and Miss Mandible" believe in abstract structures so strongly that they do not accept the evidence of their senses. Even the janitor, as the pawn of the authorities, does not know *why* Joseph does not fit his chair, only that it means something is wrong with Joseph. If this were not a radically existential story, we would learn that the authorities are wrong in their dehumanizing rationalism (we would learn that Joseph is really a man), and, too, they would most likely either triumph over Joseph or be defeated by him. Instead, it is a case of Joseph *believing* they are wrong, and at last coming to struggle against their undeniable power. "The crowd is untruth," said Kierkegaard,[8] but realizing the crowd is untruth does not entirely eliminate their power.

There is, of course, an existential metaphor in "Me and Miss Mandible" (the classroom and all that goes with it) which we have not explicitly discussed, but because of space limitations we must move on to another example, where we may perhaps be able to discuss metaphor's existential implications. In "The Balloon," we are presented with a too-obviously-deceptively-simple circumstance: a balloon is inflated in the sky over Manhattan and people react to it. As with the story just discussed, it is "The Balloon's" ontological premises that strike one as the path to critical insight, only this time the question is not so much "What can be known by us about the protagonist?" but, rather, "What can be known by the people of Manhattan about the balloon, when they know nothing of its origin?" If we ask this question, we at once see the existential metaphor: the balloon is a spheroid, patchwork object reacted to in different ways by different people, none of whom have any of our knowledge of who its creator is or what his motives (?) are for creating it. Let the balloon be the world, and this is man's condition in an existential nutshell.

Of course, *we* are aware of, and interested in, the creator/narrator. In the story's opening lines, he exerts supreme control over the balloon and also, strangely, over us, by ostentatiously selecting his revelations:

> The balloon, beginning at a point on Fourteenth Street, *the exact location of which I cannot reveal,* expanded northward all one night, while people were sleeping, until it reached the Park. There I stopped it. . . . [my italics]

We wonder why, if he can stop the balloon, the narrator "cannot reveal its point of origin. Is he not able? Or does he choose not to? In any case, the narrator enjoys a kind of supremely whimsical indifference to all the irrelevant public reactions to his "concrete particular," which he nevertheless very carefully notes:

> [The balloon] was extremely exciting for children. . . . But the purpose of the . balloon was not to amuse children.

> As a single balloon must stand for a lifetime of thinking about balloons, so each citizen expressed, in the attitude he chose, a complex of attitudes. One man might consider that the balloon had to do with the notion *sullied,* as in the sentence *The big balloon sullied the otherwise clear and radiant Manhattan sky.* . . . while this man was thinking *sullied,* still there was an admixture of pleasurable cognition in his thinking, struggling with the original perception. [narrator's italics]

> People began, in a curious way, to locate themselves in relation to aspects of the balloon. . . .

> It was suggested that what was admired about the balloon was finally this: that it was not limited, or defined.

As with "Me and Miss Mandible," "The Balloon" presents an opportunity for competing subjectivities. But whereas Joseph in "Me and Miss Mandible" could only make a decision to assert his subjectivity and could not pretend to have much control over events, the subjectivities in "The Balloon" belong to the Manhattanites, while the narrator apparently has total control. (I say that if he can stop the balloon and explain it, he can also tell us its point of origin on Fourteenth Street, and that he merely chooses not to.) He is both godlike and artistlike for he invisibly presides over an artifact of his creation, seeing the truth but waiting, at least for a while. He is not like the public, for whom the balloon is an in-itself provoking their various critical desiderata. They need to "locate themselves" in relation to it, but, for the creator/artist, it is adequate as it is:

> There were no situations, simply the balloon hanging there. . . . Having produced his own work, the artist needs no relative location; he disappears. Perhaps God does the same.

Structurally sedate, as Barthelme stories go, "The Balloon" is composed entirely of well-organized expository paragraphs with no separate dialogue and only one brief episode of fragments. Typographically these fragments imitate their (lack of) sense, an incoherence belonging to the critical interpreters of the balloon, not to the artist. We know this because the eleven incoherent snatches of language and typography—two of which seem to be drawn from literary or art criticism (references to "passages" and to "a sprawling quality") are introduced with the line, "Critical opinion was divided:". In the end, we learn that the balloon is "a spontaneous autobiographical disclosure," a manifestation of a psychosexual disturbance in the narrator occasioned by the temporary absence of his girlfriend. Implied is the absurdity of all the intellection of the people who have had to somehow interpret the balloon or make it fit into their accepted notions of what things mean. Even their consensus opinion that the balloon is admirable because "not limited or defined" seems at first to be satirized by Barthelme, for the narrator/artist/creator defines and limits its significance plainly enough.

But the existentialist would point out, first, that by not revealing his role in the matter, the artist/creator has chosen not to limit or define the public's freedom to interpret; and, second, he would ask why that freedom should be limited or defined. What ultimate difference can it make to them to *know* that the universe (or the work of art) is a disease? The question then becomes one of who is really irrelevant, the people or the artist/creator. "Not that we believe that God exists, but we think that the problem of His existence is not the issue," as Sartre said. Or, put slightly differently by Heidegger, "Why is there any Being at all—why not far rather [believe in] Nothing?"[9] In Heidegger's terms, the balloon would be the Manhattanites' *dasein,* their (yes, *their*) projection into nothingness. Of course it is a metaphor, and my point is that its meaning is not fixed, because no one person (in Manhattan) can claim the sole truth about it, and because the God of the Balloon chooses not to let anyone in on the secret. *We* know the secret, sort of, but we are outside the story.

Now, for those readers new to Barthelme who want to insist that, in the case of "The Balloon" at least, the point is not that there are competing subjectivities, but that there *is* a secret, and that I am simply imposing my own existentialist reading on Barthelme's quite different intentions, there is only the minor remedy of referring you to an interview with Barthelme conducted by Larry McCaffery in volume forty-nine of the *Partisan Review,* in which Barthelme mentions having been influenced by a professor at the University of Houston to become interested in the writings of Husserl, Heidegger, Kierkegaard and Sartre.[10]

It was, we know, a whole generation of college students who were schooled in existentialism by their professors, and one might profitably compare the existential qualities of various postmodern writers. Charles Mayer, one of the editors of this book, has suggested, for example, that I discuss the common milieu of Barthelme and John Barth as explaining what he called their "common relation to the now-traditional existentialists." But, while the suggestion is a perfectly reasonable one, I was made so uneasy by the reference to "now-traditional existentialists" that I began to imagine another way of "placing" Barthelme (*and* Barth, the beat poets, and all the other existential postmoderns)—a way that is more true to the spirit of existentialism. That way is, as you have probably guessed, to place Barthelme not within the tradition of existentialism-the-vogue, the campus phenomenon, but in the tradition of existential fiction writers from Dostoevsky on. It is not, after all, the existential condition, or the infinite number of existential responses to it, which have become "now-traditional"—although the condition, being the human one, is always the same—but rather the academic references, the clichés.

Existential literature is about non-essential people, people like Raskolnikov, Ivan Karamazov, or perhaps even someone like Don Quixote. Jacob Horner in Barth's *The End of the Road* is non-essential, like these other characters, not in the sense of being "unnecessary" (although one could also make that case) but in the sense of having no essence, in being required to define himself. In recent years, there has been a highly interesting non-essential character named "you" inhabiting the block apartments of Frederick Barthelme's short stories. (Frederick is Donald's brother, incidentally.) "You" tend to have meaningless affairs with women who live down the hall in these block apartments, and although you never say so, you feel somehow totally dehumanized and isolated in your normal American life. The variety of these characters, and of their fictional experiences, will go to show that the existential *act of art* is not "traditional" in any sense that could be construed as suggesting the predictable or the boring. One might perhaps point to the common typographical games and "spoken voice" approaches of Barthelme's stories and the pieces in Barth's *Lost In the Funhouse* as evidence of some type of uniformity, but those rather superficial qualities are precisely the ones that cling tenaciously to the nineteen-sixties, while the broader, existential view of life does not. Please remember that the existential view can drive a non-essential person to an existential God, as it did to Raskolnikov and Job. It can also produce a philosophical novel, a re-worked Greek play, or a short experimental piece of humor. It can do all of this and more, in any mode from the pseudo-heroic to the ironic.

If I may bring this point about the formulaic and the original back to a specific remark concerning the themes in Barthelme's fiction: the critic who bewildered me, back in my fifth paragraph, did make one observation that I found interesting, which was that Donald Barthelme does not often choose death as his theme.[11] It was interesting to read this, because "death," by itself, is not much of a theme. Perhaps, if one relied heavily on Tolstoy or Celine, one could name three good and important works written on a theme of "death." But it would be so much easier (no, more of a time-consuming task, rather) to index "*love* and death." *The End of the Road* is about *love* and death; so many good, long fictive works are, and there are any number of stories by Donald Barthelme in which a character's sense of the loss of love is informed by his or her sense of mortality. "Bishop," for example, or "I Bought A Little City," or even "Me and Miss Mandible," if we change the word "loss" to "momentary lack." (Joseph, while he is waiting for Miss Mandible to make up her mind, is worried about his future, about *"not getting anywhere."*) One may not want to say that "love and death" is the *major* theme of these stories, but it is definitely something Barthelme writes about. Theme is really too malleable to make hard and fast arguments about, but the fact is that Barthelme writes about the same kinds of human issues that other writers write about; his "themes" are more traditional than is often realized, while his existentialism contributes to his un-traditional quality.

Barthelme does not avoid the common themes; it is just that they are sometimes harder to pick up. For example, we have to read all the way to the end of "At the End of the Mechanical Age"—and then perhaps we have to reread it—before we realize that it is about a marriage that has failed because it was founded solely on sexual convenience, and it thus compromised the partners' deepest psychosexual needs. It was a "mechanical" marriage, which we have to "mechanically" read through to the "end" of, in order to see the metaphor. The form is innovative, but it is your basic, tried-and-true theme of failed love and compromised ideals.

As long as we have been referring to variety in form, let us be sure to note that Donald Barthelme is not Sartre, and that one of the big differences between them is that Barthelme is not as serious as Sartre, considered either as a philosopher or as a playwright and novelist. Barthelme is serious, but not *as* serious. He is a kind of humorist, after all, and claims the influences—in addition to Heidegger, et al—of S. J. Perelman and Nathanael West.[12] But this should not mean that "The Indian Uprising" is less existential than *No Exit.* "The Indian Uprising" is ontologically free and self-definitive as a work of art. *No Exit* is less so. *No Exit* simply redefines an old concept of hell, of punishment, in a sort of

Platonic symposium with passion. Barthelme's way is different. That way is, as we said earlier, to reorder our notions about fiction, and in doing so, to reorder our notions of reality. (Is the last phrase too ambitious? Would it be different to say "makes us think"?) Whether it makes us laugh or not, this, I claim, is a rejection of a type of rationalist authority, but beyond that perhaps we need not discuss existentialism at all; perhaps we may discuss the metaphor of the Indians, this rather funny metaphor that yet seems to have serious impact on us. In fact, I should like to try to look at the Indians purely as metaphor now, just in order to see if doing so yields a substantially different result than is yielded by talking about existential ontology.

The Indians in "The Indian Uprising" represent love. Not every kind of love, and not any one *very* limited kind of love, but that kind of psychosexual love that is unprogrammable, untameable, unrepeatable, primitive, and everywhere abused, threatened, and sullied by the trappings of a motley and incomprehensible supercivilization. It is a kind of love that frightens us because it disallows our comfortable rationality and our sense of control. It laughs at our coping mechanisms. It is aggressive, perhaps angry, and deceptive: we cannot understand it but can only submit to it, and when we do we are defenseless. But when we submit to it, it saves our life.

I offer the preceding interpretation of "The Indian Uprising" as one subjective response to a very rich and complex extended metaphor. It is an interpretation that can and ought to change with repeated readings. But as it changes, it will, at least for me, retain its (sorry, but we are back into it) obviously existential elements: its insistence on freedom and its rejection of formulaic rigidity; its dynamic of mortality and meaninglessness (the belt and shoelaces the narrator removes at the end of the story, for example, suggest suicide; this is only one of several permutations of the motif); the question—implied everywhere in the story—of how to live a human life in the dirty, teeming supercivilization with its useless proliferation of official authorities. Howsoever, on a given day, I may decide to interpret lines such as: " 'Call off your braves,' I said. 'We have many years left to live' " or "I decided I knew nothing" or "Not believing that your body brilliant as it was and your fat, liquid spirit distinguished and angry as it was were stable quantities to which one could return on wires more than once, twice, or another number of times I said: 'See the table?' "—howsoever, on a given day, I may interpret those lines in their contexts, it will be hard *not* to sense the profound *political* nature of this story. One might take a feminist approach to that political quality, or an anti-capitalist approach ("We sent more heroin into the ghetto"!) but what will be common to these more tendentious critical approaches will be, or ought to be, an awareness of the poetry of the philosophical imagination deeply mistrustful of scientific rationalism and the technological society. ("Have you ever tried to reason with a Convenience Card money machine?" Barthelme asks.)[13] I hope, too, that in re-shaping Barthelme's work for critical discussion, we do not lose sight of the fact that his heap of images, while they may often confuse us, never pin us wriggling to the wall.

There is, I think, little necessity to direct the reader interested in Barthelme's existential qualities to his more obviously allusive or seemingly derivative stories, such as "The Leap," "Nothing: A Preliminary Account," or "On Angels," which begins with a reference to the death of God. It is not as if one could expect to get a philosophical tract from Barthelme, even if one wanted one. I do not think the "philosophical imagination" implies that. If understood correctly, the existential elements of Barthelme's thought will be seen in most or all of his stories, however. They are not there to be turned into a tradition of clichés or a religion; they are not rules, but tendencies in the apprehension of reality that inform the experimentation. Other things inform the experimentation too, some of which we have discussed and some not: things such as a sense of humor, a critical exposure to modern art, twentieth century literature, popular culture. When I describe Barthelme as someone who creates existential acts of art, I am not describing a philosopher, but a writer and a free human being.

NOTES

[1] William V. Spanos, ed., *A Casebook On Existentialism* (New York: Crowell, 1966), pp. 2-3. Nothing is more illustrative of what Spanos is describing than a memo that recently fell into my hands while I was doing a temporary job in a giant, high-technology corporation. The memo, too long to quote in full, directs technical writers to avoid "non-behavioral" words such as "think," "learn," and "enjoy," and to use instead only "behavioral" words such as "splice," "differentiate," and "conduct." The nonbehavioral words are bad because they are "broad, vague," and they "permit a variety of interpretations." "There is no way," says the memo, "to measure these words in units of measurement." The most frightening aspect of all this is that what is being described is, are, students, human beings.

[2] Thomas M. Leitch, "Donald Barthelme and the End of the End," *Modern Fiction Studies,* 28 (1982), 136.

[3] Jo Brans, "Embracing the World: An Interview With Donald Barthelme," *Southwest Review,* 67 (1982), 132.

[4] "Implied author" is, I suppose, still Wayne Booth's term, and I do not mean to imply, by linking it to the others, that they are also his.

[5] All quotations from Donald Barthelme's fiction in this essay are from Donald Barthelme, *Sixty Stories* (New York: Putnam, 1981). The beginning page numbers for each story quoted or referred to are: "A Shower of Gold," p. 14; "Me and Miss Mandible," p. 24; "The Balloon," p. 53; "The Indian Uprising," p. 108; "On Angels," p. 135; "Nothing: A Preliminary Account," p. 245; "At the End of the Mechanical Age," p. 272; "I Bought A Little City," p. 295; "The Leap," p. 379; "Bishop," p. 444.

[6] Please see "A Shower of Gold" for an example of a story Barthelme resolves with the use of the phrase "in a sense."

[7] Spanos, p. 2.

[8] Spanos, p. 238.

[9] Spanos, pp. 297, 275.

[10] Larry McCaffery, "An Interview with Donald Barthelme," *Partisan Review,* 49 (1982), 185.

[11] Leitch, p. 129, says that Barthelme's fiction does without "such themes as love,

idealism, initiation, or death,'' which is not true; but he is closer to the truth when he also excludes from Barthelme's fiction character, plot, and setting. One would have to qualify very carefully what one meant by these latter terms in order to confirm or deny the claim.

[12] McCaffery, p. 185.

[13] McCaffery, p. 191.

Doctorow's *Lives of the Poets* and the Problem of Witness

ARTHUR M. SALTZMAN

"I believe you have to reinvent fiction with each and every book," declares E. L. Doctorow, a writer whose projects defy predictability. "You've got to take the conventions and break them down, reconstitute them."[1] Consider the range of fabrication: a tale of the rigors of the Old West (*Welcome to Hard Times*); a fictionalized history—or historically fortified fiction—of early twentieth-century America (*Ragtime*); an investigation of the Rosenberg case, with debts to Marx and Disney (*The Book of Daniel*); a proletarian satire buttressed by poetic interludes and computer printouts (*Loon Lake*); and a lyrical memoir of the author's youth (*World's Fair*). There is also a science fiction novel (*Big as Life*), to further convolute his career, but Doctorow tends to disavow the book as negligible. Each of these products is a unique assimilation of and challenge to the deeds and data of experience; and whatever their respective ingenuities of style may be, each proposes an inevitable interdependence between fact and fiction, between history and how history is rendered. "I am thus led to the proposition," Doctorow concludes, "that there is no fiction or nonfiction as we commonly understand the distinction: there is only narrative."[2]

By extension, there is no knowing apart from the contingent apparatus of storytelling.[3] This is simultaneously a liberating and anxiety-provoking situation for Doctorow's narrators, who are responsible for creating the reality they relate. One thinks of Blue in *Welcome to Hard Times* spending his waning resources on some presumed posterity as he marks down in his ledgers the catastrophic story of the town, all the while apologizing for the fitfulness of memory or castigating himself for the insufficient, and probably unredemptive, nature of "talk." "In my limits, taking a day for a day, a night for a night, have I showed the sand shifting under our feet, the terrible arrangement of our lives?"[4] If language can control anything, is Blue artist enough to do so reliably? And if language is just another pinched-out claim in this unforgiving wilderness, is Blue's narrative little more than a delirious obsession? "And it scares me more than death scares me that it may show the truth," he reflects at the close. "But how can it if I've written as if I knew as I lived them which minutes were important and which not; and spoken as if I knew the exact words everyone spoke? Does the truth come out in such scrawls, so bound by my limits?"[5]

The Book of Daniel similarly complains that the price of coherency is falsification. Because the government purveys illusion so as to reinforce a blindly patriotic faith in the American Dream, the artist must struggle against succumbing to the anesthetizing effects of an officially sanctioned manipulation of history or die from "a failure of analysis."[6] As Doctorow proclaims in "False Documents," "There is a regime language that derives its strength from what we are supposed to be and a language of freedom whose power consists in what we threaten to become. And I'm justified in giving a political character to the fictive and nonfictive uses of language because there is conflict between them."[7] Unfortunately for Daniel Isaacson, whose parents had been singled out for victimization during the Cold War paranoia of the 1950's, it is almost impossible to decipher with confidence reality from exploitative tamperings with reality. A would-be "little criminal of perception," Daniel may well be a prisoner of a crusade to rewrite history rather than reveal it. Perception is both aesthetically and politically consequential, but the welter of propaganda and manifestoes, personal memories, research material, private interviews—the general information overload—tends to obstruct his view.[8] Daniel can barely recognize his parents in the revolutionary fervor of the 1960's that resuscitates the Isaacsons as precursors, nor can he escape the suspicion that his desire to discover the conspiratorial plot against his family may have led him into a plot-making of his own that is no more trustworthy (a particularly insidious form of complicity). Even if Daniel manages to refute the charge that writing his book is politically illegitimate when compared to other more extreme strategies of protest, he cannot dismiss the feeling that narrative has its own priorities that champion the truth of design over the design of truth. Daniel intuits this deceptiveness when driving through the rain:

> . . . he fixed on one drop and followed its career. The idea was that his attention made it different from the other drops. It arrived, head busted, with one water bead as a nucleus and six or seven clusters in a circle around it. It was like a melted snowflake. Each of the mini-drop clusters combined and became elongated and pulled away in the direction of its own weight. As he accelerated the car, so did they increase their rate of going away from the center.[9]

Daniel is a victim of the artistic version of Heisenberg's Uncertainty Principle, according to which the act of measurement adulterates the operation being measured. No matter what generic method of approaching experience he tries—diary, dissertation, polemic, anecdote, or self-confessed storification of the facts—none earns privileged status. Closure, after all, is the province of the very "sanctioning authorities" against whom Daniel harbors his suspicions and whose institutionalized accounts of historical events motivated Daniel's exploration in the first place; "Doctorow and his narrator are trying to discover what kind of narrative is possible when one stands not only outside but in opposition to the regime."[10] In the end, he cannot choose among several conclusions to his book, for everything is ultimately more plausible than convincing: "Life is never this well plotted . . . ."[11]

A "Beacon of Faith in a Time of Persecution"[12] or a rampant dreamer haunted by a history from which he cannot awake—the Doctorow narrator perpetually consults his own motives and questions his own adequacy. When he does happen upon the consolations of causal sequence, narrative closure, lines of plot like underground cables, he regards these as pseudostructures—the enticements of reigning political forces or of literary habituation—and resists complicity. In other words, continuity is a convenient misapprehension of the world; coherence is a lie of fiction. And yet, even if questions of epistemology contaminate the narrative, because personal and aesthetic legitimacy are thoroughly interrelated, the questions must be asked. Or as it is put by Ralph Ellison's Invisible Man, who is something of a precursor to Doctorow's narrators by virtue of his book-long concern with creating private identity while avoiding preconceived systems that threaten to absorb him, "To be unaware of one's form is to live a death."[13]

In *Lives of the Poets,* Doctorow explores the inevitability and the necessity of imaginative imposition. These "six stories and a novella" do not constitute a novel so much as a blueprint for a novel that cannot be more than tentatively proposed; they represent a series of approximations, as engineered by Jonathan (who appears undisguised by the fictions he concocts only in the first story, "The Writer in the Family," and in the novella that titles the volume). Jonathan tries to "authorize" himself through the telling of stories that exercise various strategies for consolidating and establishing his distance from life's hard facts. Narration—specifically, the several fictional postures he adopts—affords Jonathan a qualified immersion in the world. To remain both objective and responsible, to sustain the integrity of the fictional project without avoiding the complications and contradictions of the events one addresses, to make connections without sacrificing authenticity—these are the tasks that make the act of artistic witness so problematical, and they are always imminent concerns of *Lives of the Poets.*

In "The Writer in the Family," Jonathan remembers how, urged to the deception by his aunts, he undertook the psychological, moral, and artistic challenge of protecting his decrepit grandmother from the news of his father's death by writing her letters that presumably came from Jonathan's father himself (the pretense being that he had moved to Arizona for his health). By accepting this charge, Jonathan acquiesces to "the manner of that side of the family of making government on everyone's behalf"[14]; moreover, the incorporation of his father's voice into his writing proves less a means of keeping the man alive than a grotesque refusal to bury the dead. Although he silently accuses his mother of masochism for accepting a part-time job at the hospital where his father's illness had been diagnosed, Jonathan is the greater culprit. A sounding board for the antagonisms of his mother and his aunts against one another, a buffer against their complaints and recriminations, Jonathan places the highest priority on keeping the peace: "I . . . rationalized the snubs and rebuffs each inflicted on the other, taking no stands, like my father himself" (p. 8).

Jonathan is soon possessed by the man he impersonates. He shivers in the dead man's suit, which his steadfastly practical mother wants to alter to fit him; he dreams of the living corpse taking up residence with him. Soon he begins to realize that the conspiracy of letter-writing is not really designed to calm his grandmother, who is too diminished to know the difference, but to control him as his father himself was controlled. Instead of doing his father honor, Jonathan is duplicating and perpetuating his implication into family service (p. 13). Thus, Jonathan writes a final letter in which his father confesses his dying. Art is redeemed, and it redeems the artist; he is able to exorcise his father's ghost. The writer in the family transforms himself into the writer *of* the family, and suddenly Jonathan is granted a revelation: "I thought how stupid, and imperceptive, and self-centered I had been never to have understood while he was alive what my father's dream for his life had been" (p. 17).

Having freed the man, Jonathan is able to objectify him. We are reminded of the conclusion of *Ragtime,* in which another dead father is eulogized as a failed explorer: "He arrives at the new place, his hair risen in astonishment, his mouth and eyes dumb. His toe scuffs a soft storm of sand, he kneels and his arms spread in pantomimic celebration, the immigrant, as in every moment of his life, arriving eternally on the shore of his Self."[15] The parallel goes beyond two failed dreamers, one a man killed aboard the *Lusitania* and the other leaving behind a miniscule pension from his naval service; just as it is at this late juncture that the Boy reveals himself to be the narrator of *Ragtime,* so it is now, when his father has been granted the right to die on his own terms, that Jonathan begins to achieve a more aesthetically conscionable narrative identity.

The next five stories in *Lives of the Poets* employ a variety of narrative guises, as though the artist were engaged in underground testing. "The Water Works" is a first-person account of a detective who, tracing the dark figure of an unidentified "captain" through the convoluted city water works building, is arrested by the tragic discovery of a drowned child who had apparently plunged to his death into the reservoir and been trapped at the sluicegates. The brief tale concludes with considerations reminiscent of Joyce's "The Dead": "I went back in and felt the oppression of a universe of water, inside and out, over the dead and the living" (p. 24). The captain is forgotten; instead, the narrator wonders at the ritualistic indifference to their work of the men who salvage the body, for it is directly opposed to the narrator's own efforts to know and possess the event. This characteristic is reinforced by his referring to the captain he had been pursuing as "my black-bearded captain," of whom he has spoken as a secret sharer of sorts: "I was sure he knew of my presence. Indeed, for some days I had sensed from his actions a mad presumption of partnership, as if he engaged in his enterprises for our mutual benefit" (p. 22).

What those mysterious enterprises are is never revealed, for the more prominent concern here is the continuation of the development of a narrative stance—the writer's toward his fiction, as well as Jonathan's toward his father (the unattainable captain). Guilt seems to instill conflicting motives: a desire to capture (or embrace) the subject, coupled with a reluctance to inhibit the freedom and fullness of mystery that accompanies the subject.

Similarly, the complex charge of being an adequate, conscientious witness is central to "Willi," a story in which a boy's exultation over feeling at one with nature on a marvelous spring day is nightmarishly corrupted by his seeing his mother ("on the straw and in the dung . . . a reddened headless body") having sex with his tutor. When he had been in touch with nature's pure pleasures, Willi had been "aware of my being as the arbitrary shape of an agency that had chosen to make me in this manner as a means of communicating with me" (pp. 28-29, 28); now his role of intuitive medium takes on new and serious complications. Feelings of betrayal—as a son and as a representative of nature itself—are mingled with a sense of triumph, for the artist/voyeur has seen much! Willi is understandably distressed by the fact that only he seems to have been affected by that cataclysmic scene, by the "windy universal roar" (p. 28) that resolved itself into his mother's treachery. (One thinks not only of the drowning of the boy in the previous story, but also of Faulkner's Quentin Compson trying to keep the "loud world" at bay.) Surrounded by the adults who constitute an "unholy trinity of deception and ignorance" (p. 31), and stifled by the manufactured composure of his mother, father, and tutor in the face of his intolerable knowledge, Willi traduces his mother to his father.

Thus, the story is a confession of Willi's own participation in the mechanics of betrayal, and hence, a counterpart to the conspiratorial letter-writing of the opening story. As do many young boys, Willi had imagined his father to be a mythic presence, "the god-eye in the kingdom, the intelligence that brought order and gave everything its value" (p. 32); while he suffers from having engineered his father's fall from eminence, Willi magnifies his own powers by having slain a Goliath. (Indeed, as his horror mixes with lust at the thought of his mother's adultery, he completes the Freudian wish by destroying the father.) Willi's father had been scornful of society and its expectations, and he had lived on their estate "in the pride of the self-constructed self" (p. 33). Willi deconstructs that arrogant removal from the world. The father wreaks a violent revenge against his unfaithful wife, and Willi is torn between approval and protective fury. "All of it was to be destroyed anyway," he concludes, "even without me" (p. 35). The narrator notes that this was in 1910; war, age, and forgetfulness would have eventually plunged all of them into the same indistinguishable demise. Still, he keeps witness and takes responsibility. It is an example of a boy's growth into manhood and a guilt-ridden maturation into artistry.

The next three stories in the volume all have to do with the theme of dereliction, and in this sense they are preludes to the culminating novella, in which "this mortal rush to solitude" (p. 89) is most expansively demonstrated. "The Hunter" is the story of a teacher who hopes to foster in her young pupils a sense of wonder and the world's possibility, but who finds few encouraging prospects in her town, which is consistently characterized in terms of inertia, emptiness, and desolation. Although the teacher displays a genius for turning even the musty school into a waiting adventure (she tells them they are a lost patrol "looking for signs of life" in the caves of a distant planet as they follow her through the deserted building), her world remains stubbornly unprepossessing. Moreover, the children themselves are irredeemable: "She has been here just long enough for her immodest wish to transform these children to have turned to awe at what they are" (p. 40). Movies, valium, the beery men of the town all contribute to the slow wash of despair she endures, and the story concludes with the teacher drawing the children around her for a photograph, as though shoring her fragments against the ruin, or as though trying to halt the diminishment that plagues her.

Morgan is also suffering from isolation in "The Foreign Legation." His divorce triggers a painful exploration of his failures to connect with other people, and his commentary has the tone of an autopsy: "He knew there was nothing to keep him from changing his life, but staying on suited his sense of himself as someone waiting" (p. 54); "He sincerely believed that his house was not lived in and that it needed to appear otherwise to passers-by" (p. 58); "I am the lucky one chosen for my lack of consequence" (p. 58). In short, Morgan barely occupies his own house. He tries to summon a little vitality from lascivious daydreams, but they merely emphasize his peripheral relationship to the world and the guilt he feels for having divested himself of his family. The provisional nature of his contacts is reminiscent of that described by the narrator of William Gass's "In the Heart of the Heart of the Country": "We meet on this window, the world and I, inelegantly, swimmers of the glass; and swung wrong way around to one another, the world seems in."[16] Voyeurism exposes the poverty of imagination.

When the climactic event of "The Foreign Legation" occurs—an explosion at a foreign legation that apparently claims schoolchildren among its victims—it seems an outward manifestation of the implosions Morgan has been enduring behind closed doors. Thus, he feels implicated by the tragedy, even imagining himself to be responsible for it, but he is crediting his own effects on the world too exorbitantly. We might say that Morgan is desperate to be plotworthy. But reversing the "diplomacy" of detachment remains forbidding to one whose relationship to the world has been so severely qualified.

"The Leather Man" expands the symptom of frayed contacts with the world beyond isolated cases to designate a separate species of contemporary estrangement. Ranging from hermits and street people to prisoners and astronauts, Leather Men are explorers of the outcast state; they have either been discarded by society for being superfluous or—and this is the more threatening possibility, for it indicts those of us who hold fast to the communal matrix—they opt out, turning escape into an art form in the manner of Houdini in *Ragtime.* Our narrator is some sort of surveillance man in the employ of a governmental agency, and as his official breakdown of the phenomenon progresses, he becomes increasingly anxious about the impenetrability of the people he classifies, dockets, and interrogates. The phenomenon will not be possessed through the data it affords; the proliferation of these Leather Men suggests a conspiracy of solitude. They are artisans of private order:

> But say you are some hapless fellow, you can't keep a job, the wife nags, the children are vicious, the neighbors snigger. Down in your basement, though, you make nice things of wood. You make a bookshelf, you make a cabinet, sawing and planing, sanding, fitting, gluing, and you construct something very fine, you impose that order, that is the realm of your control. You make a bigger cabinet. You make a cabinet you can walk into. You built it where nobody will watch you. When it is done, you walk inside and lock the door. (p. 70).

If the writer justifies his detachment on the grounds of improving the reliability of his perceptions, the Leather Man represents the point at which detachment is its own justification. Whether it be due to "an infrastructure of layered subversion" or "a rearrangement of molecules" (p. 74), the threat that the alien and alienated personify is a challenge to accept faiths, conventions, and duties. Our narrator's agency belongs to an invisible network—media, government, advertising, and all the purveyors of language who, like "The Writer in the Family," sell out their principles to keep the peace—whose mission it is to patrol our responses and program the significance of our experiences for us. Leather Men are shapeless people, and the closer the narrator tries to come to them, the more amorphous they become; ironically, one must maintain a discreet distance from their disturbing detachment to manage to see it at all. It is no longer just one troubled child, one harried teacher, one divorced father; it is a plague of dissociation.

The novella-length title piece extends the malaise to implicate observer and observed alike. Our narrator is a writer who has just turned fifty in a Greenwich Village garret, and from that vantage point he recapitulates the fate of past hopes and contemplates the likely demise of future prospects. Moreover, this writer—it is Jonathan emerged from behind his fictional stand-ins—speaks for a whole collection of writers who populate "Lives of the Poets," all of whom endure personal crises of faith in the legitimacy of their profession. A publication party is an opportunity to trade examples of suffering, frayed commitments, and other symptoms of paralysis. Thus, even the writers, the privileged witnesses, have started to succumb to the "creeping ruin" of contemporary urban life (p. 81). The antennae of the race are riddled with static—"I walk the streets feeling like a vagrant, I've got this stinging desolation in my eyes" (p. 90)—and writing seems to have declined into a mythologizing of isolation. Nothing is repaired because no one is available to any complaint but his own.

> We are each aloof in our private beings, our cilia wigglingly alert to those closest to us because they may without warning do us harm. My skin is my border. I may read a newspaper, but I can't think, I'm conscious of them, they flow through me, the presence of impassive strangers flows through me and shoulder to shoulder, bottom halves carefully untouching, we form in the thirty seconds between stations momentary grudging community, all dissolved and reformed as the doors open, some of us jam out and new impassivities jam in. (p. 107).

"It's life itself that seems to be wanting," the writer contends; professional impasses only imitate personal ones. The estrangement that has ravaged the marriage between Jonathan and Angel is absolutely representative, and "Lives of the Poets" is filled with examples of the physics of disaffection: husbands and wives all retreating to solitary outposts or practicing poor substitutes for intimacy. There are parties and appointments, long talks and fervid trysts, endless provocations and dull blows that leave no mark:

> On the other hand, what could be more dangerous than twenty years of marriage, where she has the same thought a few seconds after you have it, or before; or that you tell her one day how fragile your ego is, how you keep drifting in and out of yourself and don't remember who you are supposed to be, and she tells you she has the same experience, disappearing into herself, and so the two of you have been living together all these years not sure of

who you are or what you're supposed to feel, but known to one and all as the same clear couple they've always known and recognized, a flowerpot on the back of the skull may be preferable. (pp. 112-13)

Instead of love, there is the rhythm of familiar opponents stalking one another; there are also fashions and extravagant gestures, Walkman radios, shopping malls, younger lovers. Instead of purpose, there is "Stroll theater," as "people cruise for the impact of themselves, it's their art form" (p. 119). Crazies roam the streets and subways; politicians assault us, as do charitable organizations, brand names, headlines; there is a need for urban renewal, but we feel our middle age, our energies are waning, our bellies swell, and our fingers stiffen. Rumors are everywhere: a friend has reportedly moved permanently into his subbasement and padlocked the door; another is publicizing his humiliation over his wife's choice of a lesbian lover; a third has retreated into mysticism. There is the CIA to worry about. Reputation. The Russians. Reproachful children. Cancer. We pray for everything, and we are too jaded to believe.

Not flinching from his vision helps the writer to improve his vision of himself (we remember Doctorow's Daniel announcing that he would undertake the aesthetic and psychological challenge of depicting the electrocution of his parents). However, Jonathan must also address the possibility that he is really just trying to enlarge himself by granting his own anxieties societal proportions. If I cannot be consequential, at least I am sensitive—this is the logic "of simple squatting accommodation" (p. 120); all of the poets in "Lives of the Poets" are out to foster an acceptable sense of themselves, and it is predicated on the assumption that their catalogue of woes constitutes Tragic Art and not self-obsessions.[17] Still, Jonathan doubts himself. He wonders whether he has lost contact with his calling: "Oh Leo, I wanted to say, each book has taken me further and further out so that the occasion itself is extenuated, no more than a weak distant signal from the home station, and even that may be fading" (p. 142). What has happened to the commitment to delivering "the wet shining soul"? "When am I being true to myself and when am I only doing penance?" (p. 103).

So "Lives of the Poets" concludes without resolution. On the one hand, the writer is a Prufrock who cannot manage more than self-consciousness. He turns his wants, needs, and fears into universal preoccupations, in the same way Saul Bellow's Tommy Wilhelm saw fit to litanize his frustrations on behalf of the throbbing urban masses:

And the great, great crowd, the inexhaustible current of millions of every race and kind pouring out, pressing round, of every age, of every genius, possessors of every human secret, antique and future, in every face the refinement of one particular motive or essence—I labor, I spend, I strive, I design, I love, I cling, I uphold, I give way, I envy, I long, I scorn, I die, I hide, I want. Faster, much faster than any man could make the tally.[18]

Or like the alter ego of Gilbert Sorrentino who narrates "The Moon in Its Flight," only to discover that he cannot guarantee hospitable fictions for his imagined contemporary lovers, Jonathan also surrenders to the limitations of an insubstantial craft: "Art cannot rescue anybody from anything."[19]

On the other hand, there is the argument that fictional and spiritual projects coincide, that the beseiged self may be tutored by the exactitude and stability of prose. At the end of the novella, Jonathan hoists his child onto his lap:

> OK, I hold his finger, we're typing now, I lightly press his tiny index finger, the key, striking, delights him, each letter suddenly struck vvv he likes the v, hey who's writing this? every good boy needs a toy boat, maybe we'll go to the bottom of the page get my daily quota done come on, kid, you can do three more lousy lines (p. 145).

"I'll never know, in the silence you don't know, you must go on, I can't go on, I'll go on."[20] Both Doctorow's stand-in and Beckett's Unnamable swallow the paradox and urge themselves onward. But the question remains as to how to interpret Doctorow's closing passage. Has Jonathan reconciled artistic and familial duties (if only temporarily) and discovered in the little boy's fascination a way to rededicate himself? Or has what should be a tranquil, innocent moment with his son been contaminated by Jonathan's self-deprecation over the value of his "daily quota"?

The problem of witness in *Lives of the Poets* arises whenever the writer inspects his materials, his motives, or his morals; this line is all wrong, and I may be more than half creating what I perceive, and the disdainful world goes on without me, anyway. Jonathan aspires to the condition of Wallace Stevens' "Snow Man," who has the aesthetically enviable capacity to behold "Nothing that is not there and the nothing that is."[21] However, he risks succumbing to the condemnable situation detailed in another Stevens poem, "Chaos in Motion and Not in Motion": the hero, a "turbulent Schlemihl,/ Has lost the whole in which he was contained,/ Knows desire without an object of desire,/ All mind and violence and nothing felt."[22] Or, as Jonathan himself puts it, "I turn around and around and I'm alone. Is there a specific doom that comes of commitment? You cross some invisible limit, in logic and in faith, and a nameless universe blows through your eyes. It is possible I have crossed" (p. 132). Doctorow's Daniel Isaacson, we recall, could not even spell "commit," much less feel comfortable about the integrity of his methods.

In the end, trapped between fears of co-optation and ineffectuality, the writer falls back upon instinct. As Doctorow himself confides, "I always look for connections, try to synthesize and put things together."[23] "There is a theory, for instance," we learn in "The Leather Man,"

> that the universe oscillates. It is not a steady beaming thing, nor did it start with a bang. It expands and contracts, inhales and exhales, it is either growing larger than you can imagine or imploding toward a point. The crucial thing is its direction. If things come apart enough, they will have started to come together. (p. 70)

Jonathan takes his place in Doctorow's lineage of narrators who struggle to encompass, to classify, to analyze, to possess. By practicing his art, he brings imagination to bear upon the world and emerges as the hero of his own testimony.

NOTES

[1] John Blades, "E. L. Doctorow—Reinventing Fiction with Every Book," *Chicago Tribune,* 11 November 1984, Sec. 13, p. 13.

[2] E. L. Doctorow, "False Documents," *American Review,* 26 (1977), 231.

[3] This contention, as it relates to Doctorow's fiction prior to *Lives of the Poets,* guides my previous article, "The Stylistic Energy of E. L. Doctorow," in *E. L. Doctorow: Essays and Conversations,* ed. Richard Trenner (Princeton, NJ: Ontario Review Press, 1983), pp. 73-108. Here I delineate Doctorow's ability to answer to what are often mutually exclusive demands of artistic innovation and social conscientiousness.

[4] E. L. Doctorow, *Welcome to Hard Times* (New York: Simon and Schuster, 1960), p. 169.

[5] *Welcome to Hard Times,* p. 178.

[6] E. L. Doctorow, *The Book of Daniel* (New York: Random House, 1971), p. 301.

[7] "False Documents," 217.

[8] See Geoffrey Galt Harpham's "E. L. Doctorow and the Technology of Narrative," *PMLA,* 100 (1985), 81-95. Harpham argues that Doctorow's early novels in particular represent "a critique of the coercive power of the textual and ideological regime" (p. 82). Anarchy in either the artistic or the social world is threatening, so structure and systematization are often justified according to the feeling of stability they offer alone.

[9] *The Book of Daniel,* p. 55.

[10] Harpham, 84.

[11] *The Book of Daniel,* p. 262.

[12] *The Book of Daniel,* p. 12.

[13] Ralph Ellison, *Invisible Man* (New York: Random House, 1952), p. 6.

[14] E. L. Doctorow, "The Writer in the Family," in *Lives of the Poets: Six Stories and a Novella* (New York: Random House, 1984), p. 4. Subsequent references to this collection are given parenthetically within the text of the article.

[15] E. L. Doctorow, *Ragtime* (New York: Random House), p. 368.

[16] William H. Gass, "In the Heart of the Heart of the Country," in *In the Heart of the Heart of the Country and Other Stories* (New York: Harper and Row, 1968), p. 196.

[17] See Ihab Hassan's "Pluralism in Postmodern Perspective," *Critical Inquiry,* 12 (1986), 503-20. Hassan proposes a "lower case" version of authority that seems to sanction the pre-disclaimed observations of writers like Jonathan. Hassan locates its origin in the philosophy of William James, according to which "there can be only continual negotiations of reason and interest, mediations of desire, transactions of power or hope. But all these still rest on, rest in, beliefs, which James knew to be the most interesting, most valuable, part of man" (p. 515).

[18] Saul Bellow, *Seize the Day* (New York: Viking, 1974), p. 115.

[19] Gilbert Sorrentino, "The Moon in Its Flight," *New American Review,* 13 (1971), 163.

[20] Samuel Beckett, *The Unnamable,* in *Three Novels: Molloy, Malone Dies, The Unnamable* (New York: Grove Press, 1965), p. 414.

[21] Wallace Stevens, "The Snow Man," in *The Palm at the End of the Mind: Selected Poems and a Play,* ed. Holly Stevens (New York: Knopf, 1971; rpt. Random House-Vintage, 1972), p. 54.

[22] Stevens, "Chaos in Motion and Not in Motion," in *The Palm at the End of the Mind,* p. 278.

[23] Quoted in Blades, p. 14.

Cynthia Ozick and Grace Paley: Diverse Visions in Jewish and Women's Literature

JEANNE SALLADÉ CRISWELL

Historically, American literature owes its rich heterogeneity to writing that emerged from various smaller segments of our culture. In the last half of this century, contemporary American literature continues to draw on works from recognizable—if not always distinct—regional, subcultural, ethnic, racial, and sexual groups. Almost any critical survey of recent literature classifies Southern, Black, Jewish, and women's writing into separate groups or schools. In his introduction to *Jewish-American Stories,* Irving Howe loosely refers to the work of these groups as "regional literature." American Jewish writers, Howe explains, "don't, to be sure, all come from the same part of the country, yet they do come from a kind of regional culture . . . [and] their work shows major similarities and continuities with regard to subject matter, setting, tone."[1] Yet the association of writers in any of these groups can never be considered more than a loose yoking of widely divergent visions based on shared experiences, memories, traditions, values, or attitudes. Cynthia Ozick and Grace Paley, for example, may be classified as both Jewish and women writers, based on their shared experiences and backgrounds. Both women were born in the Bronx, their families being Jewish immigrants from Czarist Russia. Both attended college, married, had children, and currently teach at colleges in New York. Both write stories that rely heavily on these common backgrounds and experiences, that share certain technical approaches to their material, and that address similar thematic issues such as their views of their art (as in "Usurpation" and "A Conversation With My Father"), the exigencies of Jewish identity and the question of assimilation (as in "Usurpation" and "The Loudest Voice"), and their feminist perspectives on art and human relationships (as in "Virility" and "Goodbye and Good Luck"). Despite these similarities, any regional classification of these two authors must ultimately recognize that the visions which drive their stories remain far apart.

As Ozick explains in the preface to *Bloodshed and Three Novellas,* "Usurpation" is a story "against story-writing . . . . the point being that the story-making faculty itself can be a corridor to the corruptions and abominations of idol-worship, of the adoration of magical event."[2] So the story presents us with a series of usurpations. In a fairly convoluted plot, the writer-narrator appropriates and then alters three stories by other authors. The writer-narrator hears the first story at a public reading by a famous writer, who himself took the story from a newspaper article about a fake rabbi. The fake rabbi sold silver crowns and is now in jail. In the preface, the reader learns that this story is actually based on Bernard Malamud's "The Silver Crown." The narrator, who craves Malamud's story for her own, remarks, "It has never occurred to me to write about a teacher; and as for rabbis, I can make up my own craftily enough" (*Bloodshed,* p. 133). This remark refers to Ozick's story "The Pagan Rabbi" and is one of several references that link the narrator to the author. While she is at the reading, the narrator meets a young writer who claims he is related to the fake rabbi in the newspaper article. The narrator dubs this young writer "the goat," but eventually ends up reading his manuscript, the second usurped story, which is based on David Stern's "Agnon, A Story." This story is about an ambitious young writer's visit to a prominent religious writer (Agnon) living in Jerusalem. Partway through the manuscript, the narrator stops reading and invents her own conclusion to the goat's story. In the narrator's version, the prominent religious writer tells the young writer about his meeting with the ghost of the poet Tchernikhovsky, a pantheist whose worship of pagan gods produced his most famous poem to the god Apollo and who now admires the prominent writer's story about the disappointed Messiah precisely *because* the Messiah is prevented from coming. The prominent writer's story is actually based on Agnon's parable, so it becomes the third usurped story. During their meeting, Tchernikhovsky gave the prominent writer a box, which the latter never opened. Inside the box is a crown, which Tchernikhovsky told the prominent writer would allow its wearer to usurp the place of another writer. When the young writer puts on the crown, he grows old and later dies, and the narrator tells the reader that she killed him to punish his arrogance. Finally, when the narrator goes in search of the goat and is subsequently introduced to the fake rabbi's wife, the author's efforts to blur the line between fact and fiction and, by self-reference, to call attention in the story to the art of story-writing itself— these efforts converge as the fake rabbi's wife talks about the story in which she and the narrator are characters: "I looked up one of your stories. It stank, lady. The one called 'Usurpation.' Half of it's swiped, you ought to get sued" (*Bloodshed,* p. 175).

Embedded in this convoluted plot, some of the comments by the story's narrator also offer glimpses into Ozick's vision of her art. Toward the end of "Usurpation," the narrator says that in paradise storywriters will be put in a cage and taught that "All that is not Law is levity." (*Bloodshed,* p. 177). Without the law behind them, stories are "asur" (forbidden) (*Bloodshed,* p. 134). In Ozick's view, art for art's sake is a violation of the second commandment's warning against idolatry, and in a conclusion common to the epiphanic story, she educates the narrator to the possibility of corruption inherent in the art of story-writing. On some plane, then, Ozick's own stories must—if only indirectly—reflect the design of a moral vision consistent with Torah. Besides this central message about the storyteller's art, the narrator also claims, "All stories are rip-offs . . . . Whatever looks like invention is theft . . . . A real story is whatever you can predict, it has to be familiar, anyhow you have to know how it's going to come out, no exotic new material, no unexpected flights—" (*Bloodshed,* pp. 161, 163). According to Ozick, art should reflect a knowable truth which already exists and has existed throughout history. Since what writing is after is to rediscover what already exists, it may be innovative, but it must also exhibit an element of familiarity in making apparent, by the end of the story,

what was implicit from the first . . . . Art, in Ozick's view, tells us nothing new about [the] ontological verity [of existence]; rather, it surprises us into recalling—it evokes our memory of—this reality. This central 'secret' of existence, however, can seldom be revealed directly in a text.[3]

Like Ozick, Paley also blurs the line between fact and fiction in her story about story-writing, "A Conversation With My Father." She uses the dedication page of the volume in which this story appears to tell the reader that the character of the father is actually her father. In an obvious reference to another of Paley's stories, "Faith in a Tree," this father tells the narrator, "I object . . . to people sitting in trees talking senselessly."[4] Later, the father also describes the narrator's stories in terms applicable to Paley's own writing: "Number One: You have a nice sense of humor. Number Two: I see you can't tell a plain story" (Changes, p. 172). Like Ozick, Paley calls attention to the art of story-writing by allowing the narrator of the story to write and revise a story of her own, while both characters offer comments on the nature of fiction and its relationship to life.

There is little plot in Paley's story, unlike "Usurpation," and the story does not end in any epiphanic education of the narrator. Instead, Paley presents the narrator at the hospital bed of her dying father, and in their discussion of what a story should be, the reader is exposed to the seeming incompatibility, in contemporary fiction, of the concern for creating new forms with the desire to explore conventional themes and deal with the experiences of everyday life. The father wants his daughter to write "the kind [of story] de Maupassant wrote, or Chekhov" (Changes, p. 167). He argues that plot is the truth of tragedy, that life is tragic and poignant, and that the "enormous changes at the last minute" in her stories become evasions of what is genuine and unavoidable in life. "You don't want to recognize it," he tells her. "Tragedy! Plain tragedy! Historical tragedy! No hope. The end" (Changes, p. 173). But the narrator resists plot and the convention of closure maintained in the epiphanic story. She prefers an open-ended structure and believes her stories would otherwise seem artificial or inadequate to the possibility of change in life. "Everyone, real or invented," says the narrator, "deserves the open destiny of life" (Changes, p. 167). Although the narrator's comments do coincide with the open-ended structure of this story and other Paley stories, the father's view, too, is part of Paley's approach. His is the final comment in the story—both literally and figuratively, since Paley has couched these last words in a setting designed to remind the reader that he is, in fact, dying, and so represents the sense of inevitability in life which the narrator rejects in her fiction. Brought together in this story, the views of these two characters are separate halves of Paley's total design. In the structure of her stories, "Paley places the tragic material which interests and moves her within an antitragic structure of sudden, abrupt transformations, 'enormous changes,' but the tragic material is nonetheless left intact."[5]

These transformations, like Paley's use of inventive imagery and comic language, alleviate any sense of inevitability or sentimentality that could make this tragic material seem trivial to the reader. So while Ozick is covenanted to the moral vision of Torah, Paley is committed to what she sees as the free and open destiny of life that lies somewhere between chaos and authority.

If Ozick and Paley seem to encompass in their writing divergent views of their art—its purposes and accomplishments—they approach the traditional theme of Jewish identity and the question of assimilation from nearly antithetical perspectives. In Ozick's story, the usurpation of the three stories becomes a symbol of a larger appropriation of the Gentile culture. "Magic—I admit it—is what I lust after," says the writer-narrator. "I am drawn to what is forbidden. . . . I long to be one of the ordinary peoples . . . oh, why can we not have a magic God like other peoples?" (*Bloodshed*, pp. 134-35). Ozick draws a comparison between the Jewish writer who abandons the moral vision of Torah and tries to appeal to an alien culture and the post-holocaust landscape of the goat's neighborhood, where

> the curtain of the Ark dangled in charred shreds . . . .
> In the hollow streets which the Jews had left behind there were scorched absences, apparitions, usurpers. Someone had broken the glass of the kosher butcher's abandoned window and thrown in a pig's head, with anatomical tubes still dripping from the neck. (*Bloodshed*, pp. 160, 177).

In the character of Tchernikhovsky, Ozick presents a Jewish writer who became a pantheist, worshipped pagan gods, and wrote his most famous poem to the god Apollo. After death,

> Tchernikhovsky eats nude at the table of the nude gods, clean-shaven now, his limbs radiant, his youth restored, his sex splendidly erect . . . and when the Sabbath comes . . . as usual he avoids the congregation of the faithful before the Footstool and the Throne. Then the taciturn little Canaanite idols call him, in the language of the spheres, kike. (*Bloodshed*, p. 178)

In this last sentence of the story, Ozick drives home her view on Jewish identity and the question of assimilation—a view integral to other of her stories, such as "The Suitcase" and "A Mercenary." For Ozick, history has proven that assimilation is not possible. Even in paradise, Tchernikhovsky may avoid his obligations as a Jew and continue to associate with pagan gods, but he can never assimilate completely into any alien culture. Even in paradise, the pagan gods he worshipped call him "kike."

In "The Loudest Voice," Paley offers quite another view. The story's narrator, Shirley Abramowitz, is the daughter of Jewish immigrants, and her story is replete with the cadence and idiomatic flavor of Yiddish. Shirley attends a New York public school, and because she has a loud voice, she is chosen to narrate the school's Christmas play. Shirley's mother sees Christmas as a creeping pogrom that will undermine Shirley's religious beliefs and Jewish identity. But Shirley's father, Misha, disagrees. His view does not change throughout the story and seems to be the view with which Paley sympathizes:

You're in America! Clara, you wanted to come here. In Palestine the Arabs would be eating you alive. Europe you had pogroms. Argentina is full of Indians. Here you got Christmas . . . . Christmas. What's the harm? After all, history teaches everyone. We learn from reading this is a holiday from pagan times also, candles, lights, even Chanukah. So we learn it's not altogether Christian. So if they think it's a private holiday, they're only ignorant, not patriotic. What belongs to history, belongs to all men. You want to go back to the Middle Ages? Is it better to shave your head with a secondhand razor? Does it hurt Shirley to learn to speak up? It does not. So maybe someday she won't live between the kitchen and the shop. She's not a fool.[6]

When Shirley's father says,"What belongs to history belongs to all men," he establishes a perspective not unlike Bernard Malamud's reflection that all men are Jews because all men suffer, or Elie Wiesel's notion that with the dawning of the nuclear age, all men suddenly became Jewish because all were in danger of holocaust and extinction.

The Abramowitz's neighbors are equally confused about how they should respond, since their children also received important parts in the play. Only Mrs. Klieg and the rabbi's wife want no part of it. But Mrs. Klieg's answer is suspect, since we don't know whether she decided to prevent her son's involvement before or after he did not get an important part in the play. And anything the rabbi's wife says is suspect, because "under the narrow sky of God's great wisdom, she wore a strawberry-blond wig" (*Disturbances*, p. 58). After the performance, the parents agree that the play was a nice way to introduce their children to the beliefs of a different culture, and even Shirley's mother, though she is still suspicious, has mollified her opinion. Yet Paley gives us an ideological twist that leaves the story somewhat open-ended. Although Shirley says a Jewish prayer at the end of the story—"Hear, O Israel"— she kneels and folds her hands in the Christian attitude of prayer. Paley here recognizes that there is some alteration, that something of one's beliefs and identity is lost or subverted in this sharing process that Shirley's father so esteems. Yet Paley obviously believes that what is gained is worth what is lost. She leaves the reader in the optimistic spirit of Shirley's happiness and sense of belonging to a larger humanity and backs this up with the complicated image of "all the lonesome Christians" (*Disturbances*, p. 63). When Shirley says this, she is actually reacting to the tragic moments in the play she has narrated. But what Paley suggests is that those Christians who know only their own customs and beliefs—because these dominate mainstream society—are somehow more lonesome than Shirley, who has the advantage of knowing her own customs and beliefs and those of other people as well.

Just as similarities in their writing, backgrounds, and experiences do not prompt Ozick and Paley to depict in their fiction analogous views of the relationship between Jewish identity and the larger society, neither do these similarities engender in their work a comparable feminist perspective. Ozick claims for herself a classical feminism that denies any separate psychology on the basis of sex:

Classical feminism—i.e., feminism at its origin, when it saw itself as justice
and aspiration made universal, as mankind widened to humankind—rejected
anatomy not only as destiny, but as any sort of governing force; it rejected
the notion of "female sensibility" as a slander designed to shut women off
from access to the delights, confusions, achievements, darknesses, and
complexities of the great world. Classical feminism was conceived of as the
end of false barriers and boundaries; as the end of segregationist fictions . . . .[7]

Paley, on the other hand, writes out of what she believes is a "feminine
or woman's consciousness."[8] One critic of her work even claims that
Paley's "uncommon empathy [for her characters], which is really the
condition of adherence to subjects of everyday life, is the province of a
woman."[9] So while Ozick's "Virility" and Paley's "Goodbye and Good
Luck" share certain similarities, they also reflect these differences in the
authors' perspectives. Both stories are dramatic monologues by narrators
who are not versions of the authors, but are, nonetheless, sympathetic and
reliable characters. Both stories draw on the experiences of Jewish
immigrants from Russia. Both use humor and vivid imagery and similar
structures that allow the authors to cover nearly the entire lives of the central
characters and still keep the story open-ended.

In "Virility," a Jewish immigrant named Elia Gatoff comes to America,
changes his name to Edmund Gate, takes a job on a newspaper, and nurses
what seems a futile hope to become a poet in English. After several years
of writing atrocious poetry, his work suddenly improves, is published, and
receives wide acclaim. His work is collected in five volumes, all titled *Virility.*
He himself is described by the narrator as "a giant lingam,"[10] and the critics
all hail his work as "The Masculine Principle personified . . . . Robust, lusty,
male (*Rabbi,* p. 254). Eventually, the reader learns the reason behind Gate's
miraculous improvement—he has plagiarized the poems of his maiden aunt,
Tante Rivka, who lives in Liverpool and has sent the poems to him in letters
he never answered. Tante Rivka has been dead for three years when Gate
finally confesses. He has enough poems left for one more volume and so
makes the hoax public. These last poems are published under the title,
Flowers from Liverpool, with a picture of Tante Rivka on the cover. But
though these represent the best of Tante Rivka's writing, the critics claim
the work is "Thin feminine art . . . . A spinster's one-dimensional vision"
(*Rabbi,* p. 266). The last vision the narrator has of Edmund Gate before
he commits suicide (other than his appearance as the madman in the story's
epilogue, still defensive and insecure about his gender) is that of a wasted
man. He blames his aunt for running out on him, and gripping himself
between the legs for verification, he says to the narrator, "I am a man"
(*Rabbi,* p. 223). Tante Rivka, on the other hand, dies with quiet dignity.
Her nephew has never offered to help her, though he certainly had the
means. He never answered the letters she kept sending him until her death,
never even acknowledged receiving the poems he later plagiarized. Rather
than ask anyone for help, his aunt allows herself to starve to death.

In "Goodbye and Good Luck," Paley establishes a central contrast
between Aunt Rose's unconventional, but authentic, life and her sister's
conventional, but empty, life. Though the volume in which this story appears

was published in 1959, Paley's characters are not afraid to act out the changes in ordinary relationships that in later decades would underlie the conscious revaluation of women's experience. As Rosie tells her story, the reader encounters with her a series of deadening or debilitating experiences familiar to women: She moves in with Vlashkin, only to learn that he is a married man; Mr. Krimberg and others in the theater make advances to her; her family tries to encourage her to marry one of the boys they bring around. Yet Rosie is able to resist, or turn to her advantage, these conventional traps, recognizing as she lives that her unconventional lifestyle and her demand for more than conventional relationships have their price:

> And to myself I said further: Finished. This is your lonesome bed. A lady what they call fat and fifty. You made it personally. From this lonesome bed you will finally fall to a bed not so lonesome, only crowded with a million bones. (*Disburbances*, p. 19)

Paley also establishes the possibility of change in life as an important theme throughout the story. At the end of "Goodbye and Good Luck," the reader is prepared for the twist in Rosie's tale:

> So now, darling Lillie, tell this story to your mama . . . . Tell her . . . after all I'll have a husband, which, as everybody knows, a woman should have at least one before the end of the story. (*Disturbances*, pp. 21-22)

In this final twist, Paley works to ensure our recognition that she is not so much after verisimilitude—after all, Rosie could just as easily have remained in her lonesome bed. In fact, in allowing Rosie Leiber to say, this is the end of the story, Paley seems to acknowledge openly that if a reader is looking for mimesis, this last twist may seem stagey, or an optimistic evasion. But what she is really after is a final acknowledgement of the open-endedness of life and the possibility of change. There is no end to Rosie Leiber's story, just as there is no end to life's possibilities. And Paley thereby manages to keep the poignant material intact, while undercutting any sort of implied tragic inevitability in the story or sentimentality that could make the material trivial. Her work is very different from the classical feminism reflected in the ironies of a story like Ozick's 'Virility.''

In all of these stories, then, Ozick and Paley do rely heavily on common backgrounds and experiences. They also share certain technical approaches to their material and address similar thematic issues. For these reasons, they can be classified as both Jewish and women writers. Yet the visions behind their stories remain so far apart, such regional classifications can, at best, be considered only loose guides to the literature.

NOTES

[1] Irving Howe, ed., "Introduction," In *Jewish-American Stories* (New York: Oxford Univ. Press, 1971), p. 2.

[2] Cynthia Ozick, "Preface," in *Bloodshed and Three Novellas* (New York, 1976; rpt. New York: Plume, 1977), p. 11. Subsequent references to this volume are in the text.

[3] Catherine Rainwater and William J. Scheick, " 'Some Godlike Grammar': An

Introduction to the Writings of Hazzard, Ozick, and Redmon," in *Texas Studies in Literature and Language,* 25 (1983), 192.

[4] Grace Paley, "A Conversation with My Father," in *Enormous Changes at the Last Minute* (New York, 1974; rpt. New York: Laurel, 1975), p. 168. Subsequent references are in the text.

[5] Marianne DeKoven, "Mrs. Hegel-Shtein's Tears," in *Partisan Review,* 48 (1981), 219.

[6] Grace Paley, "The Loudest Voice," in *The Little Disturbances of Man* (New York, 1959; rpt. New York: Plume, 1973), pp. 58, 59. Subsequent references are in the text.

[7] Cynthia Ozick, "Literature and the Politics of Sex: A Dissent," in *Art & Ardor* (New York: Knopf, 1983), p. 288.

[8] Joan Lidoff, "Clearing Her Throat: An Interview with Grace Paley," in *Shenandoah,* 32 (1981), 6.

[9] DeKoven, p. 223.

[10] Cynthia Ozick, "Virility," in *The Pagan Rabbi and Other Stories* (New York: Knopf, 1971), p. 244. Subsequent references are in the text.

Cynthia Ozick, Rewriting Herself: The Road from "The Shawl" to "Rosa"

JOSEPH LOWIN

Many are the writers—both novelists and critics—who have come to the conclusion that writing is an activity based not only in reality but also on previous writing. The hero of Bernard Malamud's novel *God's Grace,* a modern rewriting of the Flood Story of Genesis, when asked where stories come from, informs his companion that stories come "from other stories."[1] In *The Anxiety of Influence,* Harold Bloom asserts that writing is always rewriting.

In "Usurpation (Other People's Stories)" (1974), Cynthia Ozick demonstrated that she had no anxieties whatever about being influenced by previous writers. To the contrary, she publicly arrogated to herself the right to rewrite other texts, basing herself on a long literary tradition that goes back at least as far as Boccaccio and Shakespeare in the Western world, and to the domain of rabbinic literature in the Jewish tradition.

"Usurpation" provides hints of a second phase to the rewriting phenomenon. In Ozick's case, rewriting does not limit itself to other people's stories but extends to her own work as well. The short story "Puttermesser and Xanthippe" is in many ways a sequel to the earlier "Puttermesser: Her Work History, Her Ancestry, Her Afterlife." Ozick's novel *The Cannibal Galaxy* is a rewriting of her earlier short story "The Laughter of Akiva," placing greater emphasis on the background of her main protagonists, emphasizing the dual role—of culture and of cruelty—that Europe has played for her Jewish heroes.

Perhaps the summit of Ozick's art as rewriter—that is to say, as writer— is attained in a pair of short stories published in *The New Yorker Magazine* between 1980 and 1983, "The Shawl"[2] and "Rosa."[3]

"The Shawl" tells the story of a woman and two girls caught up in that "place without pity" known as the Holocaust. Rosa, a mother governed by strong maternal instincts, will try to overcome a Nazi policy which dictates that infants are not to be spared. Rosa's teenage niece Stella has no motherly instincts. She will be governed exclusively by the instinct of self-preservation.

The story has two locuses: the road on which the Jews are forced to march to their final destination and the concentration camp itself, presented in miniature as a barracks and a yard surrounded by an electrified barbed-wire fence.

The story revolves about the shawl of the title, seen by Rosa as her daughter Magda's only defense against the Nazis. It is used as both a wrapping in which to hide the infant—a container—and as a security blanket with which to pacify the infant so that she will not cry out from hunger and thereby betray her existence to the oppressors. The story has one incident. One morning on the *Appleplatz* Rosa hears the cry "Maaa . . . aaa!" and notices her infant daughter, shawlless, crawling on the ground. Rosa is faced with a tragic dilemma. If she tries to run and snatch up the baby, the baby will not stop crying and the Germans will discover both "criminals." If she runs back to the barracks to find the comforting shawl, perhaps the baby will be discovered, during the brief moment of delay, by a German soldier. Rosa opts for the shawl and hurries back into the barracks. Stella, obviously in an effort to keep from freezing, instinctively trying to cling to her own life, has taken Magda's shawl and covered herself with it. Rosa grabs the shawl and runs back out into the arena. But it is too late. A German officer has picked the infant up and is heading toward the electrified fence. The maternal instinct and the instinct for self-preservation wage a silent battle within Rosa as, helpless, she observes the Nazi electrocute her infant by hurling her against the fence.

In 2,000 finely-wrought words, that is the story of "The Shawl." It is obvious, however, that the power of the story derives not merely from the plot, as starkly riveting as it may be, but from the concentrated style of the author.

Ozick, like a French symbolist poet of the nineteenth century, paints not "the thing itself" but the *effect* produced by the "thing." The effect of a concentration camp is achieved here by both indirection and concentration. How do we know that we are in a place that harbors crematoria? Ozick writes only of an "ash-stippled wind." How do we know that Magda is the fruit of an illicit liaison with a non-Jewish, "Aryan" man? Not only by her blue eyes, nor by the color of her hair which resembles the color of Rosa's star, but by the word *their* set off by italics: "You could think she was one of *their* babies."

The concentrated world of "The Shawl" extends beyond its fictional borders into other worlds. Ozick's use of metaphor here is crucial. Rosa, marching on the road with the baby in her arms, is a "walking cradle." Stella's weakened knees are "tumors on sticks," her elbows "chicken bones." Magda in the shawl is "a squirrel in a nest." The shawl's windings form "a little house." Magda's round face is "a pocket mirror" in which her ascendancy can be seen. More ominously, Magda's tooth, jutting up in her mouth, is "an elfin tombstone of white marble." Providing a moment of sad comic relief, the shawl itself, blown in the wind, is a "clown." At the end, the scream which Rosa represses is "a long viscous rope of clamor." Rosa's skeleton is not merely a frame on which her flesh is draped but "a ladder up which a scream might climb."

These images are intended to produce, by indirection, the effect of physical and mental torture. No scream is ever produced on Rosa's viscous rope, no scream climbs up her ladder. In this story there is—strictly speaking—not one word of dialogue among the protagonists. The only sound that passes anyone's lips in Magda's semi-bestial infant cry, "Maaa . . . aaa!" Aside from that one cry, even Magda is characterized by silence. "Ever since the drying up of Rosa's nipples, ever since Magda's last scream on the road, Magda had been devoid of any syllable; Magda was mute."

Of conversation between Rosa and Stella there is no indication. Stella's "I was cold" comes "afterward." In the place of dialogue Ozick puts the double voice of nature and technology. Just as the language of metaphor succeeds in dilating the scenic space and in creating a world wider than the space occupied by the text, so too the language spoken by nature succeeds in enlarging the confining space of the barracks, indicating both other places and other times.

Ozick's nature speaks in murmurs. "The sunheat [in the arena] murmured of another life, of butterflies in summer. . . . On the other side of the steel fence, far away, there were green meadows speckled with dandelions and deep-colored violets; beyond, even farther, innocent tiger lilies, tall, lifting their orange bonnets." This moment of lyricism provides relief in the tension-filled drama; it constitutes a delaying tactic at the precise moment of the greatest horror.

The language of technology performs a different function. The fence surrounding the barracks is electrified. In the deathly silence characteristic of "The Shawl" Rosa can discern its pathetic hum. "Sometimes the electricity inside the fence would seem to hum. . . . Rosa heard real sounds in the wire: grainy sad voices."

The voices within the wire are quite possibly the voices of Jewish history, the voices of those who have already gone up in fire. These are not the voices of warning; they are voices of lamentation, of poetry. They constitute a striving to turn lament into a liturgical voice of triumph. They have come to urge Rosa to act courageously. When Rosa appears on the margins of the arena, shawl in hand, she sees her infant being carried aloft by a helmeted soldier. "The voices told her to hold up the shawl, high; the voices told her to shake it, to whip with it, to unfurl it like a flag." The voices vainly urge Rosa to become a hero.

At another moment the electric voices of the fence take on the identity of the voice of the infant Magda; soon those two voices will indeed be one and the same. "The electric voice began to chatter wildly. 'Maamaa, maaa, maaa,' they all humed together." The moment that Magda "splashed against the fence, the steel voices went mad in their growling, urging Rosa to run and run to the spot where Magda had fallen."

Rosa's instinct for self-preservation overcomes both her maternal instincts and any heroic urges she may have had. Rosa does not obey the voice of the electric wires because she knows that "if she let the wolf's screech ascending now through the ladder of her skelton break out, they would shoot." Rosa's story in "The Shawl" ends with her making the same use of the shawl that Stella had done, and, incidentally, as Magda had done, as a life preserver. Rosa takes the shawl and stuffs her mouth with it. Stifling speech, she preserves life.

Because Rosa has denied the tragic, heroic moment, she has left Cynthia Ozick with a problem. Surely there is more to this woman Rosa than her actions under superhuman stress. It is on the pretext of this problem that Ozick will enter into "The Shawl" and pull out a midrash on it, the prize-winning story "Rosa," a rewriting of "The Shawl."

"Rosa" takes place approximately 35 years after the events described in "The Shawl." Both Rosa and Stella have survived the ordeal. After the war, Zionist rescue organizations had made an effort to induce teenager Stella to be rehabilitated in a Youth Aliyah setting in Palestine. Rosa, who had herself been brought up in an assimilated non-Zionist family, blocks these efforts and whisks Stella away with her to America. There, aunt and niece live what is probably no exaggeration to call an eccentric existence. Rosa is still resentful of Stella's role in Magda's death; Stella is unable to "normalize" her existence in marriage and family. This double spinsterhood is remarkable for the way Rosa Lublin chooses to earn a living: she opens an antique shop.

The shop specializes in both real and metaphorical mirrors. Every customer who enters the shop is offered not only things "used, old, lacy with other people's history" (p. 2) but also a story of Jewish suffering at the hands of the Nazis. In particular, Rosa offers to her "clientele" not the story of "The Shawl"—of that there is no direct mention—but a story of the tramcar that used to pass through the center of the Warsaw Ghetto.

Obviously frustrated by her customers' total indifference to the story she has to tell, and unable and unwilling to adapt to life after her traumatic experience, Rosa goes mad and, one day, smashes up her store. In order to save her aged aunt from prosecution and a possible sentence, Stella works out a deal with the authorities whereby Rosa will leave New York and retire to Miami Beach.

Such is the background against which Cynthia Ozick's story is set. The word "background" is used here because only at this point does "Rosa" the short story begin, in a run-down retirement hotel in Miami Beach. To the casual and disinterested observer, Rosa looks like a "madwoman and a scavenger" (p. 1), indifferent to life. She rarely ventures out into the hot Florida sun, taking her meals—a cracker spread with Welch's grape jelly or a single sardine from a tin can—standing up in her kitchen. Her shabby dress would lead one to believe that she is negligent of her person.

On the day the story begins, Rosa makes what appears to be a superhuman effort to do a wash at the local laundromat. There she meets Simon Persky, a relative of Israeli politician Shimon Peres and a near-widower whose wife has been institutionalized for mental illness. It appears that Persky, who otherwise fancies himself something of a ladies' man, has been sent by fate to rehabilitate Rosa. Although unaware of the extraordinary past life that Rosa has led and equally unconscious of the extraordinary inner life that Rosa has been leading, Persky does not treat Rosa as "the ordinary article" but rather as an individual of intrinsic worth. After her encounter with Persky, Rosa returns alone to her hotel room with her laundry—curiously, minus a pair of underpants. The missing pair of pants will become an obsession with Rosa throughout the course of the story; her suspicions will be directed at her new acquaintance.

She has another obsession, not evident to the casual observer, and that is to write letters in Polish to her dead daughter Magda. In these letters Rosa displays a cultured background, a literary style, and a vivid imagination. She conjures up Magda either as an adult woman, a professor at Columbia University, or as a 16 year old girl dressed in frilly clothes. Rosa's letters have two main themes: complaints about Stella's stubborn resistance to Magda's continued existence and reminiscences of Rosa's beautiful home life in pre-war Warsaw.

Rosa also writes to Stella, to whom she must, for appearances' sake, feign that Magda is indeed dead. In her last letter she has asked Stella to send her a package: a box containing Magda's shawl, religiously preserved all these years. Despite Stella's misgivings that her aunt is engaged in some mad form of idolatry, she informs Rosa that the shawl is under way.

Rosa receives other mail as well. This includes a series of letters and a box containing a scholarly manuscript from Dr. James W. Tree. The name is suggestive, especially in work by the author of "The Pagan Rabbi," in which the main protagonist hangs himself from a tree. A professor in the "Department of Clinical Social Pathology" at the "University of Kansas-Iowa," Dr. Tree is doing research on a theory of "Repressed Animation"—souls in hiding?—and would welcome the opportunity to make a case study of Rosa's reaction to her "stress resulting from incarceration, exposure, and malnutrition." Rosa does not respond to this cold clinical intrusion into "other people's suffering" except to burn Tree's insistent letters.

Does Rosa resist *all* intrusions? Eventually, she will not resist Persky's warm, humane, personal, value-laden intervention in her life. At the end of the story she will have the telephone in her room reconnected, symbolically renewing contact with the outside world. More importantly, she will begin to make room in her inner life for Persky's continuing presence.

While "Rosa" is many ways a continuation of "The Shawl," it is not strictly speaking a sequel to its predecessor. Both stories are independent works of art and neither "needs" the other to be considered complete. One might say, however, that once the reader has knowledge of both stories, neither story can be approached without reference to the other. Once again Cynthia Ozick has entered, and drawn the reader into, the midrashic mode.

The similarity of "Rosa" to Ozick's earlier midrashic writing is striking. Like Isaac Kornfeld, the main character of "The Pagan Rabbi," like Jimmy and Lucy Feingold, the authorial couple of "Levitation," like Hester Lilt, the "imagistic linguistic logician" of The *Cannibal Galaxy,* and like almost all of the personages depicted in "Usurpation," from the narrator, to the "goat," to "Saul-not-Tchernikhovsky," Rosa is a writer. Taken by itself, it is perhaps not significant that Rosa spends much of her life in Florida cooped up in her room with a writing board on her knees composing letters. What is significant is that these letters written to her dead daughter Magda are works of fiction. What is even more compelling is that "to her daughter Magda she wrote in the most excellent literary Polish" (p. 1). Rosa's parents, no less than Rosa's literary predecessors in Ozick's *oeuvre,* are thinkers and writers. Her father she describes as a philosopher; her mother, she reveals, published poetry. Stella, as if in criticism, calls her aunt a "parable-maker" (p. 17), but the reader attuned to nuances in Ozick will realize that that title is a badge of honor.

When Rosa was a high school student in pre-war Warsaw, she had been praised by one of her teachers for her "literary style." Ozick intervenes in the story (using a free indirect style of quotation) to comment on the linguistic power accorded to the writer. "What a curiosity it was to hold a pen—nothing but a small pointed stick, after all, oozing its hieroglyphic puddles: a pen that speaks, miraculously, Polish" (p. 19). Of course, Ozick is commenting not only on Rosa's power but on her own ability as a novelist to create a fiction in which she can write in English and force her reader into accepting that what she is reading is indeed "literary Polish." After all, says Ozick, what is writing but an "immersion into the living language. All at once this cleanliness, this power to make history, to tell, to explain. To retrieve, to reprieve!" And that is not all. Writing, she concludes, is something more: the making of fictions. In her own words, writing is: "To lie" (pp. 19-20). Rosa, for her part, explains her own fiction-making capacity to her daughter in her own way: "to those who don't deserve the truth, don't give it" (p. 19).

The fictions that Rosa creates are based in fact, located in history. Their goal is to make the past meaningful. Simon Persky, obviously in an effort at bonding, claims that his past is identical with Rosa's. After all, like her, he was born in Warsaw. More than once Rosa will protest to him vehemently: "My Warsaw isn't your Warsaw." First of all, since Persky left Europe in 1920 for America, he did not experience the degradations of the Warsaw Ghetto. In addition, Persky, insulated in Polish Jewishness, had had nothing at all to do with Polish culture. Rosa's Poland is unfathomably different:

> In school she had read Tuwim[4], such delicacy, such *loftiness,* such Polishness. The Warsaw of her girlhood: a great light: she switched it on, she wanted to live inside her eyes. The curve of the legs of her mother's bureau. The strict leather smell of her father's desk. The white tile tract of the kitchen floor, the big pots breathing, a narrow tower stair next to the attic. . . . the house of her girlhood laden with a thousand books. Polish, German, French; her father's Latin books; the shelf of shy literary periodicals her mother's poetry now and then wandered through, in short lines like heated telegrams. Cultivation, old civilization, beauty, history! Surprising turnings of streets, shapes of venerable cottages, lovely aged eaves, unexpected and gossamer turrets, steeples, the gloss, the antiquity! Gardens. Whoever speaks of Paris has never seen Warsaw. (pp. 5-6)

There are, then, two types of Warsaw, Rosa's and Persky's, and the lives lived in these two cities are not comparable. Life itself, for Rosa, can be further divided, as she puts it, into three phases: "the life before, the life during, the life after. . . . The life after is now. The life before is our real life, where we was born." (From the word "was" we know that Rosa is not speaking "literary Polish" but immigrant English, and she is speaking it to Persky.) Persky wants to know what the "life during" was. "This was Hitler," Rosa answers. This is the life of which Persky has no inkling. This is the life to which the people coming into her store were indifferent. Rosa admits that "before is a dream" and can therefore be preserved only in the fantasy world of fiction. Further, when one looks at the superficiality of modern life, and here Rosa means modern American life, one concludes that "after is a joke." What Rosa wants to force her interlocutor to understand is that "only during stays. And to call it life is a lie" (p. 28).

How is one to render an account of the "during" that "stays"? "The Shawl" is one of the stories of the enduring "during," presented as a brutal, simple truth. Rosa has another story to tell about the "during," about the time contained between the lovely "before" and the superficial "after." It concerns the tramcar that went through the heart of the Warsaw Ghetto. What was extraordinary about that tramcar was its very ordinariness. "The most astounding thing was that the most ordinary streetcar, bumping along on the most ordinary trolley tracks, and carrying the most ordinary citizens going from one section of Warsaw to another, ran straight into the place of our misery" (p. 34). Amazingly, the ordinary streetcar passengers did not even see the extraordinary setting in which they were riding. They could not imagine, much less notice, an "other" for whom an ordinary head of lettuce might take on pastoral dimensions, representing all of nature. "Every day they saw us—women with shopping sacks. Green lettuce! I thought my salivary glands would split aching for that leafy greenness" (p. 34).

"Rosa" is a story in the Jewish mode to the extent that it demonstrates to the reader the extraordinariness that lies hidden in Rosa's very ordinariness. In one of her letters to her daughter Magda, Rosa protests that Stella's accusation that Magda's father is a non-Jew, a German, and possibly a Nazi, is a slander. She does admit that after Madga's death she had been "forced" more than once by Nazi soldiers. She insists however that her relationship with Magda's father, her admittedly gentile father, was most ordinary: "Take my word for it, Magda, your father and I had the most ordinary lives—by 'ordinary' I mean respectable, gentle, cultivated. Reliable people of refined reputation" (p. 19). The ordinariness of which Rosa speaks is extraordinary on several accounts. Hers was not the life that most Polish Jews in America speak of. Persky did not know of such thorough acculturation. In addition, compared with the uncultivated "joke" that life has become in the "after" of America, the ordinary life of pre-war Europe is in itself extraordinary.

Extraordinariness may indeed be the key to "Rosa." Behind the "madwoman and the scavenger" that we see, there is a rich extraordinary background, a background that includes more than an affair with a gentile and an illegitimate child. It is a background that includes even more than the reading of an exquisite Jewish-Polish poet, Julian Tuwim. The Lublins had fine art at home, including an authentic Greek vase, no less suggestive of eternity than Keats' Grecian urn. In addition, "we had wonderful ink drawings, the black so black and miraculous, how it measured out a hand and the shadow of a hand" (p. 35).

It is in Rosa's developing relationship with Persky that "Rosa" gives further meaning to what Ozick has called "the riddle of the ordinary."[5] Before his retirement, Simon Persky had been a button manufacturer. That button is magnified by Rosa into a major metaphor for ordinariness. She compares Persky's background to her own in its terms. "She considered Persky's life: how trivial it must have been: buttons, himself no more significant than a button. It was plain he took her to be another button like himself, battered now and out of fashion" (p. 26). Time and again Rosa returns to this image, apparently mad to one who has not yet fathomed the poetry of her language. "I'm not your button, Persky! I'm not nobody's button!" (p. 30).

Rosa is unfair to Persky. He is not trivial. He, too, is not a button. Not only that, but he means to deal with Rosa as a person of intrinsic worth. He recognizes that there is something of the extraordinary in her. (He would probably believe that of everybody, like Ozick.) At one point in the story the conversation between Persky and Rosa turns to books. Persky is impressed to learn that Rosa reads only in Polish and, moreover, that she does not read mere "books" but is interested only in real "literature." Noticing that Rosa has no books in her home, Persky humanely offers to drive Rosa to the library. This gesture of warm humanity is taken as such by Rosa. "A thread of gratitude pulled in her throat. He almost understood what she was: no ordinary button" (p. 28).

If Rosa is to be admired for her extraordinariness, Persky himself is to be given consideration for the fact that his very ordinariness contains a grain of Jewish heroism. Persky's outlook on life—one is tempted to call it a philosophy—is based on his simple humanism. Persky counsels Rosa that in life what is needed is perspective, what is required is moderation. To Rosa's assessment, for example, that her quarters are "cramped," Persky answers: "I work from a different theory. For everything there's a bad way of describing, also a good way. You pick the good way, you get along better" (p. 27). When Rosa complains to Persky that Stella is trying to wipe out the memory of all that Rosa cherishes, Persky advises her to be moderate, even in her effort to do such a noble thing as to commemorate the past. "Sometimes a little forgetting is necessary . . . if you want to get something out of life" (p. 28).

It is clear that, before the encounter with Persky, Rosa will want little if anything from life. After all, life, the "life after," is a joke. Rosa does not want to be normal, like Persky. She prefers a life that is lived on an entirely different plane, a plane that involves art, creativity, the imagination, a plane that with some justification might plausibly be called pagan.

In Rosa's reminiscences of her parents' home in pre-war Warsaw, she recalls that her mother was attracted to the object of her maid's religious adorations: a statue. In Ozick's writings, this type of attraction always verges on the idolatrous. Magda's shawl becomes Rosa's substitute for her mother's statue of the Virgin and Child. The shaw is a religious icon that Rosa feels the urge to kiss. In a letter informing her aunt that the requested shawl is in the mail, Stella takes the opportunity to sermonize Rosa: "Your idol is on its way. . . . Go on your knees to it if you want . . . . You'll open the box and take it out and cry, you'll kiss it like a crazy person. Making holes in it with kisses. You're like those people in the Middle Ages who worshipped a piece of the True Cross, a splinter from some old outhouse as far as anybody knew" (p. 12). Stella's assessment of Rosa's behavior in the presence of the shawl, as brutal as it may appear in its rationality, is on the mark. Indeed, Rosa is very close to being an idol-worshipper. Even Rosa's letter-writing activity is ambiguous. On the one hand, it is an esthetic outlet for a deep emotional strain; on the other, it is the expression of a pagan mentality.

When Rosa prepares to write her highly creative letters to Magda, she first meticulously sets the scene. Is she preparing a canvas for painting or an altar for devotion? Even the act of preparing the paper with which to write Magda is an ambiguous one. The act of receiving Magda's shawl, however, is clearly idolatrous.

Rosa has gotten in the mail a package which she is certain contains her beloved shawl. Rather than rip it open victoriously, she delays opening the box as long as possible. In so doing, she makes herself into a statue:

> She put on her good shoes, a nice dress. . .; she arranged her hair, brushed her teeth, poured mouthwash on the brush, sucked it up through the nylon bristles, gargled rapidly. As an afterthought she changed her bra and slip; it meant getting out of her dress and into it again. Her mouth she reddened very slightly—a smudge of lipstick rubbed on with a finger. *Perfect, she mounted the bed on her knees and fell into folds.* A puppet, dreaming. Darkened cities, tombstones, colorless garlands, a black fire in a gray field, brutes forcing the innocent, women with their mouths stretched and their arms wild, her mother's voice calling. After hours of these pitiless tableaux, it was late afternoon. (p. 20, my emphasis)

The perfection achieved by Rosa in this tableau is that of a work of art creating other works of art. Rosa has succeeded in making herself into a *tableau vivant,* perfect, ready to investigate the contents of her treasure chest. Instead of opening the box, she dreams of her brutal past, a dead civilization, painting, in her mind's eye, *tableaux morts.* The connection between these *tableaux morts* and the *tableau vivant* that Rosa has transformed herself into is striking. One contains the other. And, although hours pass at this activity, both are frozen in time. The dreaming activity is not merely a hiatus between the desire to open the package and its opening. The dreaming activity—the artistic activity—itself becomes central, and leads to further artistic activity. Reintegrating reality after her dream, Rosa does not return her attention to the box with the shawl in it. Instead, she returns to the underpants that were mysteriously missing from her laundry.

How are underpants different from a shawl? The latter represents the life of the imagination. It represents the dangers of the life of the imagination, to be sure, but it also represents the attempt to give meaning to history. The underpants represent present reality in all its commonness, in all its ordinariness. They represent the need to regain meaning in life.

Rosa will now go out into the Miami evening in search of her underpants. She will go out, therefore, "to retrieve, to reprieve" (p. 20). On the sands of Miami Beach she will find decadent reality in the form of homosexual lovers. She will also find a way of framing her life.

One of the most vivid techniques adopted by Ozick in "Rosa" is the striking opposition between images of the "container" and the "contained." The word "container" is found only once in the entire story, applied metaphorically to Stella, but it appears to have been enough to set the image humming. Stella looks innocent on the outside; she has "the face of a little bride." Rosa, nevertheless, harbors a great deal of resentment of Stella, for a complex set of reasons, including blame for Magda's death. To Magda, Rosa writes of Stella: "you would not believe in what harmless *containers* the bloodsucker comes" (p. 2, my emphasis). The very sentence implies a distinction between the container and the contained. Miami Beach, with what Rosa calls its trivial residents, is another type of container, "a box for useless buttons" (p. 26). The button metaphor is here contained within the container metaphor. Her own place of residence, a container within a container, a single-room apartment in a Miami Beach retirement hotel, is described as "a dark hole" (p. 1). And yet, when Rosa is able to conjure up Magda's presence, the room is magically transformed into a magnificent surreal palace, in which the buttons on Magda's dress are the stars of some extraordinary heaven:

> The whole room was full of Magda: she was like a butterfly, in this corner and in that corner, all at once. Rosa waited to see what age Magda was going to be: how nice, a girl of sixteen, girls in their bloom move so swiftly that their blouses and skirts balloon. They are always butterflies at sixteen. There was Magda, all in flower. She was wearing one of Rosa's dresses from high school. Rosa was glad: it was the sky-colored dress, a middling blue with black buttons seemingly made of round chips of coal, like the unlit shards of stars. (p. 32)

When Rosa ventures out into the Sodom and Gomorrah of Miami's beachfront, the sand in which the lovers lie enveloped is compared to the volanic ash of Pompei. "The sand was littered with bodies. Photograph of Pompei: prone in the volcanic ash. Her pants were under the sand; or else packed with sand, like a piece of torso, a broken statue; the human groin detached, the whole soul gone, only the loins left for kicking by strangers" (p. 22). Time is here doubly frozen, once by lava and once by the art of photography; both of these contain time. The underpants themselves are at one and the same time the thing contained in the photograph which is conjured up and the frame for another work of art: the statue of a torso. Rosa is compelled to look for her pants in the sands of Miami Beach perhaps because she feels a need to convert them into a work of statuary.

Her suspicions lie elsewhere. She believes that Persky, in a fit of perversion, has stolen her pants. Only a sense of decorum and respect for Persky's humanity prevent her from confronting him with her suspicions. Nevertheless, her imagination will still think in terms of intertwining containers: "she wanted to tell him he was under suspicion; he owed her a look in his jacket. . . . If not in his jacket, his pants. But it wasn't possible to say a thing like this. Her pants in his pants" (p. 25).

The most striking use of the image of the container and the contained can be found in Ozick's use of the metaphor of electricity. It is on this point that the continuity of "Rosa" with "The Shawl" is most apparent. Rosa is frozen by the hum of electricity; the electrified fence of the concentration camp is the container for voices which cry out to Rosa. In "Rosa" the metaphor of electricity is extended to encompass two other types of expressiveness. When Rosa writes letters to Magda, she writes "inside a blazing flying current" (p. 35). Rosa's writing is contained and expressed by an electric hum. The second type of electric current has to do with the fact of Magda's blond hair and with the fact that Magda is the product of Jewish and Aryan strains. "She was always a little suspicious of Magda, because of the other strain, whatever it was, that ran in her. . . . The other strain was ghostly, even dangerous. *It was as if the peril hummed out from the filament of Magda's hair, those narrow bright wires*" (p. 33, my emphasis).

As with Stella, so with Magda: what is inside the container is dangerous. Rosa herself is tempted to exteriorize her feelings; it is quite likely that she fears that, doing so, she will empty herself of all content.

There are two other containers in "Rosa," the package from Stella containing Magda's shawl, and a package from Dr. Tree, containing a scholarly study of another type of "containering," called by Ozick "Repressed Animation." Dr. Tree's package comes first. Rosa mistakes its contents for those of the other package. She treats it as though it did indeed contain the object of her idolatrous worship. In order to maximize the feelings of her inner life, she delays opening the package and exteriorizing her dreams. "She tidied all around. Everything had to be nice when the box was opened" (p. 13). This retarding tactic is expanded into the episode of her foray into Miami Beach underlife.

On Rosa's return to her hotel she is greeted by the faithful Persky. In what she thinks is an act of religious self-sacrifice, she offers to Persky the honor of opening the package. "What her own hands longed to do she was yielding to a stranger, a man with pockets; she knew why. To prove herself pure: a Madonna" (p. 29). What Persky, the man with pockets, is a container for remains to be seen. Rosa wishes to display herself for the world to see; she wants to remain the statue she had created previously. The box contains not Magda's shawl but Dr. Tree's treatise.

Just as Rosa had destroyed her store—the store that contained stories—Rosa will destroy the treatise, sending the Tree up in flames. Subsequently, the "real" package from Stella arrives. Neither the container nor its contents will any longer hold any interest for Rosa. It is her own contents that interest Rosa now, and she feels she is losing hold of them. "It was not possible to be hoodwinked again, but Rosa was shocked, *depleted*, almost as if yesterday's conflagration hadn't been Tree but really the box with Magda's shawl" (pp. 30-31, my emphasis). Rosa feels empty of content. The former owner of a store which specialized in mirrors sees in Simon Persky a possible mirror for her own humanity.

Rosa's room had been tidied up, prepared for a pagan ritual, the worship of the dead. It turns out by some "miracle" to have been prepared instead for life. Persky arrives. "Her room was miraculously ready, tidy, clarified. . . . Destiny had clarified her room just in time for a visitor" (p. 27). In this encounter with the "visitor" Rosa gets a further inkling that she is quite willing to be brought back to life. One of the signs of her newly expressed "animation" is her decision to have her telephone reconnected. At first, when she hears the telephone ring (the sound coming by the way from wires, contained in them), she thinks of the telephone as a dead idol that can magically be brought to life. In a pagan gesture, she will even take the telephone and wrap it in the shawl, making the shawl a container for repressed animation.

When Persky, a gentleman come to call on a lady, has his presence announced via the telephone, the shawled telephone will be described as "a silent god, so long comatose." Like Magda, the telephone can be "animated at will" (p. 35). Unlike Magda, however, the telephone announces not a dead past but a future which contains Persky's version of life. In the closing scene of the story Rosa takes the shawl off the telephone, thus divorcing it from Magda. The shawl which contained Magda and at the same time repressed Rosa's animation will now repress Magda. "Magda was not there. Shy, she ran from Persky. Magda was away" (p. 36).

Given Cynthia Ozick's attitude toward background and history, one may be confident that Magda will not be "away" for good. Rather, having written "Rosa" as a midrash on "The Shawl," Ozick means for the two stories to stand not in a diachronous relationship one to the other, a relationship in which one story would follow the other chronologically. Rather, Ozick means for the two stories to stand next to each other in a synchronous relationship, in which one story "always" contains the other and comments on it. Just as the mirrors in Rosa's store are meant both to freeze time and to record its passing, so too these two stories, "Rosa" and "The Shawl," are mirrors of themselves and mean to give meaning to both history and life.

NOTES

[1] Bernard Malamud, *God's Grace* (New York: Avon, 1980), p. 80.

[2] Cynthia Ozick, "The Shawl," in *The New Yorker,* May 26, 1980, pp. 33-34. Superfluous here, page numbers will not be provided in the text.

[3] Cynthia Ozick, "Rosa," in *The New Yorker,* March 21, 1983, pp. 38-71. Reprinted in *Prize Stories 1984: The O. Henry Awards,* ed. William Abrahams (Garden City, NY: Doubleday, 1984), pp. 1-36. References are to this text.

[4] Polish poet Julian Tuwim (1894-1953) represents one form of the symbiosis between enlightened Jewish and western culture. His 1944 manifesto, *We Polish Jews* (Jerusalem: The Magnes Press, 1984), is required reading in this connection.

[5] In "The Riddle of the Ordinary," *Moment* 1 (1975), 77-79, Ozick asserts that the mission of the Jews is to sanctify the ordinary.

Photographs and Fantasies in the Stories of Ann Beattie

STACEY OLSTER

"You know what fascinates me about photographs?" asks one Ann Beattie character in *The Burning House.* "Did you ever notice the captions? Photographer gets a shot of a dwarf running out of a burning hotel and it's labeled 'New York: 1968.' Or there's a picture of two humpbacked girls on the back of a pony, and it says 'Central Park: 1966.' "[1] For Nick, who spends his time at Boulevard Records supplying chicken tacos to bands like Barometric Pressure, the fascination springs from a deliberate downplaying of the extraordinary. In contrast, a photographer like Diane Arbus, who did supply her studies of freaks and eccentrics with equally nondescript titles (and whom Beattie cites in her first collection of stories), saw no further explanation as necessary. "Maybe the comment has to be implicit in the pictures," she wrote. ". . . If these are shattering enough, anything like comment or judgment on the subjects would betray both them and us."[2]

Looking at the pared-down prose of Ann Beattie's stories, it is instructive to keep in mind both remarks, for together they suggest the way in which her portraits of contemporary American life should be viewed. That the short story writer has long identified his work with the visual arts is by now a commonplace.[3] Indeed, the singularity of effect provided by a painting resembles most closely the kind of effect Poe dictated for the short story when defining the genre's properties.[4] And for Beattie, who describes her own work as focusing on "small moments," and, in denying any "overall view of things to express," eschews "putting pieces together," the photograph in particular serves as the visual artifact most related to what she does in print.[5] Yet while suffusing her stories with references to photography, Beattie also populates her stories with characters who view their own experiences with respect to the same medium. Beattie's people continually take pictures, develop pictures, observe pictures, and—perhaps most important—*imagine* pictures. What distinguishes the author's perspective from that of her characters is the different purposes for which the same medium is used. For characters like Nick, the photograph provides a way of framing experience. The criticism in his remarks notwithstanding, he still composes the details of a friend's mysterious drowning into "Lake Champlain: 1978." For Beattie, like Diane Arbus, the photograph provides a harsh exposure of experience. The story in which Nick appears is entitled "Winter: 1978."

In attempting to frame their lives through the ordering lens of art, the people in Beattie's fiction are hardly unique among characters in fiction today. Whether embodied in the prospects of Skylab falling, as in *Falling in Place,* or located, more typically, in the domestic details of a dog's unaccountable barking and a pot of soup boiling over, as in "Marshall's Dog," they respond to a world whose workings seem beyond their control.

However, in resorting to the temporally limited frame of photography for comfort, Beattie's characters affirm just those strategies abhorred by other writers while rejecting the very devices which others advance. In *The White Album,* for example, Joan Didion depicts the feeling of vertigo she suffered between 1966 and 1971 as a set of unrelated snapshots: "flash pictures in variable sequence, images with no 'meaning' beyond their temporary arrangement, not a movie but a cutting-room experience." Opening the collection of essays with the statement, "We tell ourselves stories in order to live,". she proposes instead "the imposition of a narrative line upon disparate images" as the means which enable us to survive from day to day.[6] In the dedication to Miguel Cervantes which precedes his "Seven Exemplary Fictions," Robert Coover affirms a similar ameliorative function that narrative forms serve. He thus applauds Cervantes for teaching how "great narratives remain meaningful through time as a language-medium between generations, as a weapon against the fringe areas of our consciousness, and as a mythic reinforcement of our tenuous grip on reality."[7]

To be sure, Beattie's characters *do* attempt to understand their lives with respect to a governing narrative design. "Don't try to tell me any stories. I'm ten," says Lorna to her father in "The Lawn Party," to which her recently disabled father replies, "I'm thirty-two."[8] "There's a demon in the corner," declares the narrator of "A Clever-Kids Story" in an effort to get her lover to spin the kind of tales her brother did years ago (*SS,* p. 290). But, finally, the forms of children's stories prove inadequate to contain the traumas which these adult characters have experienced. When the one-armed father in "The Lawn Party" tries to tell his daughter a fairy tale with himself as prince and his dead lover as princess, he finds that the discrepancy between what should have been and what actually was—even before his crippling automobile accident—is too great to sustain the pretense: "What I'm saying is that all was well in the kingdom. Not exactly, because she wasn't my wife, but she should have been" (*SS,* p. 211). Conversely, when the brother in "A Clever-Kids Story" presumes that he can maintain as much control over his life as he can over his stories, the error literally kills him as the difference between an indestructible persona and an all-too-destructible person is made clear to him in Vietnam. Therefore, the only story-tale elements which seem at all relevant to the lives of these people are those which presage disaster. Stripped of his wife and child in a car crash, J. D. in "The Burning House" sums up the feelings which all Beattie's emotional war veterans share: "You know what I believe. I believe all the wicked fairy-tale crap: your heart will break, your house will burn" (*BH,* p. 237).

Furthermore, the kind of narrative that Didion would have imposed over experience implies the passing of time and the acceptance of change— exposition, climax, denouement—and the characters in Beattie's fiction remain incapable of admitting either one into their consciousness. After twenty-one-year old Pammy informs the narrator of "Jacklighting" that she was a speed freak in another life, she assesses the ten-year older crowd around her with the remark, "I don't get the feeling you people had another life" (*BH*, p. 21). She is perfectly correct, of course. In "Winter: 1978," the history of evolution becomes a tale of loss as transformed by Benton for his young son, a story of dinosaurs reduced in size to deer, and saddened "because they were once something else" (*BH*, p. 113). Far more comfortable with the photograph which freezes time instead of the narrative which explores time's passing, he is recalled as having taken picture after picture of his infant son when he was sleeping because the only thing changing during that time was light.

Both critics and admirers of Beattie's work assume that the particular moment of time in which her characters remain frozen is the Sixties, with the end of the world equated with the end of the decade and the Second Coming of Christ defined as the arrival of Dylan's new album to the record store shelves.[9] Nowhere might these claims have more potential validity than in discussions of *Chilly Scenes of Winter,* for the novel repeatedly draws the contrast between the Sixties and the Seventies. Burning questions of whether John Kennedy is a vegetable are replaced by idle speculations of whether Marvin Mandel cheated on his first wife with the woman who became his second wife or whether Jimmy Carter has lust in his heart (as if anyone cared one way or another). Lists of celebrities provide a running commentary of who's who in polite society (Mick Jagger married to a women with expensive tastes, John Lennon applying for U.S. citizenship) or who's where in rock 'n' roll heaven (Janis Joplin, Brian Jones, Jim Morrison, even Jim Morrison's widow). And a parade of characters confirms how low the rising stars of the best and the brightest have sunk in 1974-75: a guard at a mental hospital reads a book on seventeenth-century poetry, a Phi Beta Kappa conferee is an unemployed jacket salesman, a physics major waits tables at a place called "The Sinking Ship," and Charles—the book's main protagonist—works at a pencil-pushing government job so mundane its name is never given by Beattie (unlike James's reticence concerning the Newsome family business, which at least bespoke the energy of vulgarity).

At the same time, nowhere would the charge of "generation fiction" be more off-base. Characters in this novel who mourn the end of the Sixties mourn an era in which they never were actively involved. "I almost went to Woodstock," is the best that Charles can claim. "I wish I had gone to Woodstock."[10] Likewise, his paranoid fear of policemen has no basis in his radical acts of the decade past; given the fact that the extent of his present subversion is requisitioning unneeded paper clips, it has little to do with the decade underway. Nor does his obsession with old age have much to do with the tragedy that Elvis turning forty poses to a generation which refused to trust anyone even ten years younger. Both derive, instead, from a loss which predates the Sixties by years, namely the death of Charles's father at the age of thirty-nine and a policeman's notification of the family of the event. If Charles's sister then continually accuses him of being infantile, she has ample proof for her charge—how else should a twenty-seven year old man who still needs his jacket zipped up for him be judged?—for he has not grown past the reaction he displays upon hearing the news of his father. "He was so scared he froze. When the policeman said his father was dead he froze" (*CSW,* p. 91).

Though the loss which Charles incurs may be more dramatic than others sustained in Beattie's fiction, it exemplifies well the kind of traumas forced upon the majority of her characters who repeatedly turn to visual media in order to make sense of what has happened or presently is happening to them. When asked what he was thinking about as the automobile in which he sat was being driven off a cliff by his wife's sister, the painter in "The Lawn Party" recalls *Jules and Jim* (*SS,* p. 209). When viewing a chain formed by his lover, her child, and her ex-husband in "Vermont," Noel thinks of Death leading people across a hilltop in *The Seventh Seal.*[11] "Certification" was the name that Walker Percy gave to this mechanism of verification,[12] and Beattie's moviegoing characters make use of it in abundance in order to apprehend their experiences. Perhaps the best example of its pervasiveness occurs in *Falling in Place,* in which the same film authenticates the lives of a number of different characters. Nina sees John Knapp as John Travolta in *Saturday Night Fever,* giving away his first-place dance trophy to the couple who should have won the prize. Involved in his first serious love affair with Nina, John sees himself as Father Frank Junior, in a disco for the first time, alternately attracted and repulsed by the new encounter.[13] That John Knapp is forty and not twenty, a suburbanite instead of a Brooklynite, in advertising rather than paint (and not even a Catholic much less a priest) is beside the point, for the certification provided by movies is a wholly subjective phenomenon. The counterman John's son meets in New York slaps meat on a grill all day and shakes his hips in a club all night—and misses the resemblance between himself and Tony Manero when the Travolta film is discussed (*FIP,* p. 108).

Because the recognitions that movies facilitate involve painful realizations, however, Beattie's characters go one step further and project their experiences back into pictorial form in order to cope with the consequences they entail. Sometimes the projection is imaginative. In "Running Dreams," Lynn recognizes the discrepancy between her present ability to know "simple things" about other people and her inability at five years old to have known that her own father was dying. Aware, as well, that her present ability to do easy favors for people without her strength can never compensate for her earlier inability to have done a thing for her weakened father, and torn apart by the contrast between the two, she turns a scene from her childhood into a photo touched up by adult understanding:

> I remember that my father was bending over—stooped with pain, I now realize—and that he was winter-pale, though he died before cold weather came. I remember standing with him in a room that seemed immense as the explosion from a flashbulb. If someone had taken that photograph, it would have been a picture of a little girl and her father about to go on a walk. I held my hands out to him, and he pushed the fingers of the gloves tightly down each of my fingers, patiently, pretending to have all the time in the world, saying, "This is the way we get ready for winter." (*BH,* p. 197)

At other times, the projection back to visual form is quite literal. Fed up with the irresponsible behavior of her friends and yet aware that they are all the friends she has, Francie sees how close to death laissez-faire generosity brings her when an intruder enters her unlocked house at night and threatens her life in "Friends." Confronted by a stranger who literally demands her friendship at knifepoint, and thus faced for the first time with the dangers of naive and adolescent trust, she is forced to conclude, "It's the first time I ever wanted to be old" (SS, p. 268). Yet rather than take any decisive steps to change her life or dispense with the friends she has outgrown, she begins making sketches of them all for a painting she wishes to do at the end of the story.

Indeed, rather than serving as a means of personal exploration, the transposition of their experiences into art promotes the illusion among Beattie's characters that what can be composed in art is composed in fact. Unfortunately, nothing is further from the truth when it comes to the messy lives led by most of these people. As Peter Spangle reminds his graduate student girlfriend in Falling in Place, "What happens to characters happens to characters, and what happens to you and me happens to you and me" (FIP, p. 251). The former fall into place, the latter just in place. The difference between those who confuse the two and those who do not is a trademark of Beattie's short stories, which tend to pose people of greater and lesser insight against each other.[14] "Sunshine and Shadow" provides an especially striking illustration of the contrast that results. From the beginning of the story, the difference between Jake's and Laura Ann's conception of art is clear: he tells her to bracket her photographs, she deliberately prints her pictures with irregular black borders. "You chisel out the negative holder," she explains. "You print it exactly the way it was shot. Then there's no way you can cheat" (BH, p. 129). Jake, however, can no more deal with a sloppy photograph than he can deal with the sloppy situation in which he is involved—an affair with his wife's best friend. What he needs in his life is exactly the kind of enforced framing that the negative holder provides the photographer.

In a beautiful extension of the story's central image, this is exactly what Beattie shows Jake doing with the pattern of "Sunshine and Shadow." Introduced as a diamond-shaped design of alternating light and dark squares, this pattern for a quilt becomes an ordering device with which Jake psychologically frames those situations which have implications he cannot accept. Tormented by his present inability to choose between his wife and his lover, he recalls an earlier incident in which he was surrounded by bees as a child and was unable to make a move in any direction. His memory of the incident, however, is permeated by criss-crossing bands of light and darkness—the floor of his aunt and uncle's house on which the sun shines through a network of leaves, the netting of the bee-keeper's hat he wears which literally divides things for him into diamond-shaped forms. Moving back to the present, he looks at Laura Ann and sees her sleeping body criss-crossed by the same pattern. "The streetlight, streaming light through the curtains, blotched her body—luminous shapes that were almost a triangle, almost a circle" (BH, p. 133). Perceiving each scene in this neatly framed manner provides Jake with the illusion that he can impose upon each incident an equally neat resolution. He can believe the story that the bee-keeper made up for him years ago, that he was a gentle boy unwilling to move for fear he might hurt the bees, instead of seeing his petrified gear as the paralysis it truly was. In much the same way, he can believe the story he imagines Laura making up for him in the present, that he is unable to leave her because he loves her so much, instead of seeing his inability to decide as the emotional paralysis it really is.

In blunting the painful edges of experience in this way, the transposition of experience into art also exacts a price: it drains experience of whatever vitality it once possessed (however minimal). The painting that Francie plans to make of her cohorts in "Friends" turns them all into two-dimensional figures: "They were going to be standing on the canvas holding hands, like paper dolls. It was a realistic painting . . ." (SS, p. 270). Similarly, the photogrpahs of his travels that J. D. passes around in "The Burning House" impress by their "flatness," the "unreality" of his subjects confirming for him "the unreality of what he does" (BH, p. 239). Extended even further in Love Always, in which videotape replaces single snapshots, the successive transposition of actuality into art ascribes more life to a television soap opera than it does to the soap opera that forms the characters' real lives. "The best lack all conviction, while the worst are full of passionate intensity," quotes a doctor to the manager of the show's star. ("All that money, and he plagiarizes," says Piggy of the show's creator.)[15] And as Yeats's words steadily pass from verse to script to novel, the passion they originally contained grows less and less as the artifacts which contain them grow worse and worse. Not much intensity runs through T.V.'s Passionate Intensity—just ask any fan how long it takes for an affair to commence or a court case to adjourn on camera. The novelization under way called Barren promises even less—the title comes from a fictional book written by a fictional character on the show, which in turn is a fictionalized account of the trials and tribulations of his fabricated soap opera family. In the case of Nicole Nelson, the "centre" holding the series together, the diminution of vitality assumes a very literal form. A fourteen-year old whose moods swing from complacency to apathy, "with no real pull toward excess or passion or even the belief that something might be fun" (LA, p. 116), and already reduced in the role of Stephanie Sykes to what can fit within the size of a television screen, she undergoes still further reduction (to no more than a foot) for a doll being made in her likeness.

To her credit, Nicole constantly tries to assert the difference between herself and the character she plays. "A lot of me goes into my character, but other stuff goes into being me," she tells a smitten suitor of Stephanie Sykes (LA, p. 144). A "perfect California girl" perfectly willing to trade on her character's appeal, "lucky enough to be an object to people," as an artist who sketches her realizes (LA, pp. 14, 38), she refuses to be an object of art to herself. The same cannot be said of the rest of the book's characters, however. Hildon does not simply videotape the significant events of his life; he has other people videotape them for him so that he can appear as an actor in his own productions. (As Andy Warhol foresaw, "Everybody can be famous for fifteen minutes.") Objectifying himself in this manner does afford him certain residuals: showing the tape of the book's opening party to Lucy provides a sexual turn-on for both. The horror is that their arousal is prompted by so banal a stimulus—it *is* pornography, as Lucy expects, but not in the way she means when waiting for the film to unroll. As the novel comes to a close, and Hildon looks at the tape of himself packing up his *Country Daze* office, the testament to dullness on screen cannot escape even his eyes:

> The letters and telegrams might have been sent to anybody; the pictures were almost generic, the maps also a quite ordinary form of decoration. The view through the window wasn't special. . . . The metal file cabinets were ordinary, the Perrier bottle with dried flowers quite typical (somebody on the staff had put it there). Everything might have been anyone's. (*LA*, p. 246)

Having fallen in love with video because it allowed each person to make his own time capsule, Hildon finds it reducing his own life to the paraphernalia on a desk—a sight which does little to provoke the drunken woman lying under him who gets bored with the tape before it ends.

Celebrating, in 1928, the passing of "The Tchekhovian after-influenza effect of inertia and will-lessness," D. H. Lawrence proclaimed, "we've had about enough of being null."[16] Writing a half-century later about the mask that dullness can provide, Ann Beattie cites a different evaluator of the ordinary. In "The Lifeguard," perhaps the strongest piece in her first collection, a woman tries to make her husband appreciate the book of photographs she looks at: "she talked about Diane Arbus's being influenced by the Chinese belief that people pass through boredom to fascination" (*D*, p. 276). Reading Beattie's own work, one experiences the same progression. Rarely do characters expose themselves to the camera in the way that a former college professor once has in "Weekend," revealing in high-contrast prints "a man in agony, a man about to scream" (*SS*, p. 133). More often, characters pose in front of the camera, acting out those roles which afford them the most emotional camouflage. Not surprisingly, great men choose proportionately great poses. A final photograph of Horace Cragen in "La Petite Danseuse de Quatorze Ans" shows him playing the gentleman poet to the end—sitting in a tufted chair in a Parisian hotel lobby, "still strikingly handsome," holding "an uncharacteristic cigarette in his hand," trying to disguise the cancer which has ravaged his entire body (*SS*, p. 96). Yet even less self-conscious subjects exhibit a similar propensity for posturing. When John Knapp looks at an old family picture in *Falling in Place*, he sees *"The children: not the children as they really were, even then"* (*FIP*, p. 63).

It was Arbus's belief that *every* subject being photographed indulged in an acting out of fantasy: "The very process of posing requires a person to step out of himself as if he were an object. . . . He is no longer a self but he is still trying to look like the self he imagines himself to be.[17] Only blind people did she exempt from such make-believe; unable to know what their expressions were, they were unable to construct masks to cover them (as her March 1969 *Harper's Bazaar* pictures of Jorge Luis Borges illustrate). To peel away the masks from all the others, Arbus placed her subjects in their most natural environments and shot them looking straight ahead at the center of her lens, stripping them in a way which, in most cases, proved unflattering. As one of the nudists she shot remarked with respect to another kind of nakedness, "Let's face it . . . most people don't look so good."[18] At the same time, photographing her subjects in this manner led Arbus to achieve a leveling of her subjects. Studies of Andrew Ratoucheff, a dwarf specializing in Marilyn Monroe and Maurice Chevalier imitations, and Miss Cora Pratt, the "Counterfeit Lady" persona invented for herself by Polly Bushong, impress by the ordinariness of their details, attesting to their photographer's belief that their singular qualities were exaggerations rather than distortions. In contrast, studies of middle-class families impress by their freakishness, perhaps most poignantly seen in the 1968 pictures of "Two American Families," in which the son in one is retarded and his mother tries to look like Elizabeth Taylor.

In exposing the normal in the grotesque and the grotesque in the normal, Beattie explores similar terrain. Comparing her first collection of stories with her most recent novel shows the distance she has traveled in her concerns, a shift, incidentally, which mirrors the shift Arbus herself made in the subjects she chose to photograph. Depending for much of their effect on deliberate quirkiness and actual physical deformities, the early characters in *Distortions* form a cavalcade of curiosities—from the dwarf in "Dwarf House," to the "amazing family" ("Like a Salinger family") in "Wally Whistles Dixie," to the "Amazing Animal Woman" who travels with Hale Hardy, to the milk-swilling Martians who transform "It's Just Another Day in the Big Bear City, California" into more than just that. In *Love Always,* however, the curiosities fade into the backdrop of everyday life. Cindi Coeur, a.k.a. Lucy Spenser, "a Latter-Day Miss Lonelyhearts" (*LA,* p. 11), receives letters from a painter whose wife eats his art supplies, a woman whose break-dancing fiancé wants a trampoline instead of a water bed, and a management analyst who hangs Tampax from her ears while waiting tables at a club called "Slash." Unlike her literary antecedent who is tormented by the letters of supplication that he gets, Lucy loses not a wink of sleep over hers—and for understandable reasons. When embodied by Nathanael West in the queries of "Sick-of-it-all," "Desperate," and "Broad Shoulders," the anguished cries for help formed a study in surrealism circa 1933—how else to judge a letter written by a sixteen-year old girl born without a nose? When resurrected by Beattie in the questions of "Reluctant Rembrandt," "Boxstep Betty," and "Double Identity Dorothy," they form a cross-section of ordinary American life circa 1985. As Beattie writes, "It started as a made-up column, but the readers began to send in true stories that were better than the things the staff had been thinking up" (*LA,* p. 52).

In contrast, the stories that readers do not send in are the ones that Beattie finds more grotesque. The most wrenching letter received in *Love Always* is addressed to Lucy Spenser, not Cindi Coeur, and written by her sister on the morning of her wedding:

> I was thinking, last night, about all the hours we spent playing pretend when we were little girls. It makes me laugh now that we thought we could have any fantasy we wanted. . . . Lately there are so many fantasies thrust at us in all those articles telling us there are millions of men out there if you just become perfect that I'm just exhausted. . . . Why not just admit that things are terrible but we have no choice? (*LA,* p. 199)

Looking at the characters in Beattie's fiction who accept that conclusion as final, one understands why not. When the old man in "Victor Blue" realizes "There aren't any fantasies," he is left to itemize trivia (*D,* p. 261). When Louise Knapp cannot come up with anyone better than Donald Sutherland in *Klute* to dream about, and is forced to confess *"I don't even have fantasies anymore,"* her fate in *Falling in Place* is assured—an endless round of strawberry picking with Tiffy (*FIP,* p. 143). Therefore, characters continually engage in pretense. Some invoke the most grotesque pretext of all: if not the pretext of being perfect, the pretext of perfect control. The woman in "A Reasonable Man" pretends that being "competent" in the kitchen, serving "balanced and nutritious" meals, and following "perfectly" her husband's advice give proof that she has recovered from her breakdown (*SS,* p. 50). John Knapp pretends that playing Ozzie Nelson on family picnics will give proof there is nothing unusual about the living arrangement he has with his family—in Connecticut on weekends with his wife, his son, and his daughter; in Rye during the week with his mother, his son, and his dog.

While the flat prose for which Beattie is known conveys the composure that her characters affect quite accurately, her exposure of the crises it hides reveals conditions which are anything but flat. Nowhere is this better seen than in those works pierced by unexpected acts of violence, for what at first seems shocking is shown upon second glance to be embedded in the texts all along. Early in *Falling in Place,* Mary reads a poem "about somebody falling out of the sky while some other people worked" (*FIP,* p. 11). The poem, though not named by Beattie, is Auden's "Musée des Beaux Arts," and as the chapter comes to an end, she borrows from it in commenting upon Mary's obsession with Peter Frampton: "No point in hoping against hope for the extraordinary: a small seed exploding into a giant beanstalk; a body falling from the sky" (*FIP,* p. 13). Yet when Mary is shot by her brother, a gruesomely extraordinary fall does occur. In the words with which Mary imagines her grandmother's reaction, "She must think the sky is falling" (*FIP,* p. 217).

A similar exposure of pretense reveals the bad joke which is the put-on in "Friends." "Everybody has to be so teasing," Francie complains at the start of the story. "Nobody can talk straight" (*SS,* p. 232). When an intruder returns to her house at night, however, Francie gets a taste of what "straight talk" means, for his words make literal what before was amusing banter. Forcing her into a game of "Mother May I," he turns her central role of hostess into a travesty. Claiming to have had an affair with Freed in actuality, he takes Freed's homosexual clowning at face value. Finally, addressing the primary theme of the story, he reveals for Francie the true quality of the comradery by which she defines her role. Having entered her house with as much advance notice as the friends who freely come and go, he explains his purpose: "I wanted to come here and be friendly . . . . I thought maybe you'd act like you were, and that you might be liberal-minded about the mistake with your friend Freed's car . . . I thought, you understand—that I wanted your money more than I wanted your friendship. But then I thought I'd serenade you and you'd come downstairs and we might be friendly too" (SS, p. 264). The horror of his presence is undeniable; yet, in the context of the piece, what he exposes to Francie about her group of pals proves more unbearable. No mere perversion of the concept of friendship that binds them, the intruder exposes the perversion that their concept of friendship truly is.

Do the kind of truths unveiled in this manner make any discernible difference in the end? For most of Beattie's characters, they do not. For the reader of Beattie's fiction, they do. Casual remarks made early in her works are not passed over so lightly when repeated later on. At the beginning of Falling in Place, Cynthia can assume that her students are just stupid but not malicious, and a reader can agree completely. When reiterating her refrain in the second half of the novel, and ascribing her students' stupidity to easy lives and carefree childhoods, the reader does not comply. Cynthia may not know of Mary's shooting at this point, but the reader already has been informed. Similarly, Francie may settle back into a household of "Friends" at the end of her story and the joking can recommence once more. In the middle of a band's rehearsal, Roger can break into "Young At Heart" on his trumpet, and T. W. can threaten to stab his eyes out with a Bic pen. All can laugh. But not the reader who has come too close to witnessing a stabbing already and has learned a lesson about fantasies that most of the characters ignore: "Fairy tales can come true, they can happen to you" go the lyrics of the tune Roger plays. If you're a character in Ann Beattie's fiction, however, you'd better hope that they do not.

NOTES

[1] Ann Beattie, The Burning House (1982; rpt. New York: Ballantine, 1983), p. 92. Subsequent page references to this book will appear parenthetically as BH following quotations.

[2] Letter from Diane Arbus to Robert Benton, n.d., c. Oct. 1959, quoted in Don Arbus and Marvin Israel, eds., Diane Arbus: Magazine Work (New York: Aperture, 1984), p. 156.

[3] See, for example, Valerie Shaw, The Short Story: A Critical Introduction (London: Longman, 1983), pp. 12-16.

[4] See Edgar Allan Poe, "Review of Nathaniel Hawthorne's Twice-Told Tales" (1842), in Edgar Allan Poe: Selected Prose, Poetry, and Eureka, ed. W. H. Auden (San Francisco: Rinehart, 1950), p. 450.

[5] Larry McCaffery and Sinda Gregory, "A Conversation with Ann Beattie," Literary Review, 27 (1984), 175.

[6] Joan Didion, "The White Album," in The White Album (1979; rpt. New York: Pocket, 1980), pp. 13, 11.

[7] Robert Coover, "Seven Exemplary Fictions: Dedicatoria y Prólogo a don Miguel de

Cervantes Saavedra," in *Pricksongs & Descants* (1969; rpt. New York: Plume, 1970), pp. 78-79.

8 Ann Beattie, *Secrets and Surprises* (1978; rpt. New York: Warner, 1983), p. 207. Subsequent page references to this book will appear parenthetically as *SS* following quotations.

9 For representative examples, see Joseph Epstein, "Ann Beattie and the Hippoisie," *Commentary,* Mar. 1983, pp. 54-58; and Blanche H. Gelfant, "Ann Beattie's Magic Slate or The End of the Sixties," *New England Review and Bread Loaf Quarterly,* 1 (1979), 374-84.

10 Ann Beattie, *Chilly Scenes of Winter* (1976; rpt. New York: Fawcett Popular, 1978), p. 41. Subsequent page references to this book will appear parenthetically as *CSW* following quotations.

11 Ann Beattie, *Distortions* (1976; rpt. New York: Warner, 1983), p. 215. Subsequent page references to this book will appear parenthetically as *D* following quotations.

12 Walker Percy, *The Moviegoer* (1961; rpt. New York: Noonday, 1967), p. 63.

13 Ann Beattie, *Falling in Place* (1980; rpt. New York: Fawcett Popular, 1981), pp. 80-81. Subsequent page references to this book will appear parenthetically as *FIP* following quotations.

14 For Beattie's own discussion of this characteristic, see McCaffery and Gregory, 167.

15 Ann Beattie, *Love Always* (1985; rpt. New York: Vintage, 1986), pp. 167, 173. Subsequent page references to this book will appear parenthetically as *LA* following quotations.

16 D. H. Lawrence, *Selected Literary Criticism,* ed. Anthony Beal (London: Heinemann, 1967), p. 288, quoted in Shaw, p. 133.

17 Diane Arbus to Barbara Brown, quoted in Patricia Bosworth, *Diane Arbus: A Biography* (New York: Knopf, 1984), pp. 131-32.

18 Diane Arbus, "Notes on the Nudist Camp," unpub., 1966, in *Diane Arbus: Magazine Work,* ed. Doon Arbus and Marvin Israel, p. 69.

Neorealism, Postmodern Fantasy, and the American Short Story

LANCE OLSEN

> "As the Chinese used to say when they wished to curse someone: May you live in an interesting age.' "
>
> —Umberto Eco[1]

Over the last thirty years or so—and especially within the last ten— there has been a tremendous revitalization of realism in the American short story. I am thinking of projects by literary superstars working in the nineteenth-century tradition of William Dean Howells such as John Cheever, whose *The Enormous Radio and Other Stories* appeared in 1953; John Updike, whose *Pigeon Feathers and Other Stories* appeared in 1962; and Bernard Malamud, whose *Idiots First* appeared in 1963. But I am thinking as well of those projects by a new generation of minimalist writers working in the early twentieth-century tradition of Ernest Hemingway such as Jayne Anne Phillips, whose *Black Tickets* received an extremely positive review by John Irving in the *New York Times Book Review* when it saw print in 1979; Raymond Carver, whose *What We Talk About When We Talk About Love* made a splash upon its publication in 1981; and Bobbie Ann Mason, whose *Shiloh and Other Stories,* many of which first appeared in *The New Yorker,* was acclaimed in 1982. I should like to begin my discussion of this neorealism—this third or fourth generation of American realism—by asking two questions: 1) what is the narrative strategy of such fictions? and 2) what metaphysical strategy does that narrative strategy suggest?

To answer these, let us briefly explore the passage that opens Mason's "Shiloh," and one which could serve as an emblem for the rest: "Leroy Moffitt's wife, Norma Jean, is working on her pectorals. She lifts three-pound dumbbells to warm up, then progresses to a twenty-pound barbell. Standing with her legs apart, she reminds Leroy of Wonder Woman."[2] This is the fiction of a middle-class. It taps into contemporary fashion, into America's obsession with looking good and being healthy, into the trendiness of the superwoman image fostered by magazines such as *Cosmopolitan,* into the current media, here television, with the reference to Wonder Woman), and into a universe of details. There isn't just a woman working out, but a woman named Norma Jean who is also a man named Leroy Moffitt's wife. Nor is she just working out; rather, she is working on her pectorals; she doesn't just lift weights, but lifts three-pound dumbbells to warm up, then a twenty-pound barbell). This fiction is also into a narrative discourse that believes in a world *out there,* an empirical world that the reader can smell, see, and touch. Moreover, it believes in logic, in chronology, in plot; *first* Norma works on the dumbbells, *then* on the barbell. And it is *Norma Jean* who works out— a character who already begins accruing gestures, interests, a certain quirkiness, who already begins taking on the resonance of a fully rounded fictional figure; and her working out is seen through the eyes of another character, Leroy ("she reminds Leroy of Wonder Woman"), who also has begun to take on personality. A narrative strategy that builds character so early, even as the first brush strokes are applied, suggests a metaphysical strategy that believes in a stable identity; that is, a sense of self; that is, a certain psychology. Readers know that there are no narrative or metaphysical surprises in store for them. They are in the universe of communal reality, in the realm of common sense associated with American pragmatism. And they are in a realm where content is privileged over form, where language is transparent, where style is secondary, where it is assumed that the word mirrors the world.

Perhaps it is not such a long jump to suggest at this point that I sense in the Mason passage a gentle desire that in some world life might be like patterned fiction: coherent, interpretable, unified. That is, it strikes me that ultimately this so-called "*neorealism*" is really just a longing for the old realism of a Hemingway and of a Howells before him. It is a longing for the empiricism and pragmatism of the nineteenth century and early part of our own. Neorealism is, then, in its purest sense a *conservative* vision of reality—a vision, in other words, that wishes to *conserve* a way of writing, a way of seeing, a moral and humanist optic through which one looks backwards rather than ahead. It is the vision of the American settlement, not of the American frontier. And I should also like to suggest that it is no wonder that such neorealism finds such a comfortable and congenial home in the neoconservative sociohistorical context of contemporary America, an America where the E.R.A. has a miserable time passing, and anti-abortionists gain increasing political power, and Ronald Reagan is serving his second term as one of the most popular presidents in the history of the United States.

Alongside this essentially stable and compensatory voice in America and in the American short story, however, has surfaced a dissident one which has come to be called the avant-garde, the innovative, and, recently, the postmodern. In a word, postmodernism is that mode of consciousness which has deconstructed the notion of the transcendental signified. It is that mode of consciousness which has turned the universe from—to use Roland Barthes' terms—a work into a text. "We know now," claims Barthes, "that a text is not a line of words releasing a single 'theological' meaning (the 'message' of the Author-God) but a multidimensional space in which a variety of writings . . . blend and clash." When the Author-God has been removed from the text (and remember that the world is a text), all limits on the text are abandoned. When all limits are abandoned, the text ceases to possess only one meaning. The textual universe opens into a multiplicity of meanings. Hence, the postmodern "liberates what may be called an anti-theological activity, an activity that is truly revolutionary since to refuse to fix meaning is, in the end, to refuse God and his hypostases—reason, science, law."[3] The work (a macronarrative) is thus transformed into a text (a series of micronarratives).

One strategy that has been employed frequently by postmodern fiction as a way to liberate this "anti-theological activity," to free up the gravity of mimesis, is the fantastic. For Tzvetan Todorov, "the fantastic . . . lasts only as long as a certain hesitation" in the text and in the reader between the uncanny where "the laws of reality remain intact and permit an explanation of the phenomena described" and the marvelous where "new laws of nature must be entertained to account for the phenomena."[4] That is, fantasy is a narrative strategy whose goal is to dislocate and destabilize. In its purest form, it is hostile toward anything static, rejecting any definitive version of "reality" or "truth." Fantasy is a mode designed to surprise, to question, and to put into doubt. Consequently, if neorealism is the expression of the conservative side of American consciousness, postmodern fantasy is the expression of the dissident side of American consciousness. If neorealism expresses the need for settlement, postmodern fantasy expresses the need for frontier—for expansiveness, for extreme freedom, even for subversion. Postmodern fantasy is a radical vision of reality-as-fantastic. It is an amoral and posthumanist vision that looks ahead rather than backwards.

Little wonder, then, that such a vision finds itself continually marginalized in contemporary America's neoconservative climate. Rather than finding extensive expression in the major commercial magazines (*The New Yorker, The Atlantic,* even *Esquire*) and publishing houses (Random House, Dutton, Simon and Schuster), as was the case in the late sixties and early seventies, postmodern fantasy now finds expression as a secondary voice in literary journals (*Tri-Quarterly, The Paris Review, Chicago Review*) and the small presses (New Directions, Grove Press, The Fiction Collective). And little wonder that the third edition of R. V. Cassill's *The Norton Anthology of Short Fiction* has dropped stories by John Barth, Donald Barthelme, Mark Costello, and several other postmodern "fantasts" that appeared in earlier editions, only to replace them with pieces by Raymond Carver, James Allen McPherson, and Bobbie Ann Mason.

Interestingly enough, the textual father of postmodern fantasy is not an American, but a Czech: Franz Kafka. Allen Thiher uses as a spring board Jorge Luis Borges' comment in his essay "Kafka and His Precursors": "the fact is that every writer *creates* his own precursors. His work modifies our conception of the past, as it will modify the future."[5] Thiher then notes: "We read Kafka though the lens of intertextuality, in the sense that our contemporary fictions have taught us to read what Kafka's immediate contemporaries could not see. To reverse what Borges said about Kafka . . . we must read in turn most of our contemporary writers by making of the Czech writer their precursor, perhaps the most important precursor for what many now call postmodern fiction."[6] Just at the moment of modernism's apex, when Joyce, Proust, Rilke and the rest were achieving their most famous texts, Thiher argues, Kafka entered and ruptured modernism's security and sense of power by generating a mode of discourse that "puts constantly into question its own quest for representation, revelation, and meaning" (Thiher, p. 546). That is, Kafka's project becomes an emblem to postmodern consciousness of literary autism, language-in-crisis, ontological and epistemological uncertainty, anti-logic, and unfulfilled desire.

His impulse enters into his textual children in a number of ways. Thomas Pynchon, for instance, wrote what he called his "entry-level fiction"[7] in the late fifties and early sixties. His third published story, "Entropy," appeared in 1960 and, according to Pynchon, "is a fine example of a procedural error beginning writers are always being cautioned against. It is simply wrong to begin with a theme, symbol or other abstract unifying agent, and then try to force characters and events to conform to it" (SL, p. 14). Be that as it may, it was a text often anthologized during the early seventies, and one that holds within itself the core of Pynchon's postmodern vision which manifests itself in his three later novels. Downstairs in an apartment in February of 1957 Meatball Mulligan holds a lease-breaking party which is moving into its fortieth hour and, at the same time, toward maximum chaos and minimum available energy: "Ambiguity. Redundance. Irrelevance, even. Leakage" (SL, pp. 90-91), one of Meatball's friends says. Upstairs in the same apartment an intellectual named Callisto and his girlfriend Aubade try to warm a freezing bird in a "hermetically sealed" "hothouse jungle it had taken him several years to weave together," a "Rousseau-like fantasy" filled with other birds, philodendrons and small fan palms. Callisto's is the antithesis of Meatball's universe; it is "a tiny enclave of regularity in the city's chaos" (SL, p. 83).

Meatball's universe is a text, Callisto's a work. As a young man at Princeton, Callisto thought the universe could forever remain a work, unified, coherent, intelligible, but now in his fifties he has come to realize "that the isolated system—galaxy, engine, human being, culture, whatever—must evolve spontaneously toward the Condition of the More Probable" (SL, p. 87), toward entropy. Meatball by the end of his tale decides "to try and keep his lease-breaking party from deteriorating into total chaos"; he decides to try ordering his universe into a work, but the last we see him he fails since "most of the revellers had passed out and the party trembled on the threshold of its third day" (SL, p. 97). At the same time, however, Aubade smashes the window in the upstairs apartment, literally deconstructing the stability of the sealed room, and waits for "the final absence of all motion" (SL, p. 98). Active or inactive, the characters cannot stop the conservative from giving way to the anarchic, the sealed to the open, the ordered to the disordered, the unified to the multiplied.

What Pynchon transforms into concrete metaphor, John Barth eight years later discusses as an abstract concept in his essay-like metafiction "Life-Story," which is about a failed writer who, on the day before his birthday in June, 1966, sits down to rewrite a piece of prose: "Whereas his earlier version had opened in a straight-forward documentary fashion and then degenerated or at least modulated intentionally into irrealism and dissonance, he decided this time to tell his tale from start to finish in a conservative, 'realistic,' unself-conscious way." What he realizes almost immediately, though, is that "his own life might be a fiction, in which he was the leading or an accessory character."[8] In other words, he tries to write in a compensatory mode, but realizes almost immediately that his universe is one of intertextuality where his life is simply one more micronarrative among a web of micronarratives. He attempts creating the world according to Callisto and Aubade, but finds he can do no more than exist in the world according to Meatball. What the reader receives is a hyperironic fiction: "self-conscious, vertiginously arch, fashionably solipsistic. . . . Another story about a writer writing a story! Another regressus in infinitum!" (LF, p. 114).

Barth's subtext here is a painful acknowledgement of universal entropy, or exhaustion as he calls it: "He rather suspected that the medium and genre in which he worked . . . were moribund if not already dead. . . . He rather suspected that the society in which he persisted . . . was moribund if not et cetera. He knew beyond any doubt that the body which he inhabited . . . was et cetera. The idea et cetera" (LF, p. 118). At a personal, textual and cultural level a rupture has surfaced, a "dissonance" (LF, p. 113)—a word that echoes Pynchon's metaphor of white noise in information systems—that refuses to be silenced. Such dissonance produces in the writer the Barthesian insight that "the old analogy between Author and God, novel and world, can no longer be employed unless deliberately as a false analogy" (LF, p. 125), and points to a universe where we are the protagonists in a game whose rules we do not know.

In the same year that Barth published *Lost in the Funhouse*, in which "Life-Story" appeared, Donald Barthelme published *Unspeakable Practices, Unnatural Acts.* Now what Pynchon makes into concrete metaphor, and Barth discusses as abstract concept, Barthelme enacts on the page. "The Indian Uprising," for instance, opens thus:

> We defended the city as best we could. The arrows of the Comanches came in clouds. The war clubs of the Comanches clattered on the soft, yellow pavements. There were earthworks along the Boulevard Mark Clark and the hedges had been laced with sparkling wire. People were trying to understand. I spoke to Sylvia. "Do you think this is a good life?" The table held apples, books, long-playing records. She looked up. "No."[9]

The first sentence announces a story about war, but even with the second the story is knocked off trajectory: "The arrows of the Comanches came in clouds." What city would Comanches be attacking? A greater hesitation surfaces in the next line, where war clubs "clattered" on "yellow pavements." We are, then, in a modern city lined with sidewalks. A contemporary war with indians? And where exactly? The next line subverts the original seemingly realistic impulse even further. In this city there are "earthworks," and streets named after modern war heroes like Mark Wayne Clark, who as commander in chief of the United Nations forces in 1953 signed the truce that ended the Korean War. Consequently, we are in a postmodern fantasy whose goal is to place mimesis and its assumptions under erasure. In this way, the following line, "People were trying to understand," refers not only to the universe of the story, but to that of the reader. The text has begun commenting on its ability to thwart reader expectations, has announced itself in the middle of its own progress as the decomposition of a work. On the heels of this floats up the line, "I spoke to Sylvia"—but who is the protagonist, and who is Sylvia? Gaps have been provided that call for supplementation, but with what should we supplement them? The narrative strategy also raises the question of a metaphysical kind ("Do you think this is a good life") which is negated by the paragraph's last word, after the disjunctive image of the table (an image of stability; an object the narrator likes working on, we find later, at times of personal crisis) filled with the detritus of our culture.

The battle between the Comanches and city dwellers continues throughout the rest of Barthelme's metalogical text. The indians infiltrate the ghetto, and the ghetto-dwellers join them. Miss R., an "unorthodox" teacher, "successful with difficult cases" (*UPUA*, p. 5), seems to join in the battle against the Comanches, and delivers a soliloquy in a "dry, tense voice," explaining that "the only form of discourse of which I approve . . . is the litany" (*UPUA*, p. 8)—a form, that is, of order and certainty that runs against the "more and more unpleasant combinations" (*UPUA*, p. 9) she finds in our society. Jane, perhaps a one-time lover of the narrator, is attacked by a dwarf. Comanches are tortured. The officer in the garbage dump reports that the garbage has begun moving. And finally the protagonist finds himself in an interrogation room before the Clemency Committee, apparently about to be tortured by Miss R., who asks him to remove his belt and shoelaces; he does so as he looks "into their savage black eyes, paint, feathers, beads" (*UPUA*, p. 12). But what does this series of nonsequiturs and absences add up to?

Through one optic it adds up to a satiric indictment against our contemporary society that has gone crazy with its barricades made out of the essence of middle-class values, its pollution ("there was a sort of muck running in the gutters" [*UPUA*, p. 6]), its drugs ("we sent more heroin into the ghetto" [*UPUA*, p. 6]), its collapse of middle-class morals ("and when they shot the scene in the bed I wondered how you felt under the eyes of the cameraman, grips, juicers, men in the mixing booth" [*UPUA*, p. 4]), its serial relationships ("I had made after all other tables, one while living with Nancy, one while living with Alice, one while living with Eunice, one while living with Marianne" [*UPUA*, p. 4]). Through another optic it adds up to an allegory of the Vietnam conflict, since the indians come from the north, and "we killed a great many in the south suddenly with helicopters and rockets but we found that those we had killed were children and more came from the north and from the east and from other places where there are children preparing to live" (*UPUA*, p. 11). Through a third optic it adds up to a story about the irruption of the unconscious forces into everyday reality, through a fourth to an inversion of American history where native Americans strike back against foreign imperialism, through a fifth to a struggle between Miss R.'s authority and the anarchism of the invaders, through a sixth to a story of deception where the enemy (Miss R.) turns out to be among us, through a seventh to a story about telling stories and about how "strings of language extend in every direction to bind the world into a rushing, ribald whole" (*UPUA*, p. 11); and it is in this way that what Miss R. says is true, that "there is enough aesthetic excitement here to satisfy anyone but a damned fool" (*UPUA*, p. 9), and so on, and so forth.

It is finally a story about how meaning is generated. Like sacred texts, it exists in order to be interpreted, and there is no limit to the possibilities of interpretation. In this way the reader becomes the ultimate protagonist of the story or storylessness. At the same time, however, as Maurice

Blanchot points out in his seminal essay of Kafka (and here we are back to the textual father of postmodern fantasy), "the true reading remains impossible. Whoever reads Kafka is thus necessarily transformed into a liar, and not entirely into a liar."[10] If readers choose to enter a text (and, again, the universe is a text) with the intent to discover "the true meaning," they instantly become prevaricators of meaning. They may create their own "meaning," but will never create the text's. Close to center, then, is Thomas M. Kavanagh's insight about Kafka's project: that it uses the form of a parable. The whole of postmodern fantasy uses the same form, and "the parable itself becomes a set of semes from which an infinite number of possible subsets can be successively generated."[11] I am reminded of my college biology textbook with its outline of the human body on which one placed an overlay that showed muscle structure atop an overlay which showed circulation on top of an overlay which showed the respiratory system, and so on. Every overlay, in one sense, was "correct," in another "incomplete" without the complex of other overlays. And in the end one realized that every overlay could be broken down further, made into subsets of a more general overlay, and that the process could continue *ad infinitum.*

At this turn I could explore the phenomena I have been discussing with respect to other seemingly divergent writers, such as Robert Coover, Joyce Carol Oates, Mark Costello, T. Coraghessan Boyle, Ronald Sukenick, William Gass, perhaps Renata Adler, certainly Walter Abish. But I imagine I have made my points: that such a thing as postmodern fantasy exists, that it exists as a dissident response to the neorealist impulse, that it is a mode of radical skepticism that challenges all we once took for granted about language and experience. Before closing, however, I should like to make one more point, one that again momentarily places postmodern fantasy in a larger sociohistorical context.

Unlike the neorealist impulse which expresses that element of a culture that is fairly content with itself, postmodern fantasy expresses that element of a culture that believes itself *in extremis.* Postmodern fantasy is the voice of that part of a culture that views culture as a whole to be in crisis, at its limit, perhaps even in the midst of decomposition. To put it another way, then, postmodern fantasy is the mode of discourse for a consciousness that believes we are in a between-times, what Umberto Eco calls "a new Middle Ages" (Eco, p. 488). For Eco, in both the original and this Middle Ages "a great Peace . . . is breaking down, a great international state power [i.e., America] that had unified the world in language, customs, ideologies, religion, art and technology, and which at a certain point, by its actual ungovernable complexity, collapses" (Eco, p. 490). Eco cites what he calls the theme of "the Vietnamization of territories, theatres of permanent tension due to the breakdown of consensus . . . (Eco, p. 495); ecological deterioration in "the large city, which today is not invaded by warlike barbarians and devastated by fires, suffers from water shortages, power failures and traffic jams" (Eco, p. 495); "insecuritas," for the recurrent themes of nuclear holocaust and ecological disaster . . . are enough to indicate strong apocalyptic currents . . ." (Eco, p. 497). Clearly with America in mind, Eco speaks of "vagantes," of "broad areas in the grip of insecurity" through which "wander adventurers, mystics, and bands of the dispossessed" (Eco, p. 498); of "auctoritas" because "the search for sacred texts (be they Marx or Mao, Guevara or Rosa Luxemburg) has first of all this fuction: to re-establish a basis for common discourse, a body of recognizable authorities on which to initiate a play of differences and proposals for conflict" (Eco, p. 500); and formalism in thought because "Nothing is closer to the medieval intellectual game than structuralist logic, just as nothing is closer to it, after all, than the formalism of logic, physics and contemporary mathematics" (Eco, p. 500). Finally, Eco clinches his analogy by references to "art as Bricolage," with "the operation of composition and collage that high culture carries out on the debris of the past" (Eco, p. 501); to the "monasteries": "Nothing more resembles a monastery (lost in the countryside, walled, surrounded by alien and barbarian hordes, and inhabited by monks who have no contact with the outside world and pursue their own private researches) than an American university campus; and to a state of permanent transition (Eco, p. 503).

Of course, what is important about Eco's highly imaginative claims is not whether they are correct or incorrect. What is important is that one set of voices in our culture feels the need to make such claims. In other words, at the core of at least one subset of the American short story pulses the expression of unsteadiness, of challenge, even of a kind of narrative terrorism. Ultimately such an expression is a healthy one since its goal is to interrogate the aesthetic and political assumptions of the dominant mode of discourse in our contemporary culture, to generate a dialectic that refuses to be silenced, and to create a dazzling vitality that has always beat at the heart of American consciousness.

NOTES

[1] Umberto Eco, "Towards a New Middle Ages," in *On Signs,* ed. Marshall Blonsky (Baltimore: The Johns Hopkins Univ. Press, 1985), p. 504. Hereafter cited parenthetically within the text as "Eco."

[2] Bobbie Ann Mason, "Shiloh," in *Shiloh and Other Stories* (New York: Harper and Row, 1982), p. 1.

[3] Roland Barthes, "The Death of the Author," in *Image-Music-Text,* trans. Stephen Heath (New York: Hill and Wang, 1977), pp. 146-47.

[4] Tzvetan Todorov, *The Fantastic: A Structural Approach to a Literary Genre,* trans. Richard Howard (New York: Cornell Univ. Press, 1975), p. 41.

[5] Jorge Luis Borges, "Kafka and His Precursors," in *Labyrinths,* trans. James E. Irby (New York: New Directions, 1964), p. 201.

[6] Allen Thiher, "Kafka's Legacy," *Modern Fiction Studies,* 26 (1980-81), 543. Hereafter cited parenthetically in the text as "Thiher."

[7] Thomas Pynchon, "Entropy," in *Slow Learner* (Boston: Little, Brown, 1984), p. 4. Hereafter cited parenthetically in the text as *SL.*

[8] John Barth, "Life-Story," in *Lost in the Funhouse* (New York: Bantam, 1969), p. 113. Hereafter cited parenthetically in the text as *LF.*

[9] Donald Barthelme, "The Indian Uprising," in *Unspeakable Practices, Unnatural Acts* (New York: Farrar, Straus and Giroux, 1968), p. 3. Hereafter cited parenthetically in the text as *UPUA.*

[10] Maurice Blanchot, "Reading Kafka," trans. Glenn W. Most, in *Twentieth Century Interpretations of "The Trial,"* ed. James Rolleston (Englewood Cliffs, NJ: Prentice-Hall, 1976), p. 14.

[11] Thomas M. Kavanagh, "Kafka's *The Trial:* The Semiotics of the Absurd," in *Twentieth Century Interpretations of "The Trial,"* p. 91.

The Freak Endures: The Southern Grotesque from Flannery O'Connor to Bobbie Ann Mason

LINDA ADAMS BARNES

An ugly fat girl views a hermaphrodite on exhibit in a freak show, an escaped convict murders a matronly grandmother and her vactioning family in cold blood, a pornography-viewing Bible salesman steals the wooden leg of a Ph.D. who calls herself Hulga: this is the stuff of Flannery O'Connor's short stories. Grotesque it is, any way you look at it. But a thirty-seven-year-old unmarried woman having a baby? A man in mid-life crisis who drives a bus for mentally handicapped adults and lives with a twenty-year-old who is currently acting in a production of *Oklahoma*? A disabled truck driver building a miniature house out of popsicle sticks? This is the stuff of Bobbie Ann Mason's short stories. While it is more quietly grotesque than Flannery O'Connor's fiction, it is grotesque nonetheless. In fact, it is grotesque in a manner uniquely fitting the age in which she is writing, an age that has ceased to be shocked by hermaphrodites and escaped convicts, not to mention pornography-reading Bible salesmen. It is a grotesque without the consolation of O'Connor's Christian faith, written for an age that readily accepts neither consolation nor faith. The things that shake the foundation of the South in the 1980's are marriages breaking up, identity crises disrupting retirement years, and shopping centers taking over farmland. Certainly, these things are more mundane than the grotesque elements of Flannery O'Connor, but perhaps are more grotesque by their very mundaneness.

I believe that the grotesque of Bobbie Ann Mason is firmly rooted in the tradition of Flannery O'Connor. Since the grotesque has come to mean so many things in the past three decades, it is helpful to isolate three elements of Flannery O'Connor's creation of it, gleaned from her short stories and from her essays, which are representative of her grotesque and her attitude toward it. O'Connor has an instructional purpose in her use of the grotesque; she is a writer of realism who is a spokesman of and to her age, and, despite the weighty purpose of her grotesque, its effect is often comic. We will then trace the erratic path of the grotesque—as defined by these key elements—and examine how it arrives in the 1980's to rear its ugly head in the fiction of Bobbie Ann Mason.

A primary feature of the grotesque of Flannery O'Connor is its instructional purpose. In pointing out that Southern writers are able to recognize a freak when they see one, O'Connor said, "To be able to recognize a freak, you have to have some conception of the whole man, and in the South the general conception of man is still, in the main, theological."[1] By exaggerating the spiritual deficiency in man, by making him a freak, she can emphasize his need for morality, and in her own words, for "grace." She implores us to look not for the dead bodies in her fiction, though there are plenty to be found, but for the "action of grace" in the souls of her characters (*MM*, p. 113). Her characters are saved from eternal grotesquerie, then, by the possibility of grace, which could encourage a movement toward spirituality.

Although her purpose is largely instructional, the short stories of Flannery O'Connor are far from being didactic abstractions. Her stories are a rich mixture of the most minute realistic detail and loftiest ideal. Much of the vivid grotesque quality has come from the marriage of these elements, as Marshall B. Gentry suggests when he speaks of O'Connor's "positive grotesque": "the ideas are wed to misunderstanding, banality, even cruelty, so that the characters are oppressed by degraded ideals."[2] Largely because of the complexity produced by this mixture O'Connor is a spokesman for and to her age. Her grotesque characters are firmly rooted in the world she saw around her. The incongruity resulting from the conflict between the ideal held by the freak and his actual deformed condition helps to account for the "strange skips and gaps" that O'Connor told us to expect from grotesque fiction:

> In these grotesque works, we find that the writer has made alive some experiences which we are not accustomed to observe every day, or which the ordinary man may never experience in his ordinary life. We find that connections which we would expect in the customary kind of realism have been ignored, that there are strange skips and gaps which anyone trying to describe manners and customs would certainly not have left. Yet the characters have an inner coherence, if not always a coherence to their social framework. Their fictional qualities lean away from typical social patterns toward mystery and the unexpected. (*MM*, p. 40)

Despite her mention of mystery, O'Connor was careful to link the grotesque with realism, often substituting the phrase "this kind of realism" (*MM*, p. 40, 44) for the grotesque, and much of the realistic quality of her stories comes from her careful use of detail. She explained in her essay, "Some Aspects of the Grotesque in Southern Fiction," that because a writer claims to be a writer of the grotesque, he or she is not allowed "in any sense to slight the concrete. Fiction begins where human knowledge begins—with the senses—and every fiction writer is bound by this fundamental aspect of his medium" (*MM*, p. 42). An example of this brand of realism is found in the grandmother in "A Good Man Is Hard to Find," a comically "hypocritical old soul" (*MM*, p. 111) as O'Connor called her, grotesque because of the incongruity between her vigorous espousal of Christianity and her actions. O'Connor chided the overzealous teacher who made the grandmother into a symbol of evil, "because [the students] all had grandmothers or great-aunts just like her at home" (*MM*, p. 110). How can anyone be a symbol of evil who sports an artificial flower pinned to her bosom and wears a dress so that anyone who should find her dead along the roadside would recognize her as a lady?[3] The mixture of concrete reality and grotesqueness is always there in O'Connor, leading Walter Sullivan to say that it was Flannery O'Connor's contention that the strange characters who populate her world are essentially no different from you and me. That her characters are drawn more extravagantly, she would admit, but she claimed that this was necessary because of our depravity: for the morally blind, the message of redemption must be writ large.[4]

Painful though it is to see ourselves as freaks, at least we have the consolation that we are funny ones. The effect of the grotesque relies heavily on the delicate balance between the terrible and the comic; Walters explains, "we are often still laughing as the victims expire before our startled eyes. The grandmother is funny until she drops in her own blood."[5] Despite the violent end to which the grandmother comes, it is impossible to forget the hilarious, almost madcap adventure which precedes it. In the middle of Georgia, children beg to detour on their way to Florida to see the big white house with the secret panel inside it; the grandmother has a "terrible thought"; and when the cat, Pitty Sing, springs upon Bailey—none too happy about this side trip to begin with—the car dives into the ditch. We are then told quietly that "the horrible thought she had had before the accident was that the house she had remembered so vividly was not in Georgia but in Tennessee."[6] C. Hugh Holman sees comedy in O'Connor not as merely relief from the tragic elements with which it coexists, but as central to O'Connor's vision of mankind:

> Her vision of man was not of a cloud-scraping demigod, a wielder of vast powers, but of a frail, weak creature, imperfect and incomplete in all his parts. To embody such a vision calls for either comedy or pathos, and pathos was alien to Flannery O'Connor's nature and beliefs.[7]

The South changed in the decades that followed Flannery O'Connor's lifetime, and the Southern grotesque changed with it. Writers of the grotesque had to reflect the changing reality of the South as they saw it if they were to remain true to the standards for grotesque fiction set forth by its master, Flannery O'Connor. In a 1967 essay entitled "The Grotesque in Recent Southern Fiction," Lewis A. Lawson sought to dispel some of the misconceptions about Southern grotesque and to clear the pathway for the generation following O'Connor. He criticizes writers who include grotesque elements in their fiction in attempts to capitalize on the sensationalism that is an effect of the grotesque gone awry: "murders, suicides, rapes, castrations, and self mutilations" perpetrated by "the insane, the idiotic, the obsessed, the freakish, the incestuous, and the perverted."[8] In effect, he is admonishing writers who have failed to conform to O'Connor's standards for a moral purpose and a reflection of reality in the use of the grotesque, but he goes on to say that the Southern grotesque is alive and well because it changes in imitation of the ongoing transformation of the South. Lawson's premise is that the grotesque in fiction flourishes during times of cultural crises, and that the South has been forced into a cultural crisis more intense than that of other regions because it is faced with keeping pace with the rest of the country economically and culturally, while striving to maintain its identity.[9] He agrees with Allen Tate's comment that it was not the Civil War which doomed the South, but the highways.[10] He concludes by saying that Southern grotesque, in its role as a mirror of society's painful transformations, will survive as long as the South continues to evolve. Lawson proves his assertion with the publication in 1984 of *Another Generation,* a collection of essays on Southern writers since World War II. This era has been trying for the Southerner, he believes, "a period when southern writers have been torn between their responses to the continuing southern presence and their awareness that a southerner must now be depicted as having pretty much the same range of emotions as anyone else."[11] The role of the Southern writer, as Lawson sees it, is to be true to the South as a unique region, to preserve its identity, while presenting characters who respond to the pressures of modern life that afflict all men of our time. This inevitably leads to some pretty grotesque characters in the short stories of the 1960's, '70's, and '80's.

In a section of his book on the American short story entitled "A Mad World, My Masters," William Peden chronicles the use of the grotesque in these decades. Peden finds grotesque characters to be archetypes rather than mere freaks or biological mistakes, "and so are suggestive of the disorder of our times."[12] He expresses dismay at the key element he finds missing in the grotesque of the two decades following O'Connor, the compassion "that gave meaning to the twisted lives of so many . . . earlier misfits, grotesques, and freaks."[13] Flannery O'Connor had a good bit to say about compassion as well, insisting that legitimate grotesque always stems from moral power rather than sentimentality:

> It's considered an absolute necessity these days for writers to have compassion. . . . Usually I think what is meant by it is that the writer excuses all human weakness because human weakness is human. The kind of hazy compassion demanded of the writer now makes it difficult for him to be anti-anything. Certainly when the grotesque is used in a legitimate way, the intellectual and moral judgments in it will have the ascendancy over feeling. (*MM*, p. 43)

We can see that critics call for the same kind of moral purpose in the grotesque that O'Connor demanded, rather than sensationalism or a kind of "hazy compassion." And the writers who have been praised the most during these years are those who conform to O'Connor's standard for the grotesque. Peden, writing in 1975, predicts a growing preoccupation with the grotesque, saying that as a society becomes more complex, its literature must grow to reflect it, and citing as some of the reasons for the growth of grotesque fiction,

> Concern for the emotional complexities of the human experience; the revolt from tradition of all kinds; three major wars; unparalleled political scandals and the increasing disillusionment with big government, big business, big anything; the loss of individuality in an authority-dominated society. . . .[14]

Peden finds the short story "particularly compatible with the temper and temperament of the present age" because of the "fragmented nature of contemporary life."[15] And the grotesque in the short story has proven to be particularly compatible with the present age. Walker Percy, for instance, reflects his generation's frustration with the complexities which confront them—the breakdown of social interaction, alienation and loss of identity, the lack of values in the face of annihilation—in his *Love in the Ruins,* in which civility has been given over to chaos, and reason to insanity. Another writer, Harry Crews, not finding meaning in traditional values, substitutes martial arts for love in *Karate is a Thing of the Spirit.* And just as O'Connor used humor in the face of disaster, so do these later writers.

The Southern grotesque is kept alive in the 1980's by Bobbie Ann Mason. Mason's grotesque is a grandchild of the grotesque as described and practiced by Flannery O'Connor: it has an instructional purpose, it reflects the tenor of the times, and it is often comic. Furthermore, and most significantly, Bobbie Ann Mason's grotesque is particularly suited to its time and to its audience. Because of this, it may not be as recognizably grotesque as some of the works that precede it; a generation jaded by daily accounts of murders in the local newspaper and years of violent racial upheaval is not shocked by a roadside multiple murder or a country boy encountering his first black man. This is not to diminish the universality of O'Connor's short stories, but rather to point out that if the grotesque is to work at all, it must reflect the society that it depicts; it may distort that reflection to make its point, but the ideal that it seeks to examine must be firmly rooted in contemporary life experiences if the grotesque extreme of that idea is to be meaningful at all. It must combine realism with exaggerated extremes of that realism, or, as Flannery O'Connor said, "a literature which mirrors society would be no fit guide for it" (*MM,* p. 46); grotesque literature must be a sort of cloudy mirror.

Bobbie Ann Mason's short stories were first published in magazines, as Flannery O'Connor's were. Since the beginning of this decade, her stories have appeared regularly in *The New Yorker, The Atlantic,* and *Redbook,* and this has undoubtedly influenced Mason's choice of subject matter. Her audience was fairly well defined by the readerships of these magazines, and she could feel confident that her readers would identify with the situations that appear in her fiction—ex-hippies struggle to bring up their son in the 1980's, a young woman tries to make a living after her husband left for Texas to become a cowboy—and with the details which pepper her work: K Marts, Toni twins, and Crisco cans.

Bobbie Ann Mason's short stories hinge on the immediate relationship of story and reader that results from her publishing in magazines, and the grotesque elements in her work are uniquely fitted to this immediacy. She achieves the kind of realism of which Flannery O'Connor speaks when she refers to the grotesque as "this kind of realism," and when she refers to the writer of grotesque as a "realist of distances": "prophecy is a matter of seeing near things with their extensions of meaning and thus of seeing far things close up" (*MM,* p. 44). One of the most prominent features of Bobbie Ann Mason's short stories is her painstaking use of detail. The theme of modern life encroaching on traditional Southern lifestyles dominates her work: family farms have to be sold, malls replace corner grocery stores, fast food replaces home-cooked meals. Mason makes the reader feel this clash intensely by employing vivid, true-to-life detail in depicting the incongruous elements that result from this transition in the

South. The stores are not just department stores, they are K Marts; families do not watch just television, they watch "Charlie's Angels." Certainly this is the kind of concrete detail called for by Flannery O'Connor:

> . . . the world of fiction is full of matter, and this is what the beginning fiction writers are very loath to create. They are concerned primarily with unfleshed ideas and emotions. They are apt to be reformers and to want to write because they are possessed not by a story but by the bare bones of some abstract notion. They are conscious of problems, not of people, of questions and issues, not of the texture of existence, of case histories and of everything that has a sociological smack, instead of with all those concrete details of life that make actual the mystery of our position on earth. . . . Fiction is about everything human and we are made out of dust, and if you scorn getting yourself dusty, then you shouldn't try to write fiction. It's not a grand enough job for you. (*MM,* pp. 67-68)

Bobbie Ann Mason definitely gets herself dusty, and very often the effect of this realistic use of detail is grotesque, as it is in O'Connor.

In the opening scene of the title story of Mason's collection, *Shiloh and Other Stories,* Norma Jean Moffitt "is working on her pectorals."[16] In her quest to find herself as a woman in the 1980's, she has taken up body-building. The image Mason offers us, though, is not merely a vague one of a young woman exercising, or a person practicing self-improvement; Norma Jean Moffitt is Wonder Woman (*Shiloh,* p. 1). She is contrasted with her husband, disabled from an accident in his tractor-trailer. In a grotesque kind of role reversal, Leroy sits on the couch with a steel pin in his hip, smoking marijuana and needlepointing Star Trek pillows while watching Norma Jean lift weights and cook "unusual foods—tacos, lasagna, Bombay chicken" (*Shiloh,* p. 11). The effect of the grotesqueness of this relationship is heightened by the use of these details. At the heart of Mason's story "Old Things" is the degradation of the traditional family. Cleo Watkins' daughter, Linda, and her children have moved in with Cleo following the breakup of Linda's marriage. Cleo struggles to reconcile this situation with her view of the traditional family; she winces at her daughter leaving her children to go to a nightclub and at her grandchildren's perference for pizza over catfish and hush puppies. The grotesque lifestyle that has forced itself into the habits of Cleo Watkins is emphasized by the details chosen to describe it. In the background of the story is Cleo's past filled with quiet evenings spent at home, but her current household is bombarded by "The Tonight Show"—complete with John Davidson as guest host and Phil Donahue interviewing former dope addicts. Cleo spends her time cutting out hamburger casserole recipes in *Family Circle* magazine. The children play with Star Wars toys and Minute Maker cameras. Cleo thinks of buying a Winnebago and going out West. The story ends with Cleo finding a moment of consolation in her lately hectic life; at an antique sale she discovers an old miniature whatnot that she thinks once belonged to her dead husband. She is comforted by this link with her past; a simple object free from K Mart pricetags and "Made in Taiwan" stickers, just simply "imitation mahogany" (*Shiloh,* p. 92). The careful details of Cleo's new lifestyle contrast strikingly with the vague abstractions of her past, and the dreamy quiteness of her past is much more attractive than the grotesqueness of her current life, with its blaring television sets and droning washing machines.

Much of the grotesqueness in Mason's short stories arises from the problem of the South's identity being submerged into contemporary American life. Many of her characters find themselves to be Displaced Persons, having been forced to move from their farms into the city, or having their conventional family disrupted by divorce or death. Often the characters are disoriented by the facts of modern life which besiege the South, such as new products and conveniences, or by mores untraditional in the South. One character, for example, says that she has taken a lover, "to her own surprise" (*Shiloh,* p. 121). In this respect, Mason is a spokesman for her age. Her moral intent is not so apparent as that of O'Connor, but perhaps she offers her generation the only kind of morality that it will accept by merely dramatizing the incongruities resulting from the clash between traditional Southern life and encroaching modern life. Her stories are instructive for no other reason than that they imply the inevitability of this conflict, and her characters are survivors; no matter how grotesquely they are forced to compromise, adjust, and conform, they somehow cope, so that Mason's ultimate message is "Do the best you can." Her "Drawing Names" depicts a family drawn together by Christmas dinner, an idyllic-sounding scene, but the family is beset by many problems common in contemporary life. Because of financial pressure, the family is forced to break with tradition by drawing names for exchanging Christmas gifts rather than buying gifts for everyone; the parents' small farm, for example, "had not been profitable in years" (*Shiloh,* p. 95). One daughter, Carolyn, is divorced and anxiously awaits the arrival of her lover. Her sister confides that "Ray and me's getting a separation," (*Shiloh,* p. 101), and a third daughter arrives accompanied by her boyfriend with whom, the mother says, she is "stacking up" (*Shiloh,* p. 96) and who brandishes a bottle of Rebel Yell, much to the discomfort of the family. Carolyn's lover never shows up, but Christmas dinner goes on, despite the discomfort and the compromise that the family has had to effect. And we are left with the expectation that it will go on next year, and the next, altered as it may be by new divorces and still newer boyfriends.

"Detroit Skyline, 1949" examines many of the issues that are pressing the contemporary South. Central to it is the conflict of urban and rural life, which Lewis Lawson has offered as one of the reasons why the South has been a fertile milieu for the grotesque, stemming from its provincial, insular, conservative culture.[17] "Detroit Skyline, 1949," depicts a farm girl's first visit to Detroit, where she goes with her mother to visit her aunt. Once there, she is barraged with things which are to her unfamiliar and bizarre. Her father had warned her before she left, "Don't let the Polacks get you" (*Shiloh,* p. 34); indeed, her relatives in Detroit live in fear of the "reds," who seem to the child to be "little devils in red suits, carrying pitchforks" (*Shiloh,* p. 40). She is confused by everything in the North and is chastised for her confusion. When her uncle asks her how she likes Howdy Doody and Gorgeous George, she can only answer that she doesn't know, to which her uncle replies, "This child don't know nothing. . . . She's been raised with a bunch of country hicks" (*Shiloh,* p. 38). This story ends with the consolation of the return trip to the South, but the other stories, set in the 1970's and '80's, do not allow this comfort; the North has come to them.

Mason's stories are not devoid of characters experiencing O'Connoresque redemption. "The Retreat" is the story of a zealous fundamentalist preacher and his not-so-zealous wife, Georgeann. Georgeann is struggling for an identity of her own in a world of preachers' wives who "pray and yak at each other" (*Shiloh,* p. 132). A classically grotesque manifestation of Georgeann's dissatisfaction with her life is that she becomes infested with lice while nursing a sick chicken. And her redemption—her resolve to be responsible for her own life—is symbolized by her chopping the chicken's head off. Like O'Connor's characters who redeem themselves, Georgeann has realized "that not all forms of oppression can be banished," but that she can "take control of one form of degradation, make it more important than other forms, and then transform that grotesquerie into a form for redemption."[18]

Many of Mason's characters have physical diseases or deformities, which not only signify the internal degradation or turmoil of the character, but also operate on a literal, realistic level as indications of the times in which we live. Often these disabilities are indicative of the encroachment of modern life. In "Detroit Skyline, 1949," the mother has a miscarriage when she leaves the South. The mother in "Drawing Names" has a friend with the unlikely moniker of Pee Wee McClain, who has undergone an unsuccessful stomach by-pass operation, and Pappy is disabled by a stroke. A character in "Offerings" has had a hysterectomy. Imogene in "The Ocean" finally takes her long-dreamt-of retirement trip to the ocean, only to discover that she is gravely ill. The physical problems serve to indicate the difficulties of modern life while still operating on a realistic level, just as the obesity of O'Connor's Mrs. Greenleaf suggests moral obtuseness as well as being a realistic detail.

Comedy weaves its way in and out of the stories of Bobbie Ann Mason. She often strikes the same chord of comic detachment mingled with sympathy that critics detected in O'Connor's prose.[19] For instance, amid the pitiable and pathetic lack of communication at the Christmas dinner in "Drawing Names," a child tries to converse with her parents:

> "Dottie Barlow got a Barbie doll for Christmas and it's black," Cheryl said.
> "Dottie Barlow ain't black, is she?" asked Cecil.
> "No."
> "That's funny," said Peggy. "Why would they give her a black Barbie doll?"
> "She just wanted it." (*Shiloh,* p. 103)

And in "Graveyard Day," the single mother Waldeen contemplates remarriage while picnicking in the graveyard. She describes to her friend Betty how she would like to be happily married, and to be buried alongside her loved one. "Ooh, that's gross," says Betty (*Shiloh,* p. 177).

Bobbie Ann Mason is a writer firmly rooted in the grotesque tradition of Flannery O'Connor. But she has used the grotesque to speak to and about her own generation. She has in many ways fulfilled O'Connor's prediction that "the individual writer will have to be more than ever careful that he isn't just doing badly what has already been done to completion" (*MM,* p. 45). So the characters of Mason aren't fanatical preachers, but the wives of those preachers; they don't have wooden legs, but stomach by-pass operations. By depicting her generation as being made into freaks by being forced to conform to untraditional lifestyles, Mason is the kind of handmaid of her age, who, as O'Connor says, puts the "public's luggage down in puddle after puddle" (*MM,* p. 47). Lewis A. Lawson has said that the grotesque thrives in times of cultural confusion.[20] This, coupled with William Peden's assertion that the short story has an inherent flexibility that makes it especially suited to the "rapidly changing climate of the times"[21] would seem to ensure that the grotesque short story is here to stay. And, for now, its handmaid is Bobbie Ann Mason.

NOTES

[1] Flannery O'Connor, *Mystery and Manners,* ed. Sally and Robert Fitzgerald (New York: Farrar, Straus & Giroux, 1961), p. 44. All subsequent references to this volume will be noted as *MM* in my text.

[2] Marshall Bruce Gentry, *Flannery O'Connor's Religion of the Grotesque* (Jackson: Univ. of Mississippi Press, 1986), p. 5.

[3] Flannery O'Connor, "A Good Man Is Hard to Find," *Three by Flannery O'Connor* (New York: NAL—Signet, 1983), p. 130.

[4] Walter Sullivan, *Death by Melancholy: Essays on Modern Southern Fiction* (Baton Rouge: Louisiana State Univ. Press, 1972), p. 28.

[5] Dorothy Walters, *Flannery O'Connor* (Boston: Twayne, 1973), pp. 30-31.

[6] O'Connor, "A Good Man is Hard to Find," p. 136.

[7] C. Hugh Holman, "Detached Laughter in the South," in *Comic Relief: Humor in Contemporary American Literature,* ed Sarah Blacher Cohen (Urbana: Univ. of Illinois Press, 1978), p. 103.

[8] Lewis A. Lawson, "The Grotesque in Recent Southern Fiction," in *Patterns of Commitment in American Literature,* ed. Marston LaFrance (Toronto: Univ. of Toronto Press, 1967), p. 165.

[9] Ibid., p. 178.

[10] Ibid., p. 177.

[11] Lewis A. Lawson, *Another Generation* (Jackson: Univ. of Mississippi Press, 1984), p. xvii.

[12] William Peden, *The American Short Story* (Boston: Houghton Mifflin, 1975), p. 70.

[13] Ibid., p. 83.

[14] Ibid., p. 113.

[15] Ibid., p. 6.

[16] Bobbie Ann Mason, *Shiloh and Other Stories* (New York: Harper & Row, 1982), p. 1. All subsequent references to this volume are noted as *Shiloh* in my text.

[17] Lawson, "The Grotesque in Recent Southern Fiction," p. 175.

[18] Gentry, p. 15.

[19] Holman, p. 89.

[20] Lawson, "The Grotesque in Recent Southern Fiction," p. 165.

[21] Peden, p. 4.

Narrative Displacement and Literary Faith: Raymond Carver's Inheritance from Flannery O'Connor

BARBARA C. LONNQUIST

In their respective introductions to *The Best American Short Stories* published annually by Houghton Mifflin, guest editors of recent years, Anne Tyler (1983) and Raymond Carver (1986), have affirmed their faith in the vitality and durability of the short story as an art form all its own. Tyler asserts that the most appealing short story writer is somewhat of a "wastrel" who "neither hoards his best ideas for something more 'important' (a novel) nor skimps . . . because this is 'only' a short story," and she suggests that this perhaps explains why Raymond Carver, a short story writer and poet, but not yet a novelist, has consistently produced top quality short fiction.[1] Carver's output of short stories testifies to his belief in the efficacy of the genre, and *Cathedral,* his most recent collection (1984), offers in itself a program for the reappreciation of the capacity of this smallest member of the fiction family to embody what, in this post-modern period of life and letters, is still worthy of the name art.

In her exploration of the qualities that distinguish a truly good short story, Tyler offers an insight into the elusive power of Carver's art that manages to confer a sense of newness upon a traditional story form and aspires to lyrically despite a spareness of prose style at times verging on silence. ". . . every really lasting story," she believes, "contains at least one moment of stillness that serves as a kind of pivot." She describes a truly satisfying story as "spendthrift," as having "a strange way of seeming bigger than the sum of its parts. . . . Even the sparest in style implies a torrent of additional details barely suppressed, bursting through the seams."[2]

A first encounter with Raymond Carver's "A Small, Good Thing," the O. Henry Award winning story from his collection, *Cathedral,*[3] gives one the very impression Tyler describes of a story that has gone beyond itself to create a life or truth that is somehow bigger than anything said or done in the story. The "small, good thing" that occurs, in what is literally a profound moment of stillness near the end of the story, leaves one with a sense of simultaneous recognition and discovery. The recognition occurs as a remembered feeling, as if the story has tapped into one's memory of what real short stories do, while at the same time one has an initimation of something new happening.

The sense of newness, however, is so subtly registered that it seems to arise almost more as a vague intuition on the reader's part than as his trained perception of an author's literary innovation. In fact, in his introduction to *The Best American Short Stories, 1986,* Carver disclaims all interest in short fiction that purports to be innovative. "I'm drawn toward the traditional (some would call it old fashioned) methods of storytelling," he says, and expressed the desire that "stories, like houses, or cars for that matter, be built to last," adding that, "Along with Flannery O'Connor, I admit to being put off by anything that looks funny on the page."[4] Although Carver's own stories bear out this editorial preference for the "realistic" or "lifelike," his seemingly flat rejection of fiction based on experimental technique could be, to a degree, misleading. For despite an obvious straightforwardness of style and structure in *Cathedral,* underlying the stories in that collection is a deft handling of narrative strategy which forms the heart of Carver's craft and vision.

This essay will argue that in his paradoxically sparse, yet "spendthrift" way, to use Tyler's term, Carver develops a narrative strategy in *Cathedral* that works within the traditional story form, but allows him to exploit that form and go beyond the very tradition he supports. The architectural metaphor of Carver's title, a cathedral whose buttresses support its solidly rounded structure, but whose spires seem to transcend that roundedness, provides an apt figure for the paradoxical art form he creates. I suggest that Carver inherits this subtle power from the obvious male precursors of this clean style and keen slice-of-life vision like Hemingway and Chekhov, both of whom were deeply respected by Carver and whose work within traditional story form made much from little.[5] I also suggest that he inherited it, in another way, from the very author with whom he claims to share his mistrust of the innovative, namely Flannery O'Connor, whose most powerful work also lies within the realistic tradition of the short story.

The reader of Carver's essays soon begins to notice that he rarely discusses writing short fiction without some reference to O'Connor.[6] In his essay "On Writing," (a title emulating the simplicity he admired in O'Connor's title "Writing Short Stories"), he confesses that not until he read her essay did he meet anyone who shared what he had thought was his "uncomfortable secret" of not knowing often where a story was going, and he acknowledges being greatly heartened by O'Connor's belief that the writing process is itself an "act of discovery."[7]

Such remarks, however, underestimate the extent of Carver's respect for the intensity of O'Connor's vision and the sophistication of her narrative artistry. An examination of how he invokes patterns and images from O'Connor's fiction in his own stories offers a more telling indication of her powerful presence. The stories in *Cathedral* are laced with signs of her spirit. Carver's use of the grotesque in "Vitamins," in which a Viet Nam veteran returns with a cigarette case containing a severed human ear hooked to a key chain, resembles the traveling salesman in O'Connor's "Good Country People" whose wares include a glass eye and a wooden leg stolen from the women he defrauds. In both stories, moreover, these sinister collectors of body parts become what O'Connor calls "agents of grace" for the unsuspecting protagonists in the stories. The young woman in Carver's story, shocked into self-awareness by her encounter with the ex-soldier, says, "I take what happened back there as a sign" (p. 108). And Carver's war veteran, a black man named Nelson, shares his name with the grandson Nelson in O'Connor's "The Artificial Nigger," another story using the image of an artificial or mutilated body part (this time the plaster figure of a Negro with a chipped eye) to represent broken human connections, a major theme in both Carver's and O'Connor's fiction.

Even the peacock, the key image in O'Connor's "The Displaced Person" and the virtual trademark of the moments of sudden revelation in her stories, makes its way into *Cathedral.* The peacock is, in fact, the cover illustration of both *Cathedral* and O'Connor's collection *A Good Man Is Hard to Find.* In a recent essay on Carver in *Studies in Short Fiction,* Mark Facknitz does indeed compare those moments when Carver's protagonists are "taken from behind by understanding" to the moments of revealed grace in Flannery O'Connor's stories, but distinguishes that for Carver grace is always "bestowed by other mortals . . . it is what grace becomes in a godless world."[8]

The obvious thematic links between O'Connor's and Carver's fiction suggest an even closer affinity between their narrative forms. "The Displaced Person," the final story of O'Connor's *A Good Man is Hard to Find,* serves, like Carver's "Cathedral," as a summarizing metaphor for all that has preceded it in the collection. In O'Connor's case the metaphor of displacement reveals the narrative strategy she has used to bring her characters to their moments of epiphany. One after another, the proud and self-righteous among her protagonists suffer an experience of geographic and psychological displacement leading to an epiphany in which they are dislodged from falsely assumed positions—spiritual as well as territorial. A haughty grandmother topples into a ditch to be confronted with her own fallen nature; a bigoted grandfather wanders hopelessly lost in the confusing maze of a big city before recognizing his own darkness; stern farm women who see the land as "theirs" are edged off their property in order to be dispossessed of their pride; and an atheist who zealously upholds her dependence on "nothing" must be left stranded in a neighboring hay loft, deprived of her eye glasses and her wooden leg before she might see the pseudo-loftiness of her own creed.[9]

The dramatic structure of Carver's stories suggests that he has appropriated the method O'Connor uses to bring her characters to an epiphany, but Carver applies this method of displacement to the narrative strategy itself, thus causing not only his characters, but his readers as well, to be in Facknitz's words "taken from behind by understanding." Carver begins with a narrative situation common or familiar enough to evoke an automatic set of expectations in most readers' minds (readers who like O'Connor's characters think that they have the lay of the literary land at least). He then puts that situation through a series of dislocations that "displace" the readers' expectations at each critical juncture until the final story is not the story that even the most savvy audience would have been plotting.

A clear example of this strategic maneuver occurs in "A Small, Good Thing." Early in the story, Scotty, the son of Ann and Howard Weiss, on his birthday is struck by a car on the way to school. Seeming unharmed at first, he walks home to his mother but suddenly loses consciousness and is taken to the hospital, where he lapses into a sleep that the doctors will not call a coma. "It's not a coma yet, not exactly," the doctor said.

"I wouldn't want to call it a coma. Not yet, anyway" (p. 66). The doctor's verbal hedging with his diagnosis reflects the reader's own uncertainty at this point. Like the mother who intuits the discrepancy between what she is told and what is really happening, the reader begins to suspect that the terms of the story are shifting. When the child dies suddenly of a "hidden occlusion" that x-rays had failed to show, the physical stoppage in the passage of an artery is analogous to the closing off of the narrative flow thus far. The narrator has by this time focused briefly on the Weisses' marital relationship, enough at least to arouse the reader's suspicion that the real story is not going to be the fate of the child, but the effect of his death on his parents' marriage. This is the first displacement in Carver's literary strategy: the modulation from suspense to tragedy.

For a time, the action bears out such a diagnosis. After the grief-stricken parents leave the hospital without their son, the narrative fixes on the efforts of the couple to confront catastrophe, share their sorrow, and gather up the fragments of the life that remains to them. As they "get the coffee-maker going" and Howard begins to pick up Scotty's things scattered about the living room, Ann assesses the situation: "He's gone and now we'll have to get used to that. To being alone" (p. 82). But an exploration of marital emptiness is not, after all, the subject of Carver's story. Faced with another narrative occlusion, the reader, who has perceived the agenda to be the familiar turn from suspense plot to tragic drama, recognizes that he has been caught in a cliché and has underestimated the integrity and resilience of Carver's method. This second displacement of literary strategy draws attention to what has seemed to be an odd and somewhat gratuitous motif spreading through the story, a series of mysterious phone calls inquiring about Scotty that the parents assume to be a heartless joke on the part of the hit-and-run driver. Because they receive the calls separately while home from the hospital in shifts, they do not make the connection, already made by the reader, that the baker from whom Ann ordered a cake for Scotty's birthday is making the calls. However, during a call that comes in the middle of the night, Ann recognizes the sound of the machinery in the background, and Howard and she rush to the bakery shop to confront the caller.

Here, the most dramatic shift in the narrative strategy occurs. Anger suddenly wells up within Ann, "making her feel larger than herself, larger than either of these men" (p. 85). After she subjects the baker to a tirade of abuse, her anger subsides. "Just as suddenly as it had welled in her, the anger dwindled, gave way to something else . . ." (p. 86). Her cathartic outburst is not, however, the climax of the story; the transfer of emotions signals one more transformation of the narrative into "something else." As if directing the reader's line of vision toward the final literary displacement, "Ann wiped her eyes and looked at the baker," who, in turn, "had cleared a place for them at the table" (p. 87).

> "Please sit down," he said. "Let me get you a chair," he said to Howard. "Sit down now, please." The baker went into the front of the shop and returned with two little wrought-iron chairs. "Please sit down, you people." (p. 87)

From this moment, the narrative becomes the baker's story. In the almost sacramental exchange that follows, the baker asks for forgiveness:

> "Forgive me, if you can," the baker said. I'm not an evil man, I don't think. Not evil, like you said on the phone. You got to understand what it comes down to is I don't know how to act anymore, it would seem. Please," the man said, "let me ask you if you can find it in your hearts to forgive me?" (p. 88)

Although Carver does not share Flannery O'Connor's sacramental view of life and literature, the religious overtones of the baker's human penitential rite prepare the reader for the special dramatic moment that follows. Carver did, no doubt, assimilate O'Connor's idea of what she believes "makes a story work":

> . . . I have decided that it is probably some action, some gesture of a character that is unlike any other in the story, one which indicates where the real heart of the story lies. This would have to be an action or a gesture which was both totally right and totally unexpected; it would have to be one that was in character and beyond character; it would have to suggest both the world and eternity . . . . It would be a gesture which somehow made contact with mystery.[10]

The gesture in Carver's story is the "small, good thing" the baker does when he clears a space at the table of his own existence, offers the couple hot rolls, and pronounces, in what is the ultimate plain-song of this ritual, the simple mystery at the heart of the story:

> "You have to eat and keep going. Eating is the small, good thing in a time like this," he said.
> He served them warm cinnamon rolls just out of the oven, the icing still runny. He put butter on the table and knives to spread the butter. Then the baker sat down at the table with them. He *waited*. He *waited* until they each took a roll from the platter and began to eat. "It's good to eat something," he said, watching them. (p. 88)

The narrator's repetition of the word "waited" (emphasis mine) signals that the baker takes up the action formerly belonging to the parents as they watched over their son in the hospital, an action Ann had named in her initial outburst at the baker: "My son's dead," she said with a cold, even finality. "He was hit by a car Monday morning. We've been waiting with him until he died" (p. 86). The couple then repay the baker's gesture of clearing a space for them by suspending the expression of their own sorrow to listen to the story he tells of his own childlessness, his decision to be a baker, and his doubts and limitations in this "necessary trade" (p. 90). Although the "necessary trade" is a literal reference to the baker's occupation, it also defines the action at this moment, which is another "necessary trade," the exchange of human stories. Furthermore, the phrase describes the activity of the reader, who, at each successive displacement of the narrative line, has traded expectations of one story for another.

The understanding achieved at the end of the story between the couple and the baker, as well as that between reader and author, necessitates a similar willingness on the part of both characters and readers to be dispossessed of previously held and quite stereotyped views—literary and human. The communion experienced between baker and bereaved at the end contrasts sharply with the meager exchange between baker and customer at the beginning, in which Ann not only misjudges the baker but misapprehends the very nature of their connectedness:

> There were no pleasantries between them, just the minimum exchange of words, the necessary information. He made her feel uncomfortable, and she didn't like that. While he was bent over the counter with the pencil in his hand, she studied his coarse features and wondered if he'd ever done anything else with his life besides be a baker. She was a mother and thirty-three years old, and it seemed to her that everyone, especially someone the baker's age—a man old enough to be her father—must have children who'd gone through this special time of cakes and birthday parties. There must be that between them, she thought. (p. 60)

The irony of her mistaking the baker's pleasure in life is analogous to the reader's initial failure to locate the real heart of the story. Carver reminds us, however, that the most ordinary human exchange still has the potential for delivering the pleasure of small, good art. For despite the aching loneliness the story evokes, the author leaves us with the "dark bread" of Ann's and Howard's sorrow transubstantiated into the rich "taste of molasses" of the baker's comfort (p. 89).

Part of the pleasure experienced in reading "A Small, Good Thing" derives from Carver's ability to move beyond the larger-scaled actions we have come to expect in traditional fiction (i.e., life, death, marriage, birth, separation) and to locate in the smallest gesture, which is, as O'Connor says, "both totally right and totally unexpected," the moment that is ripe for art. Carver describes this source of "artistic delight" himself:

> It's possible, in a poem or a short story, to write about commonplace things and objects using commonplace but precise language, and to endow those things—a chair, a window curtain, a fork, a stone, a woman's earring—with immense, even startling power. It is possible to write a line of seemingly innocuous dialogue and have it send a chill along the reader's spine—the source of artistic delight, as Nabokov would have it.[11]

In "Cathedral," the title story of the collection, Carver applies the same displacement and refocusing of the narrative strategy that we have examined to produce a commentary on both the pleasures of a small, good story and its value when viewed against the historical backdrop of "high art." As with O'Connor's "The Displaced Person," the title of Carver's final story in the collection provides a summarizing metaphor for the narrative mode employed throughout. As previously observed, the image of the cathedral describes Carver's method of working within a traditional framework and yet "a-spiring" beyond the limits of that tradition.

The donnée of the plot, neatly spelled out on the first two pages of the story, augurs a conventional narrative form. The husband, in the middling stage of a marriage (his wife's second) of apparently diminished passion, awaits, without pleasure, the arrival of an overnight guest, an old friend of the wife, a blind man to whom she used to read before her marriage. The husband-narrator's blunt conclusion to the opening paragraph, "A blind man in my house was not something I looked forward to" (p. 209), suggests the outlines of a narrative shape familiar to most readers. What transpires, however, is anything but the traditional convention of the romance triangle. By using again his technique of displacing the expected narrative strategy, Carver converts the action, instead, into an exchange between the two men, climaxing in a gesture, at once both utterly simple and profoundly exhilarating, a gesure that O'Connor would deem both "totally right and totally unexpected."

After the rising action of dinner, a few rounds of drinks, and the small talk preliminary to retiring—amenities similar to those assumed to be part of standard reading fare—the story deftly short-circuits the reader's expectation for the narrative line to move in a romantic or erotic direction. When, after having fallen asleep on the couch, the wife moves upstairs to bed, leaving the two men behind to face the literal and figurative dark, the triangle neatly collapses. (Did not Flannery O'Connor's artful bible salesman also thwart romantic development in "Good Country People" by the simple removal of a leg?) What follows by necessity, according to geometric principle, is that the two men must meet on the same plane. For such human congruence to be achieved, another, psychological dislocation or "necessary trade" must occur. Before the two can inhabit a common space, the emotionally short-sighted host has to admit that his "idea of blindness came from the movies" (p. 209) and that the thought of the man's loving a wife "without his having ever seen what the goddamned woman looked like" is beyond his understanding (p. 213). Having made those admissions, he then has to quit the world of physical sight and enter imaginatively into the inner reality of his guest.

Carver sets the scene: the two men stay up, exhaust their conversation, empty their drinks, smoke a little marijuana, and finally resort to late night television. After the news, they resign themselves to the only program the husband can find on the TV, "Something about the church in the Middle Ages," he says (p. 222). After trying unsuccessfully to transcribe what the camera depicts, the narrator, whose limited vocabulary reflects a similarly restricted empathetic range, suddenly asks the blind man, "Do you have any idea what a cathedral is? What they look like, that is? Do you follow me? If somebody says cathedral to you, do you have any notion what they're talking about? Do you know the difference between that and a Baptist church, say?" (pp. 223-24)

This uncharacteristic rush of questions from a laconic speaker, whose syntactical range rarely surpasses the bluntly declarative statement, signals the beginning of the narrator's dislocation. As if sensitive to the husband's inability to help him, Robert, the blind man, proposes that they draw a cathedral—together. The husband returns with some ball points and a brown paper bag, spreads the bag out on the coffee table, and tries to smooth out the wrinkles, a gesture bearing iconographical resemblance to the baker's act of clearing a space in "A Small, Good Thing." In a motion that collapses the planes of their physical separateness, Robert moves down from the sofa and sits on the carpet with his host. Then in a gesture reducing still further the distance between them,

> He closed his hand over my hand. "Go ahead, Bub, draw," he said. "Draw. You'll see. I'll follow along with you. . . . You'll see. Draw," the blind man said. (pp. 226-27)

Paradoxically, the movement from verbal to tactile communication, a seeming reduction, is actually a movement upward, to a higher level of communication between the two. This is doubly ironic, given the generally reductive nature of the narrator's speech. The action also evokes the second, surprising rush of energy from the otherwise languid host:

> So I began. First I drew a box that looked like a house. It could have been the house I lived in. Then I put a roof on it. At either end of the roof, I drew spires. Crazy. . . .
> I put in windows with arches. I drew flying buttresses. I hung great doors. I couldn't stop. The TV station went off the air. I put down the pen and closed and opened my fingers. The blind man felt around over the paper. He moved the tips of his fingers over the paper, all over what I had drawn, and he nodded.
> "Doing fine," the blind man said.
> I took up the pen again, and he found my hand. I kept at it. I'm no artist. But I kept drawing just the same. (p. 227)

Gradually, the creative energy gives way to a stillness, much like the stillness at the end of "A Small, Good Thing" when the couple sit silently enclosed in the warmth of the baker's gift. When the blind man asks the husband to close his eyes, a moment of human, almost sacred communion ensues, collapsing distinctions between time and space:

> So we kept on with it. His fingers rode my fingers as my hand went over the paper. It was like nothing else in my life up to now. (p. 228)

Even after Robert bids him to take a look, the narrator wants to prolong the effect:

> But I had my eyes closed. I thought I'd keep them that way for a little longer. . . .
> My eyes were still closed. I was in my house. I knew that. But I didn't feel like I was inside anything. (p. 228)

The rhythm of contraction and expansion registered here though images of spatial and geometric configuration underscores a paradoxical movement throughout the story. Playing on the architectural principle that "less is more," Carver adopts a modality that not only moves from one pole to the other, but exploits their very connectedness. At the moment, for instance, that his language seems reduced to its simplest form, he explodes that simplicity and elevates it to the lyrical: "His fingers rode my fingers as my hand went over the paper. It was like nothing else in my life up to now" (p. 228). Earlier references to poetry in the story reinforce the connection. The narrator had mocked his wife's habit of writing poems and taping them to send to the blind man. Poetry, like a blind person's love for a woman he could not see, was beyond the narrator's understanding.

What Carver celebrates in "Cathedral" is the ability of the limited person, like his counterpart the limited reader, to go beyond himself in an act of human empathy. (The reader's sympathy for the narrator is an equivalent act of going beyond one's former understanding; as the narrator reaches out in empathy, the reader develops sympathy for him.) In the narrator's moment of communion with the blind man, which constitutes the poetry of the story displacing our more conventional expectations of poetic moments in fiction, Carver also celebrates the power of short stories to locate and give artistic form to the lyricism of ordinary life.

One story after another in the collection demonstrates this power as, in different ways, Carver displaces former expectations of what a short story does, and yet pushes beyond the exhaustion that such displacement was thought to cause. One leaves *Cathedral* with a heightened sense of the perils and the possibilities that face those who live, or read, or create in this world. The image of the cathedral recalls the high peril encountered and the even higher possibility entertained by the builders of medieval cathedrals. The positive juxtaposition of his collection of small, good stories against so massive an art form reveals most of all the depth of Carver's belief in the short story form. Perhaps his final inheritance from Flannery O'Connor has been her invincible faith, after all. Her belief in the regenerative nature of human beings has become his belief in the equally regenerative nature of short stories.

NOTES

[1] Anne Tyler, ed., with Shannon Ravenel, *The Best American Short Stories, 1983* (Boston: Houghton Mifflin, 1983), p. xiv.

[2] Tyler, pp. xiv-xv.

[3] Raymond Carver, *Cathedral* (New York: Random House, 1984). Hereafter quotations identified parenthetically in the text.

[4] Raymond Carver, *The Best American Short Stories, 1986,* ed., with Shannon Ravenel (Boston: Houghton Mifflin, 1986), p. xiv.

[5] See "On Writing" in *Fires: Essays, Poems, Stories* (New York: Random House, 1984), pp. 13, 14. Also see Carver's review of two biographies of Hemingway, "Coming of Age, Going to Pieces," in The Review of Books, *The New York Times,* November 17, 1985.

[6] See "On Writing" and "Fires" in *Fires,* pp. 16-17.

[7] "On Writing" in *Fires,* p. 16.

[8] Mark Facknitz, " 'The Calm,' 'A Small, Good Thing,' and 'Cathedral': Raymond Carver and the Rediscovery of Human Worth," *Studies in Short Fiction,* 23 (1986), 295-96.

[9] Flannery O'Connor, *A Good Man Is Hard to Find and Other Stories* (New York: Harcourt, Brace, Jovanovich, 1976).

[10] Flannery O'Connor, "Writing Short Stories," in *Mystery and Manners: Occasional Prose,* ed. Sally and Robert Fitzgerald (New York: Farrar, Straus and Giroux, 1969), p. 111. p. 111.

[11] "On Writing," p. 15.

Contributors

LINDA ADAMS BARNES is a graduate student at Vanderbilt University, where she is specializing in Southern Literature.

JEANNE SALLADÉ CRISWELL has a Master of Fine Arts degree in creative writing from Indiana University in Bloomington, Indiana, where she was formerly employed as an instructor of creative writing and literature. A number of her short stories have appeared in various literary journals, and she has recently completed work on two critical essays on Saul Bellow.

JOHN L. DARRETTA is Professor of English and Communication Arts at Iona College. He teaches courses in American literature and specializes in modern fiction. As a Fulbright Teaching Fellow (1975-76), he lectured on American literature in Milan, Turin, and Rome, and did extensive research on Italian cinema. His most recent book, *Vittorio De Sica,* was published in 1983. He is currently co-editing a book of essays on Joyce Carol Oates and completing a book on the novels of Flannery O'Connor.

RICHARD GIANNONE is Professor of English at Fordham University. He has published *Music in Willa Cather's Fiction* in 1968 and *Vonnegut: A Preface to His Novels* in 1977.

HELEN JASKOSKI is Professor of English at California State University at Fullerton. She published *The Tar Pit Murders* in 1983, an essay on native American women in 1980, and "Notes on a Competency-Based Curriculum in Poetry Therapy" in 1984. She is currently doing research on American Indian literature, and she is a regular reviewer of mystery/crime/spy novels for *As Crime Goes By.*

BARBARA C. LONNQUIST is a Graduate Teaching Fellow at the University of Pennsylvania and a part-time lecturer at Chestnut Hill College. She is currently working on the connections between women and architecture in fiction and poetry of the nineteenth and early twentieth century, and on revisionist mythologies in Modernist and contemporary poetry and fiction.

JOSEPH LOWIN is presently teaching in Jerusalem. He has published studies of Primo Levi, Cynthia Ozick, Herman Wouk, and Joseph Heller. The current essay will appear in a book on Cynthia Ozick to be published in Twayne's United States Authors Series.

LANCE OLSEN is Assistant Professor of English at the University of Kentucky. He published a book on Postmodern Fantasy in 1987 and numerous short stories, essays, and reviews in a wide variety of journals. He is working on a book on postmodern humor titled *Circus of the Mind in Motion.*

STACEY OLSTER is Assistant Professor of English at the State University of New York at Stony Brook. She published an essay on *The Tin Drum* in 1982, and her essay "The 60's Without Apology" has been accepted by the *Minnesota Review*. She has also completed a book-length study entitled *Reminiscence and Re-Creation in Contemporary American Fiction: "Subjective Historicism" and the American Idea of History.*

CLARKE OWENS is a Lecturer in English at The Ohio State University.

ARTHUR M. SALTZMAN is Associate Professor of English at Missouri Southern State College. His special interest is contemporary American fiction, and he has published studies of the fiction of Gass, Doctorow, and Barth. His latest book, *The Fiction of William Gass: The Consolation of Language* was published in 1986. His current research is on the anti-epiphanic nature of recent fiction.

E. P. WALKIEWICZ is an Associate Professor of English at Oklahoma State University. His book on John Barth was published by Twayne in 1986, and his essays on Ezra Pound, William Carlos Williams, and James Joyce have appeared in various journals. He is currently working on an article on Barth and producing, with Hugh Witemeyer, an annotated edition of the correspondence between Ezra Pound and Bronson Cutting.

SALLY WOLFF works as an editor for a Vice President of Emory University and teaches courses in American literature at Oglethorpe University. In 1985 she published an essay on the stories of Eudora Welty and Elizabeth Spencer in *The Journal of the Short Story in English.* She is assisting in preparing a Norton Critical Edition of *The Sound and the Fury,* and she is working on articles of Faulkner and Welty.

The editors are both long-term members of the English Department at Western Illinois University. **LOREN LOGSDON** has been fiction editor of *Mississippi Valley Review* for the past thirteen years, and **CHARLES W. MAYER** has been American literature editor of *Essays in Literature.*